SABLE ISLAND

ALSO BY THE AUTHORS

Sahara: The Extraordinary History of the World's Largest Desert

SABLE ISLAND

THE STRANGE ORIGINS AND CURIOUS HISTORY OF A DUNE ADRIFT IN THE ATLANTIC

Mary de Villiers & Sheila Hirtle

WALKER & COMPANY

NEW YORK

First published in the United States of America in 2004 by Walker Publishing Company, Inc. Published simultaneously in Canada by McClelland & Stewart, Ltd. with the title *A Dune Adrift: The Strange Origins and Curious History of Sable Island.*

For information about permission to reproduce selections from this book, write to Permissions, Walker & Company, 104 Fifth Avenue, New York, New York 10011.

Library of Congress Cataloging-in-Publication Data

De Villiers, Marq.
    Sable Island : the strange origins and curious history of a dune adrift in the Atlantic / Marq de Villiers and Sheila Hirtle.
        p.   cm.
    Includes bibliographical references (p.).
    ISBN 0-8027-1432-3 (hardcover : alk. paper)
    1. Sable Island (N.S.)—History.   2. Natural history—Nova Scotia—Sable Island.   I. Hirtle, Sheila.   II. Title.

F1039.S13D4 2004
971.6'99—dc22

2004052049

Book design by Maura Fadden Rosenthal/mspace

Frontispiece map, Sable Island, Nova Scotia, Known Wrecks Since 1583, used by permission of the Maritime Museum of the Atlantic in Halifax, Nova Scotia.

Visit Walker & Company's Web site at www.walkerbooks.com

Printed in the United States of America

2   4   6   8   10   9   7   5   3   1

CONTENTS

ACKNOWLEDGMENTS

For their help and their always cogent advice, our grateful thanks to Silver Donald Cameron, Norman Campbell, John Wesley Chisholm, Borden Conrad, Roberto Dutesco, Derek Fenton, Gerry Forbes, Ralph Getson and the Fisheries Museum of the Atlantic, Bill Gilkerson, Marcia and Craig Harding, Terry Hennigar, Barry Hiltz of Ross Farm Museum, Clem Hiltz, Ned King, Peter Landry (BluPete.com), Zoe Lucas, the Niagara Historical Society, the Nova Scotia Historical Society, John and Gerry Mader, David and Sharon Morse, Lynn Richard of the Maritime Museum of the Atlantic, Halifax, Allan Ruffman, Robert Rutherford, the Sable Island Preservation Trust, Wayne Walters, and Hal Whitehead.

vessels, small specks of white on the sea, heading for the fishing grounds of Banquereau (or Quero, as it is called on the eastern seaboard) and the vanishing cod. The water below is neither blue nor green, but a kind of steely gray roiling sea that could just as easily be magma.

An hour out, the first smudge of Sable will appear over the hump of the nose, just a blurred line on the far horizon, slowly resolving from the brume. As it grows, the curious nature of the island becomes ever clearer. It is a crescent, a deep curve, with its arms, at the east and west, reaching out to the north, the bottom of the bowl sagging toward the equator. There is nothing else showing above the sea—nothing between you and Europe, nothing between you and the Caribbean but Bermuda, nothing between you and the Arctic but the bleak and windswept Rock of New-foundland and the ancient ice sheets of Greenland, and the mass of con-tinental North America to the north and west.

If you head in from the northwest, as you would flying from Halifax, the island at first gives an illusion of surprising massiveness. It is a hun-dred miles or so out into the ocean; the island itself is more than thirty miles long if you measure along the arc, and it is easy to interpret what you see as just the beach of a much larger smudge beyond. But with in-creasing resolution the illusion vanishes, and it becomes apparent that what you had seen as just a beach was, in fact, the whole island, less than a mile wide at its middle, and shading off into western and eastern arms, each no more than a small boy's stone's throw across. If there is sunshine when you fly in, the island can look oddly tropical, a delicate sliver of so-lidity, a brilliant white beach in a glittering emerald sea, topped with dunes and greenery and dotted with ponds. Some of the dunes are bald, but most are covered in vegetation. If you didn't know the frigid tem-peratures of the water or the island's latitude, you could image that the greenery was palm trees or mangrove thickets and the air on the beaches was bikini-balmy. But, of course, there is not a tree on the island, or any growth more than a few feet high, and what you might take at first as sunbathers on the beach are really gray seals, resting after a meal of halibut or pollock in a place safe from sharks.

From a few miles out, the true fragility of this delicate crescent is only too apparent. In places the sandbanks keeping the ocean to the south from dashing itself into the ocean to the north are less than ten feet high, a quarter the height of the Fundy tides and a puny thing in relation to the waves whipped up by the Atlantic gales—in a good blow, fifty-, sixty-footers are not at all uncommon, and even on the mainland, storm-generated waves have been known to roll over cliffs fifty feet high. In a tale from the great August gales of 1927, a fisherman off Sable recounted how he had lost sight of the hundred-foot topgallant of a neighboring schooner, which disappeared entirely from his view, he being in one trough and the schooner in another.

So why doesn't the ocean simply obliterate this delicate little presence, just wash it away? It's only sand, after all, nothing much more than a dune, and in the pounding swells of the big storms the whole island quite literally shivers in the onslaught.

In fact, the fragility of Sable is in some ways an illusion. It's just sand, yes, and it moves, as though it were itself a slow and ponderous schooner on the sea, seeming to breathe as schooners do, rising and falling on the very breast of the planet, but it could be the shape-changer and face-dancer of aboriginal legend, yielding in order not to yield. There are great forces at work around the island, planetary forces that are at once forming and destroying it, and you can't understand its presence without some sense of what they are.

Even as you sat on the runway in Halifax awaiting permission to take off, you will have had conversations with Sable

Station, which knows you are coming. Indeed, if it didn't know, if you'd not already been vetted by the coast guard, you'd not be allowed to land, since the island is a protected area. In any case, Gerry Forbes, head of the station, and in 2004 one of only two full-time residents of Sable, will have had to head out to the beach in his tracked pickup to see to its state; the beach is the Sable landing strip, and if it is too soggy or recently saturated with rain, you will have to abandon your plans. Otherwise Gerry will be there as you head in, his vehicle doubling as a portable terminal, wind sock on its aerial and handheld radio its traffic-control technology. He is a large man with the hands of a mechanic and a slightly scruffy and weather-beaten nonchalance, who exudes a no doubt justified air of competence. In addition to serving as station chief, he is head meteorologist, agent of the Sable Island Preservation Trust, agent of the Canadian Coast Guard, part-time agent of the petroleum drilling rigs (some of which can be plainly seen from Sable's beaches), chief mechanic, radio and computer operator, head of rescue services, tour guide, horsemaster, and propagandist-in-chief of Sable. All these roles he fulfills with occasionally gruff good humor but scant tolerance for loud louts and litterers, of which he has seen far too many. Even if you merely want to fly down to the east end of the island and back, which you will probably want to do before landing, since that way you get the best possible overview of the island, you will need Gerry's approval. Without it, the pilot will deposit you on the beach without further ado.

From just a few hundred feet in the air, you can clearly see the island's basic configuration: beaches to the north and south, each with a bank of wind- and sea-created dunes and, in between, freshwater ponds and undulations of grass and heath. Lake Wallace (no one seems to know who Wallace was) is the largest of the ponds. It's on the western third of the island but is much smaller now than it once was—not much more than five hundred yards long and maybe fifty feet wide, where once it was closer to fifteen miles long. Other small ponds are dotted about the interior, most of them with folksy names from early inhabitants, like Paul and Myrtle Pond; others are just called West Pond or No. 3 Pond, and so on. The cluster of buildings that is Sable Station is just to Lake Wallace's west. Protruding from each of the crescent's arms are the spits, low sand fields diminishing to sea level but extending as submerged bars many miles farther out. It is these bars that so often surprised the unwary and made Sable so dangerous to mariners.

Along the beaches, the harbor seals bask, unmoved by the landing aircraft; indeed, so unwary are they that the aircraft will sometimes have to delay its takeoff or landing as a line of seals humps its way across the beach to higher ground, or back to the ocean to feed, paying no attention to any human presence. Gerry Forbes calls them "the commuters." It's one of the island's rules that humans and their vehicles always give way to the commuters.

At frequent intervals throughout the island are little bands of feral horses, families mostly, and clusters of bachelors. Their presence on Sable was for a long time a mystery, and they have added over the years a treasure of romantic stories to the already rich stock of island legend. They, too, pay little attention to human activity. They stand, gaze, loll, play, splash in the ponds, graze, and gallop along the beaches, manes flying, a grand sight to see there in the open Atlantic.

Days like this find Sable in an unusual good mood: calm and orderly, the winds manageable, the surf (water temperature aside) suitable for a child's splashing, the air, if not exactly balmy, at least temperate. So it is not surprising that one emotion experienced is that of astonishment. *This* is the "deadliest piece of real estate in the country"?[1] *This* is the "graveyard of the Atlantic," storm central, locus of two hundred,

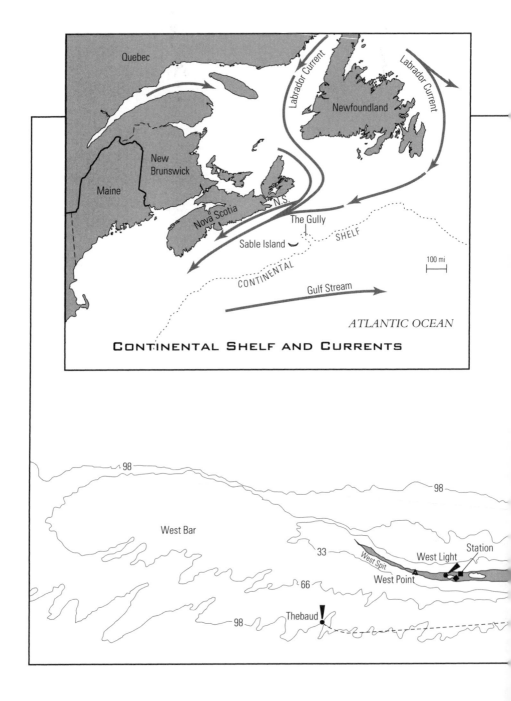

Quebec

Labrador Current

Newfoundland

Labrador Current

New
Brunswick

Maine

Nova Scotia

N.S.

The Gully

Sable Island

SHELF

100 mi

CONTINENTAL

Gulf Stream

ATLANTIC OCEAN

CONTINENTAL SHELF AND CURRENTS

98

98

West Bar

33

West Spit

West Light

Station

West Point

66

98

Thebaud

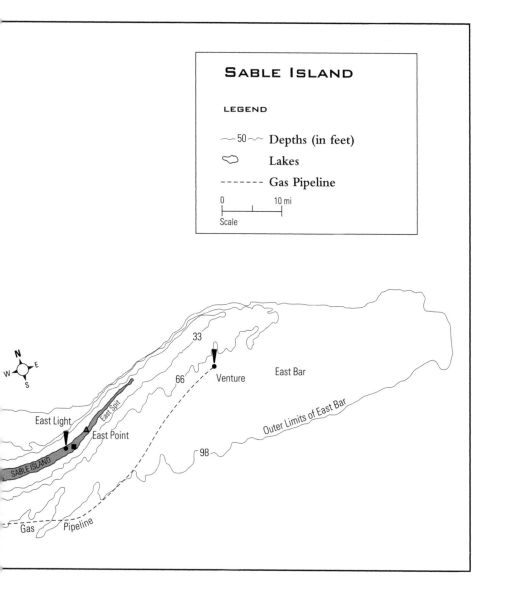

SABLE ISLAND

LEGEND

—50— Depths (in feet)

Lakes

------- Gas Pipeline

0 ⊢——⊣ 10 mi
Scale

33

66

Venture

East Bar

Outer Limits of East Bar

East Light

East Spit

East Point

98

SABLE ISLAND

Gas Pipeline

N
W E
S

three hundred, five hundred shipwrecks and the miserable deaths of thousands of sailors, their bones buried by the drifting dunes? *This* is the ever-shifting sandbar that terrorized mariners for four hundred years? *This* is the remote island that would have been an instant front-page sensation in London, had there been tabloid front pages in 1583, when Sir Humphrey Gilbert's 120-ton vessel *Delight* was wrecked on its shores "with the loss of an hundredth of men," not even the first and far from the last such disaster recorded there—to date, fully ten wrecks for every mile of coastline? Is this pretty little curving crescent of peach-tinted sand really the remote and desolate isle that so filled the imaginations of European adventurers—that infected minds with such dreams of folly and avarice that jumped-up aristocrats and would-be colonial kinglets attempted to set up seigneuries there? *This* is the dumping ground for convicts and misfits and lunatics and scavengers for more than three hundred years, as one settlement scheme after another went awry, the often-unwilling colonists starving or shivering to death? Is this the place so battered by gales and savage storms that it often radically changes shape in a single night, confusing sailors who thought they knew where the sandbars were to be found? Is this the place of mountainous waves that could tear a vessel asunder, to such an extent that the "Humane Establishment" put out on the island in later years to succor the castaways could only look on helplessly as they watched people drown in front of their eyes? Sometimes those gales can seem playful—if you're not at sea. When the winds are gusting to eighty or ninety miles an hour, scudding along the beach, Sable Station staff have been known to go out into the gale, spread their coats into the wind, and bound down the sand in strides that are thirty or even forty feet long, without effort, the nearest thing, Gerry Forbes says, to flying. ("Of course, you then have to crawl back.") At sea the gales are much more terrifying; in the stormy winter of 2002–3, a container ship facing such a gale to Sable's north had fifty containers torn from its deck and dashed into the sea. The seven-hundred-foot vessel limped into port at Halifax a day or so later, wreckage still hanging over its gunwales.

The answer to all of these questions is: Yes, this *is* the place. This gently curving sandbar, this wild island where the horses run, is and was all of those things, appearing on a succession of charts in fearful or angry guise (or even in deeply mistrustful ones). A rudimentary 1755 chart of the peninsula of Nova Scotia by surveyor Charles Morris shows the Isle of Sable Bank with an ominous round, dark eye in the western end called My Lady's Hole, a nicely misogynous insult.[2] It's deadly, yes: Sable Island is the exposed portion of a vast shoal on the outer edge of the continental shelf, with long, shifting, and barely buried sandbars on all sides, with no harbors, prone to fogs and storms, with irregular ocean currents of great strength sweeping around it, low in profile and of a color that makes it very hard to pick out. Still, the technology of navigation has, essentially, ended the era of Sable's shipwrecks. The last serious wreck was in 1947, a grim little steamer called *Manhassett,* its rusting carcass soon swallowed by the sands. (Well, we should say the era has *almost* ended. In 1999, the yacht *Merimac* went aground on the north beach; its bewildered crew, lost in the fog, apparently had no idea where in the wide Atlantic they had found themselves and were only relieved to be ashore—*somewhere.* Their bewilderment was compounded, no doubt, by seeing a truck looming out of the fog along the beach—with Texas license plates. It had been loaned to Sable Station by oil drillers on the Sable Bank.)

Sable remains an enigma. This hell's beach, this wild node of wind and water and sand and grass, wallowing in the turbulent waters and thick fogs created by the confluence of the Gulf Stream and the Labrador Current, may be shrinking and drifting eastwards. *How can a whole island move?* Four hundred years ago, Sable was a hundred miles long, and maybe much more—or at least that's what the early charts said—and, while we should acknowledge that the mapmakers may have been seduced into exaggeration out of respect for the island's fabled savagery (one such map shows it guarding most of North America), there is considerable evidence that it was once much larger and higher than it is today. Does Sable itself have a death wish? One year soon—or not so soon—will its drifting take it to the edge of the continental shelf, tipping it down into the abyss, itself wrecked as it has wrecked so very many mariners' lives? Or is it—and here's a tantalizing idea!—now actually *growing*?

Little Sable Island is besieged and beset by the great planetary forces that made and shape the continents. Yet it is just a sand dune, heaped up in the ocean by the retreating glaciers, shaped and carved and cut away and added to and moved and kept in place by water and wind in all their many incarnations. It is, in its way, a curious metaphor for the way the planet governs itself, because to understand Sable properly you must understand the great ocean currents, including the mighty North Atlantic gyre; as well as the winds and their ferocious offspring, the North Atlantic gales. And the converse is true too. By understanding Sable you can begin to grasp the mechanisms of planetary survival, to get some feel for entropy and entropy's children, randomness and chaos.

CHAPTER ONE

Its Disputed Discovery

Vikings and Basques appear, the

first shipwreck is recorded, and

"cattel & swyne" are deposited there

When Europe was overrun by the Celtic and Hunnish barbarians, its inhabitants sank back into the cultural stupor now known as the Dark Ages and seemed to lose all interest in geography, as they did in the physical world itself, steeping themselves instead in religion, into which were stirred purgative doses of superstition and the mysteries of magic. The geographic knowledge of antiquity was fortunately transferred to the Islamic world, where it was preserved and embellished—the Arabs of the eighth to the twelfth centuries were great travelers and indefatigable mapmakers. As the Middle Ages waned, around the end of the twelfth century and at the beginning of the thirteenth, this repository of knowledge was gradually reintroduced to western Europe by translation from the Arabic treatises, and from the remaining Greek texts, into Latin. It was part of an intellectual revival that was to persist for centuries, and it renewed western Europeans' interest in geographic exploration and expanded their knowledge of the physical world. "Distant islands, which had remained hidden from view because of the terrors of the ocean, now began to be revealed. Chronicles of visits replaced recollections of occasional chance encounters. By 1350, almost all the Atlantic islands were known to the historians and geographers of western Europe, though their information was vague, often confused, and lacking in precise detail."[1]

Even now, however, the identity of whoever first saw Sable Island remains shrouded in a fog of doubt. It wasn't the indigenes of America, who never ventured that far from the coast. Most writers assume it was the Portuguese, who were commonly fishing in these waters in the fifteenth century. But it could have been the Basques. Or even the Vikings.

There is no hard evidence that any of the Vikings encountered Sable Island. We know, of course, that they colonized Greenland and reached the coast of Labrador and the island of Newfoundland, from which it would have been a short hop to Sable. But no record exists that they went that one step farther.

The Viking colonization of Greenland itself had been something of a confidence trick by an Icelandic renegade called Erik the Red and his son Leif the Lucky. Erik was, according to contemporary accounts, a volatile character with scant regard for convention or for law—the Norse equivalent of a Wild West outlaw. Erik and Leif had left Norway around 960 "because of some killings," a phrase suggesting that Erik had made it to his longboat just before the posse. As a refugee in Iceland, he seemed at first to prosper. He made a good marriage and settled down to farm in the gentle valleys of Haukadale, in the south of the island. But his bad temper got him into trouble again, and there was more violence. With yet another gang of aggrieved relatives sworn to vengeance on his heels, he set sail for a land far to the west that had never been settled, but which had been described a century earlier by a storm-swept sailor called Gunnbjorn Ulfsson. Ulfsson had painted vivid verbal pictures of mountains of ice, towering seas, and ghastly storms, none of which seem to have deterred Erik in the least. Sailing west on the sixty-fifth parallel, Erik finally caught sight of an 8,200-foot ice mountain (the Ingolsfjeld Glacier). He turned south, rounded what is now Cape Farewell, and explored the much less savage west coast. Liking it well enough, he returned to Iceland for one more skirmish with his enemies and to round up a few colonists, ambitious outsiders like himself. To persuade them to depart for parts unknown, he was careful to counteract the grim tales of Ulfsson, and prudently called the new country Greenland, giving it a nicely bucolic sound. A contemporary, under no illusions about Erik's character, left a record of his reason: "He said that people would be much more tempted to go there if he gave it an attractive name."[2]

In the summer of 985, the colonists had duly signed up, and a fleet of twenty-five ships set sail from Iceland to the newly named Greenland. Erik's con game notwithstanding, Greenland was clearly more temperate than it is now. There was sufficient grassland on the western coastal strip to permit the cultivation of grains and the raising of sheep, goats, cattle, and pigs. Modern excavations of the settlement show that it had been reasonably prosperous. Erik's own farm had four barns and room for forty head of cattle, and the remains of a stone cathedral one hundred feet long have been uncovered. The Icelanders, and therefore the Greenlanders, were resolute Christians.

For the next few centuries the settlements were stable. That the Greenlanders explored the Arctic regions is known from the discovery of a stone cairn in Greenland, dating from the fourteenth century, at almost seventy-three degrees north latitude, bearing the runic description *Erling Sighvatsson and Bjarni Thjordarson and Eindridi Jonsson built these cairns.* That they also went west and south is not disputed, and the remnant of their camp at the northern tip of the island of Newfoundland, at L'Anse Aux Meadows, is now a Canadian national monument. They also found what they called Vinland, though the exact location of this land of flowing streams, majestic trees, and wild grapes is still a matter of acrimonious academic debate. It was unlikely—*pace* the grapes—to have been Newfoundland or Labrador, and still less Baffin Island, but it could have been Nova Scotia or even the New England states.

In the fifteenth century, the outlying colonists either went home or perished. It was about this time that the climate of the region began rapidly and terrifyingly to deteriorate. For a while, ships still made their way west along the sixty-fifth parallel, but ever since the middle of the fourteenth century they had had to skirt the increasing pack ice and make a difficult circuitous route along more southerly latitudes. By 1400 the Inuit, who had migrated north in Greenland after the previous ice age, began to be forced south by the cold, and there were repeated clashes with the Norsemen. A decade into the fifteenth century, the Greenland colony was completely cut off from the rest of the civilized world. The last reference to Greenland was in the Iceland annals for 1410, when an Icelander returning home left a laconic account of his sojourn, a last elegy for a hardy and energetic people now defeated by nature. His was the last ship out; winter had abruptly shut down Greenland.[3]

Sometime during the Norse sojourn on Greenland, a sailor called Biom (or Bjiorm) Heriafson,

> after making the coast of Newfoundland and sailing towards the setting Sun, came upon a sandy land, which, from its position, must have been Sable Island. In his meager chart of a new world its sands have but scant mention; but it must have been that this hardy Dane from the undecked

poop of his miserable shallop was the first European that sighted this terror of all future navigators."[4]

Possible. But this is pretty thin evidence.

As for the Basques, there is no doubt that their journeyings in these waters go back before the Portuguese, though their tales of discoveries far to the west were at first dismissed in Europe as sailors' boasting. Even now, their claims are supported by anecdotal evidence only, just as the Viking claims were, before the remains of the Norse settlement of L'Anse Aux Meadows were found a few decades ago. Still, according to those who have made the Basques their field of study,

> the more widely believed and more carefully reasoned theory is that the Basques arrived in North America, along the Newfoundland or Labrador coast in the fourteenth or fifteenth century, that they visited, perhaps with some regularity, perhaps even had people working there, substantially before John Cabot's 1497 "discovery" of Newfoundland and Christopher Columbus's 1492 Caribbean find.[5]

Well before these dates, the early skepticism in Europe about Basque exploits diminished, and there were persistent rumors that Basque fishermen had found a land across the sea, perhaps only an island, perhaps more. Certain Bretons even attempted to follow Basque fishermen to find out where they were going and what they were doing there, but without success. In the early fifteenth century, a story was current among European mariners that two Basque ships from Guipúzcoa, one captained by Juan de Echayde and the other by Matais de Echeveste, had reached land across the Atlantic at the end of the previous century, but there is no proof. Recently the ruins of extensive Basque whaling stations have been found in New-foundland and on the Labrador coast, but these date back only to about 1530, not the 1390s. Still, a mere three decades after that, the Basque population of North America may have been as high as two thousand.

Mark Kurlansky, author of *The Basque History of the World*, an engagingly Basque-positive polemic, has adduced two arguments for placing Basques in America before Columbus. The first is the sheer volume of their catch. Basque fishermen were landing enormous quantities of cod and whale products for a century or two before 1492, and their competitors were convinced that the already-discovered fishing grounds alone could not explain the number of fish they brought to European markets. Only the banks off Newfoundland and the Scotia Shelf could do that, although of course they were not known to the competition at that time.

The second argument is the improbability that the best sailors, with the best ships, the best navigators, and a tradition of sailing the longest distances could have missed North America during centuries in which they were clearly so close.

> There is evidence of the Basques in the Färoe Islands as early as 875. This was a 1,500-mile journey, which, if they did not make landfall along the way, was a remarkably long distance to sail at that time. Is it possible that in all the following six centuries, working in the narrow area of the North Atlantic where the continents are not far apart, having known and learned from the Vikings, that the Basques never ventured the relatively shorter distance to North America? In 1412 an Icelandic account records that twenty Basque whalers passed by the western tip of Iceland off Grunderfjord, which is a 500-mile crossing to Greenland. From there another 1,200-mile voyage would have taken them to Newfoundland. . . . Most fishermen had little reason to cross the Atlantic, since the catches vanish with the end of the European con-

tinental shelf and do not pick up again until the other side. But the Basques chased whales that traveled to sub arctic waters and then dropped down along both coastlines.[6]

This is better evidence that the Basques had sailed in Sable waters than that adduced for the Vikings, perhaps. But is it persuasive?

Basque threads can be found in many a Spanish and Portuguese sea-faring tale, too. For example, Juan de la Cosa, a Spanish explorer usually known as Juan Vizcaíno, or John the Basque, is famous in cartographic history for his maps. Vizcaíno may have been with Columbus on his first voyage and was definitely on the 1493 second voyage. Afterward, he continued to explore the Caribbean basin, and in 1500 drew the first map of the world to include all the Americas. It contains a number of phantom islands, any one of which could be Sable. His 1506 world map, a somewhat embellished version of the first, with a more detailed Caribbean, was scarcely any more definitive about Sable.

Which leaves us with no real evidence that the Portuguese weren't the first to discover Sable, although they are plausible candidates. Portuguese mariners were, after all, as intrepid as the Basques, if not as experienced. The Azores, for example, were discovered about 1427 by Diogo de Senill (or Sevilha), a pilot of the king of Portugal.

Some writers have suggested, without providing evidence, that the island was first sighted by John Cabot in 1497.[7]

But Sable Island itself appears definitively for the first time on a map drawn by Pedro Reinel in 1502. Unfortunately, Reinel's map shows two possibilities. Most historians consider his San João Island to be Sable, though a few dissenters have nominated his Island of Santa Cruz as their candidate. Coincidentally, Santa Cruz is what Sable was called, just a few years later.

The early Portuguese and Basque mariners faced the open ocean and the prospect of exploiting the apparently endless lands beyond it with a shifting mix of hardheaded practicality and largeness of vision. Sometimes they just seemed to want victualing stations near the cod banks; at others their imaginations were filled with spiced dreams of personal empire and of great estates bearing their names; at still others, the sheer visceral thrill of being there first was apparently enough. Often whole families were infected.

One of the earliest known stories of familial fascination started in the north of Portugal, near the border with Galicia. Two mariner brothers, Gaspar and Miguel Corte Real, set off into the Atlantic to look for . . . for *something*. Adventure? Land? Fish and therefore wealth? The fabulous Indies? The thrill of discovery? Perhaps all of these things. What they found, we don't know. They set off in 1472, twenty years before Columbus arrived in the West Indies, but they never returned. Their older brother, Vasqueanes Corte Real, sought permission from King Manuel I to go in search of his two lost brothers, but he was denied a charter.

There things rested for a while. In 1520 Vasqueanes's son, Manuel Corte Real, joined with the Portuguese adventurer João Alvares Fagundes, after whom Sable Island was briefly named in 1540, on a voyage of discovery and subsequent colonization in the North Atlantic.

Fagundes was a shipwright from the little maritime fishing village of Viana do Castelano, also near the Galician frontier. He had become obsessed with what his contemporaries were already calling the Île de la Morue (Cod Island, now the island of Newfoundland, whose importance in those days was that it was located north of the Grand Banks cod-fishing grounds). He and Manuel Corte Real were given a charter to explore and establish colonies in the region by King Manuel, and the following year

outfitted an expedition to do just that. In his exploration around Newfoundland, the Gulf of St. Lawrence, and the coast of mainland Nova
Scotia, Fagundes discovered—or at least recorded—dozens of other islands: the Îles de la Madeleine (Magdalen Islands); St. Paul's Island off the
tip of Cape Breton, a place almost as treacherous for mariners as Sable itself; Penguin and Burgeo Islands; and the archipelago of St.-Pierre and
Miquelon, which he called, for no surviving reason, the Archipelago of
the Eleven Thousand Virgins.[8]

Among his discoveries was the island he coincidentally called Santa
Cruz, now known as Sable Island. He dismissed it as nothing much more
than a bank (of sand). But he discovered it in the worst possible way,
thereby setting a precedent for so many others: One of his groups of vessels lost two of its three ships by running aground on Sable's western bar.
What could be salvaged was loaded aboard a small caravel for settlement
elsewhere; the animals he had brought with him (cows, goats, sheep, and
pigs) were abandoned on the island.

There was no reference to horses, but in any case that would have been
unlikely. The Portuguese were carrying animals to be eaten, not ridden.

The Fagundes colonies failed, partly because of a lack of enthusiasm on
the part of his creditors at home—what we would now define as cash
flow—and partly because of what was blandly called "the hostility of the
indigenes" on the island of Newfoundland. By century's end, all the names
Fagundes had given to his discoveries—including the colorful Eleven
Thousand Virgins (a great loss for map lore) and Santa Cruz, which subsequently became Sable Island—had disappeared or been supplanted.

Fagundes and the Corte Reals were not the only
Portuguese or Basques interested in colonizing the New World. After the
Azores were settled, plenty of sailors on those rugged islands turned their

gaze westward, to the cod-fishing grounds. One of them was a member of the Barcelos family, which persisted in its colonizing efforts for at least three generations. The family came from the town of Barcelos, north of Oporto on the Portuguese mainland, but sometime in the last quarter of the fifteenth century, Pedro Pinheiro, scion "of one of the most noble families of Barcelos," migrated to the Azorean island of Terceira. He was nicknamed Barcelos after he had migrated to Terceira, and the name stuck.

In 1492, Pedro Pinheiro de Barcelos made his first voyage to the western Atlantic, and specifically to Newfoundland, under a charter granted by the Portuguese king John II. He was authorized, in the manner of the time—kings were very casual with territory not their own—to set up colonies there. (His partner on that first voyage was João Fernandes Labrador, who later gave his name to the Labrador peninsula.)

Pedro Pinheiro died in 1507, colony-free but still working at it. His son, Diogo Pinheiro de Barcelos, continued in the family tradition. He sought and was granted a colonizing charter by King Manuel I that encouraged him to continue his father's uncompleted work.[9] We know this mostly because the family was a fractious one, and some of the details emerged in a lawsuit begun shortly thereafter. Diogo had a brother, Afonso, who had been given equal rights to the plunder (profits) in the charter granted to them by the king, but also equal duties (expenses) "in the colonization of the lands of Bacalhaus." Afonso, however, apparently wanted the profits but not the duties, and failed to pay his share. Diogo therefore petitioned the royal court to obtain sole rights to the lands he had colonized. The hearing took place on October 7, 1531, and five witnesses testified that they had seen on the Island of Barcelona (Barcelos, another name at that time for Sable) cattle, sheep, goats, and swine taken there by Diogo's ships, and that all the animals were well fed and had multiplied. This was enough for the court: It found for

Diogo and obliged Afonso and his wife to relinquish all the rights stated in the charter.

Sable might be seen as an unlikely spot to launch an effort at colonization, but to experienced sailors it had several advantages as a supply station on which they could leave the same domestic animals they were then breeding at home—without fear they'd be stolen or wander off, and with some confidence they'd survive. Sable was central to all the great codfish banks; it was less rugged and much less cold than the continental coast, because it was closer to the Gulf Stream; it contained no predators; and it had fresh water and pasture in abundance.

In 1550, Manuel Pinheiro de Barcelos (son of Diogo and grandson of Pedro) took with him still more domestic animals and settlers to continue the colonization of Barcelona island. His colony, too, collapsed and was abandoned. But the animals survived.

That they did so we know from the testimony of those who later depended on them. The Englishman Sir Humphrey Gilbert, who journeyed to St. John's, Newfoundland, in 1583, reported that he'd come across "a Portugal" in that city

> who was himself present, when the Portugals about 30 years past did put into the same island both meat and swine, to breed, which were since exceedingly multiplied. This seemed unto us a very happy tidings to have on an island lying so near into the main, which we intend to plant upon, such store of cattle, whereby we might at all times conveniently be relieved of victual, and served of store for breed.

These were happier tidings than Sir Humphrey realized, for later that year, on August 29, one of his little ships, the 120-ton *Delight*, was wrecked on Sable, its seams split in the pounding surf, and though "an hundredth soules" perished, fourteen men survived, and kept themselves alive by killing those among the herd of large red cattle that they could catch.[10]

According to other testimonies of the time, "cattel & swyne" had been landed at Sable prior to 1550.[11] So eminent a person as Samuel de Champlain, the first French explorer of North America (1603) and the founder and governor of Quebec (1633), reported in the first edition of his *Voyages* (1613) that "bullocks and cows [were] taken there [Sable Island] over 60 years ago by the Portuguese," that is, sixty years prior to 1613 and therefore before 1553. Champlain left a spare description of the island: "It is about 15 leagues long and contains a small lake. The island is very sandy, without any mature trees, only coppices and pastures for the cattle." He also made reference to the "large quantity of beautiful black foxes" in the interior, and the dozens of walrus on the beaches.[12] John Winthrop, the first governor of Massachusetts Colony, in his *History of New England* (1630–49) gives an account of one John Rose's description of Sable Island after he was forced to land there: "The Island is 30 miles long, 2 miles broad in most places, a mere sand, yet full of fresh water ponds, etc. He [John Rose] saw about 800 cattle, small and great, all red, and the largest he ever saw."[13] Rose apparently had no theory as to the origin of all those red cattle, but by then it was already clear that the Portuguese had landed them on the island. Large red cattle were typical of those bred on the Azores and in Portugal itself. Rose mentioned no foxes.

The comings and goings of livestock were always a good clue to the settlements—and abandonments—by humans in Sable's complex history.

CHAPTER TWO

Its Glacial Origins

The island is mapped and placed in its

ocean neighborhood, along with the

curiosity called the Gully

What they found, these early explorers, was an errant island that was by planetary standards young and still somewhat shiftless. They didn't know it at the time, of course, but the Sable Island they ran across was very likely a mere fifteen thousand or so years old, and a very peculiar piece of real estate indeed. It moved across the surface of the ocean, for one thing, and changed its shape and its "reach." As indeed it still does.

In 1967, more than four hundred years after it was discovered, a drilling rig was towed out to Sable and dragged through the dunes into the island's interior; no one much cared, in those eco-innocent days, about the possible effect on Sable's delicate environment or on the vegetated dune system that was essentially holding the island together. The Mobil Oil Sable Island No. 1 Well, as it was called in the logbooks, was sunk near the island's center, its declared purpose to assess the undersea potentials for oil and gas in Sable and its neighborhood. The well bottomed out, inconclusively for the oil prospectors and fortunately for the island's ecosystem, at 15,106 feet in Cretaceous sediments. (The Cretaceous era followed the Jurassic, starting about 144 million years ago, and finishing around 66 million years ago.) Although the well was a bust as a moneymaker, its core turned out to present a nice story-pole of the island's geologic history.

On the top were one thousand feet of modern (Quaternary) sediments. How modern is modern? Figuring the age of Sable's surface, or beach, sand accurately presents certain problems. Carbon-14 dating depends on organic material being present, but the only organic material available in sand are shells, and the ever-shifting, churning sands of Sable mean that older shells are commonly found at shallower depths than much younger ones, making an accurate chronology very difficult. But a newer technique, using the optically stimulated churning luminescence of quartz grains, shows that much of the sedimentary sand around Sable was established a mere three or four thousand years or so ago, and that the morphology hasn't changed in the last thousand years.[1] The upper layer has been tracked backward, through its composition and structure, to the continental mainland, and is assumed to have been pushed to its present location by postglacial currents; that is, it got where it is through erosion and drift. In the jargon of geologists, it is "a redistributed deposit produced by a transgressing sea across former subaerially reworked glacial deposits."[2] In plainer English, the sand was dumped there by rivers and currents in the aftermath of the glacial retreat.

Below the most recent geologic layer were three thousand feet of Tertiary sediments,[3] and below that no less than eleven thousand feet of Cretaceous sediments—the total depth of the sedimentary layers on top of the so-called basement rocks from the Devonian and Cambro-Ordovician eras (that is, older than 70 million years, and possibly as old as half a billion years) was estimated at twenty thousand feet.[4]

In all these thousands of feet, the core showed only one tiny deposit of organic life, the sole evidence that any living things had existed in the region. A thin layer of sandy peat was found around the sixty-foot level; radiocarbon dating put its age at around 10,900 years, which coincides closely with the accepted date for the ending of the last ice age. Something was either growing in the region then, or dead vegetation in huge quantities was brought down by the rivers. Both theories have their champions.

Apart from this one fleeting layer of bygone life, Sable Island and its underpinnings consist of nothing but sand. *Sable,* of course, is the French word for sand, and the island was justly named. There are no rocks on Sable, no craggy cliffs, no bedrock outcroppings, no shale or slate, no boulders, not even stones of any consequence, no soil. Just very fine gravel and sand, "Quaternary unconsolidated sands" to its very fundament, just a pile of sand, sitting in a very large puddle of water. How did it get to be there, in such a peculiar form? How is it maintained? *And why doesn't it just wash away?*

A partial answer can be found in the last glaciation and its aftermath. That glaciers can massively change the landscape is, of course, a commonplace of geology, and it is known that much of the North American continent, at least that part of it in higher and middle latitudes, was remade and reshaped by glaciers. The glaciers were so immense, and their reach so great (covering not just the poles but the temperate regions too) that the weight of the ice actually compressed the Earth's crust and the mantle beneath, squishing the globe at the poles and making it bulge at the equator. The glaciers absorbed so much ocean water that the sea level fell about four hundred feet. Even now, ten thousand years later, the last of the glaciers are still retreating, and in places the earth is still rebounding, at the fairly rapid rate of more than an inch a century and in a few places— around James Bay, for example—faster than that, faster even than the sea level is rising. Because of this, although the water is rising, it actually seems to be falling, as more and more land is exposed. Around Sable, by contrast, the rebounding has finished, and the earth is once again slowly relaxing, making it "sink" faster than the sea is rising.

As the glaciers moved across the landscape, the ice sheets carried with them huge volumes of sediment and ground up massive sections of the continental bedrock.[5] They also ground up any material trapped between the moving ice and the bedrock. Sometimes, if the original material was clay, it was ground into sand as fine as flour, which was then compacted. This deposit the geologists call lodgment till. Till is merely anything laid down or reworked by a glacier.[6]

Most glacial deposits were left on the margins. This is obvious enough: Glaciers work like bulldozers. When they advance or retreat, they shovel whatever loose material they find (or create) into a jumbled ridge of debris that follows the shape of the glacier's nose. If the glaciers are heavy enough, they can also "squish" material to their margins, and there's some evidence that this is what happened at Sable. The most recent ice there was "late ice," and therefore warmer, with more meltwater, which contributed to the outflow of sandy material from beneath the glacier.[7] These accumulations of till, whether simply piled into a ridge by the glacier's movement or revealed after it melts, are called moraines. There are all kinds of moraines; those at the end of the glacier's farthest advance are called, obviously enough considering their placement, terminal moraines. Smaller moraines, formed during periods when the glacier is hardly moving, or during smaller advances or retreats, are called recessional moraines. Glaciers are heaviest—again, obviously enough—at the center, where they are thickest and the weight of the ice will grind away almost any obstruction. At their fringes, where the ice is thinner and its weight therefore less, even smallish hills or valleys can divert their progress.[8] Plotting and dating terminal moraines is how geologists reconstruct the ebb and flow of the ice sheets.[9]

The continental shelf is, for the sake of convenience, usually divided into three main regions: an inner shelf along the coast; a central shelf of depressions and isolated banks; and an outer shelf, or outer banks, region, where Sable squats. Sable is heaped up on the very edge of the outer shelf, just before it becomes the continental slope and then the deeps, about thirty or forty miles to the island's south.

In the case of Sable Island, some things are still unknown. The geologist Lewis King tracked what he called the Scotian Shelf Drift, an extensive deposit of glacial till that overlies the central shelf in much of the Halifax–Sable Island area. King argued that the end, or terminal, moraine did not, however, reach all the way to Sable Island. Only its by-products (drifted sand and gravel) did that. To confuse matters somewhat, he did find evidence that earlier ice sheets in fact reached as far as modern Sable Island. He found evidence on the outer shelf of one or more Pleistocene-era ice sheets that had apparently covered the whole shelf, Sable included. "Multiple glaciation might have occurred, but the evidence is not clear."[10] Glaciers formed Sable therefore, but which glaciers remains unknown. It's still not known whether the deposit that now has Sable Island at its apex represents a local re-advance during a general retreat of ice from the entire shelf, or whether it marks the southern margin of the last major advance across the Maritime Provinces. Sable might therefore be a by-product of the original advance of glaciation, or its retreat, or merely a stutter in that retreat. Lewis King's son, Ned, a scientist at the Bedford Institute of Oceanography, subsequently accumulated considerable evidence of multiple generations of glaciation and is now convinced that, at least once, the Sable Island area did, in fact, represent the terminal moraine of a glacier's advance.

As the most recent ice age lowered the sea level about nineteen thousand years ago by trapping the water in continental ice sheets, the profile of the shoreline would have been very different. The inner part of the continental shelf, the relatively shallow plateau now adjacent to the mainland, was then part of the mainland itself. Many of the central and outer parts of the shelf would have protruded above the water as islands. One of these, and perhaps the largest, would have been an island that incorporated the modern Sable Bank and Emerald Bank areas. A few thousand or so years later, the ice melted and the sea level began rising again, and this much larger island began to shrink. Perhaps it still is shrinking; the sea level has continued to rise, slowly, since the end of the glacial period, and Sable Island, in turn, has been slowly submerging. As Ned King put it, "[By now] Sable should be drowned, but actually it is fairly stable and the dune system and shore-face system of supply sand is enough to keep it in equilibrium. But in the long term we know that it's losing ground, because once the island was the size of the whole bank."[11]

The material that now makes up Sable Island was carried there by meltwater, by erosion, and later by the ocean's currents. In the long glacial aftermath, these deposits—still as much made up of small rocks and gravel as of sand—were shifted and sifted, worked and reworked, by currents and tides, with the finer and more easily moved particles being carried farther and farther outward toward the edge of the shelf itself, where Sable now sits. Samples taken from the ocean floor show the progression clearly: The coarser gravel remained near the mainland shoreline, and the finer fractions of sand were deposited on the Sable Island Bank.[12]

Why did the sand stop where it did? Why didn't it continue until it reached the edge of the deeps, and itself drift into the abyss? Possibly, of course, some of it did—as indeed some of it is still doing. Or maybe the meltwater simply ran out. And perhaps the pattern of the ocean currents set up in the aftermath of the glaciation has conspired to keep Sable Island where it is, and what it is: the very edge of a glacial rubbish tip, dumped on the margins of North America as the planet retreated from its deep freeze and began, once more, to thaw.

Fifteen thousand years later, give or take a couple of centuries, tough-minded mariners began nibbling away at the awesome blanks still existing on the *mapa mundi*. For these early explorers, tracing the coastline of northeastern North America was more difficult than delineating coastlines elsewhere. Not only was the instrumentation primitive—that was true everywhere—but the weather was uncertain, prone to fog and sudden storms. The vanished glaciers had left the coast itself scored with bays and inlets, some of them deep and pocked with islands, reefs, bars, and "rackets" (shoals) to trap the unwary. By the sixteenth century, the shape of the continental shelf had been only roughly sketched in. The various underwater banks were generally known, mostly by the rich hauls of fish they yielded up, but why they were there, how deep they were below the surface, and what caused them and sustained them, were questions still without answer. Not surprisingly, the early maps were pretty hazy as to the continent's real shape and dimensions; sometimes the distance between Newfoundland and Nova Scotia was shown to be almost as great as that between Maine and Florida, with Cape Cod and Long Island showing as little protrusions, just barely south of Yarmouth.

What went for the coast as a whole went in spades for the still-more-mysterious sandbar that popped up off the ocean floor a hundred miles east of the continent. There are no points of reference, for one thing. No other land is in sight. And the weather is more than ordinarily atrocious—months can go by with a gale every day. Or, on the contrary, fog can settle in, and the sky can be blotted out for another six weeks. In between, gales and zero visibility can somehow be contemporaneous.

Mariners were running aground on Sable before real maps existed, of course. No one knows which vessel was the first, because the dead kept no records. Fagundes himself, after whom the island was briefly named, lost two vessels of a group of three to its sandbars, as we have already seen. The story was told only because of its unusual outcome: Some men survived.

No two of the early maps agreed on exactly where Sable was, or how it was oriented, or how big it was. After Pedro Reinel's 1502 map, the island made regular appearances in explorers' sketches, which were often rendered into splendid works of art by royal cartographers back home. It appeared on the maps of João Freire in 1546. It was there again on charts made by Lopo Homem (1540 and 1554), although he called it Fagunda Island, an homage to the family friend João Alvares Fagundes, Sable's most probable "discoverer." Just a few years after the Fagundes expedition, in 1548, the map by Giacomo Gastaldi, which was published in Europe, depicted Sable as a lengthy rampart guarding most of the eastern coastline of North America.[13] The same name, Fagunda, was adopted by the cartographers André Homem (1559) and Diogo Homem (1565). In his later maps, Diogo changed his mind and called it Santa Cruz (1565). It was shown as Isola della Rena (rena is Italian for sand) on a map of New France dated 1556, and as Y. Darena in 1566. Most of these maps showed the island at least a hundred miles from tip to tip, and sometimes considerably more.

Finally, in 1601, mapmakers agreed on a name: Isle de Sable, Sable Island,[14] though they did not yet agree on its size, or where, exactly, it was.

The closest mainland landfall to Sable Island is White Head, just south and west of Canso, at the strait between mainland Nova Scotia and Cape Breton Island. The port of Canso is 112 miles to the north-northwest of Sable, and occasionally, in the melancholy past, wrecked mariners succeeded through diligent rowing in a salvaged ship's boat to make their way to shore there. In 1737, for example, the *Boston Weekly News-Letter* reported that

> on July 17, the Catherine, 110 tons, Ireland bound for Boston [with] 202 persons, 98 [of whom] perished in the mighty water, 3 or 4 more died in the struggle to gain the beach, the master, mate, freighters, and five more of this sorrowful company ventured in her long boat to Canso which is about 32 leagues distance.[15]

Sable is due east of Halifax, the Nova Scotian capital, by 179 miles—the coastline of Nova Scotia runs not north-south but in a northeasterly and southwesterly direction. The coastline between Halifax and Canso and its Cape Breton extension is ragged, with deep inlets and many islands.

Between the island and the continental slope, and thereafter the deep ocean, are a series of contour ridges on the ocean floor, each about five or six miles apart, through which the seabed slopes steadily downward. Near Sable, the depth is about 100 feet. Thirty miles out it is somewhere around the 330-foot mark, and then it drops another 650 feet within six miles. Traversing these contours is the Harcourt Cameron Spur, due south of Sable, a drift of sand at around the 120-foot level, extending a shallower finger toward the edge of the continental shelf[16] Somewhere around forty to fifty miles south of the island, the seabed drops sharply; just a few miles farther south, soundings will not touch bottom before 6,500 feet, and sometimes a great deal more; 16,000 or 20,000 feet is not an uncommon depth only a hundred miles farther into the ocean. The seabed stays that deep until it rises again in the Mid-Atlantic Ridge.

The most dramatic feature of the ocean in Sable's neighborhood is without doubt the Gully, as it is simply called, a massive canyon cut sharply into the continental shelf. It almost touches the tip of Sable Island's eastern bar, before dropping away dramatically to the 1,300-foot line, then a lesser slope to 1,650 feet, and then even more sharply to 6,500 feet and beyond, deep into the abyss. It is so close to Sable that, geologically, it is the island's twin. In the wider world, the Gully's status, and therefore its fate, is still unclear; political promises were made at the start of the millennium to declare it (together with Sable Island itself) a Marine Protected Area, but there were countervailing pressures from the oil and gas companies operating nearby to allow exploratory drilling close to the Gully itself. Finally, in the spring of 2004, the declaration was made, but it left most stakeholders dissatisfied—long-line swordfishermen, gas prospectors, and environmentalists alike.

The Gully is the largest submarine canyon in the western North Atlantic and one of the deepest, about twenty-five miles long, ten miles wide, and more than eight thousand feet at its deepest. It is a huge gash in the shelf that pushes through the outer banks and into the middle shelf itself. At the head of the canyon is the Trough, a forty-by-twenty-mile shallow basin that links the canyon with inner regions of the Scotia Shelf.[17]

The Gully was chiseled out in the sediment and rock when much of the present shelf was above sea level. In preglacial times, at least thirty million years ago and perhaps much earlier, it would have been a drainage system for major continental rivers, including the ancestor of the much-punier modern St. Lawrence. But millions of years of geologic processes have dramatically changed its shape since then, deepening it considerably. Like the rest of the shelf, the Gully was carved out, as the ice ages receded, by the cutting action of trillions of tons of glacial ice. Eventually, it was no longer draining continental rivers but an enormous quantity of meltwater from the retreating glaciers. Also, judging from the scars on its sides, it was the erosional channel for ice as well as water. Several smaller feeder canyons penetrate the western side of the Gully, providing drainage channels into

This was the definitive version of Sable Island for more than a hundred years. Only those who stumbled ashore knew how wrong it really was.

De Laet notwithstanding, the early explorers would have seen no trees, no hills, no rocks, no inhabitants, no fauna but the birds and sea creatures like walrus and seals. What they saw would have been pretty much what is there today—except for the still-disputed matter of the island's actual size. Had they landed on the western end of the north beach, they would have been able to see the arc of the island through the ever-present, thin haze of spray and wind-blown sand, curving away to the left, fading into the horizon, toward the easternmost dunes. The sand on that beach is coarse, with a scattering of gravel and small pebbles, no bigger than a fingernail. Though rougher underfoot than the south beach, it is soft and curiously yielding to walk on, and makes for a difficult slog. Not quite as difficult a slog perhaps as the present road across the island, whose loose sand can be utterly exhausting, but difficult enough, much more difficult than simply traversing the gorse and grasses of the interior, which would have been easy then and still is, if you are careful of the horse dung.

The beach between low water and the highest storm surge is narrow on this side of the island, often no more than a few yards wide, and the dunes are tall and steep. A few have marram grass growing down almost to the beach level, and there are dozens of dramatic blowouts, deeply carved holes in the dune line, some of them filled with water. A typical walk along the beach will be a zigzag affair, veering inland to skip the lick of the surf, and to round clusters of seals. Most of the usual beach forms found universally on tidal sands are there, such as oscillation ripples and swash, or rill, furrows.[20] There is seldom seaweed, just pieces of driftwood, and even in the seventeenth century, there were spars and wrecked timbers from vessels gone aground and broken up. In modern times there is more clutter: posts from broken wharves and tree trunks that have drifted out here from the mainland, and bits of broken and torn fishing gear, floats, net fragments, chunks of formed Styrofoam of unknown purpose.

In the world of oceanographic studies—and in the much less formal world of beachcombers and thong-wearing beach-strollers—there are, classically, three kinds of beaches: a strip of sand along a rocky or cliff-ribbed coast; the outer margin of a marine or riverine accumulation, which is called a free beach; and the bars or sediment barriers that sometimes stretch for dozens or even hundreds of miles parallel to the coast, separating lagoons from the open sea and usually cut through by tidal inlets. Other beachlike formations—spits, points, and tombolos (which connect islands with the mainland)—also exist, but as subsets of one of the other main kinds.

But there is also a fourth kind of beach: Sable Island.

This is just a beach in the middle of nowhere attached to nothing and apropos of nothing, a beach attached to nothing but beach.

If it resembles anything at all, it resembles the dozens of phantom islands that populated mariners' maps from the very earliest days—rumors of islands, hints of islands that in reality had only a tenuous existence. Some were inspired by the numberless offshore banks and seamounts found everywhere in near-coastal oceans, extending from the Faeroe Islands to Spain, protrusions that bedeviled early sailors equipped with only rudimentary navigation gear. Occasionally, some portions of these underwater landscapes surfaced, however temporarily, just as portions of the seafloor now occasionally subside, submerging existing islands and alarming the mapmakers.[21] Phantom islands are mostly dismissed as the delightful, if innocent, visions of early mapmakers confronted with a blank sheet of paper on which nothing was securely located, but they are also sometimes real, if just as piquant. In living memory, for example, a Sable-like island appeared between Martha's Vineyard and Nantucket. It was big enough and sturdy-looking enough to hint at a future as a secure tax base, and occasioned an argument between the two communities as to which of them was the legitimate owner. Alas, before the squabble between the indignant selectmen could be resolved, the island vanished.

Some of the nearby fishing banks are could-have-been Sables—also glacial moraines, but drowned in the rising seas. At Quero Bank (latitude forty-four degrees, longitude fifty-seven degrees) is a large, narrow, submerged ridge forty miles long, which in form and direction is a counterpart of Sable Island. And at the summit of the Grand Bank of Newfoundland is a very dangerous shoal known as the Jessie Ryder, with only 3.25 fathoms (19.5 feet) of water.[22] There are also hints of a Sable-like presence in some of the easternmost Magdalen Islands, which are essentially an extension of the Gaspé Peninsula at the mouth of the St. Lawrence River—but only a hint, for those islands are rooted in rock and don't shift in the currents. And, of course, there is a resemblance, however fleeting, to the tip of Cape Cod (about which Henry David Thoreau wrote in 1865, "To the people of Provincetown at the tip of the Cape [Cod], the sea is their garden and the dog that growls at the door is the Atlantic Ocean").[23]

All beaches, Sable's included, share certain characteristics. The "swash line" is the upper limit reached by the highest sea level during big storms. The lower beach margin is beneath the water surface, either where sedimentary sand yields to rock—which does not apply in Sable's case—or, if the sediment cover extends into deep water, as the line where the strongest waves no longer sort and move the sand. Conventionally, this occurs at a depth equal to one-third the wavelength or ten times the wave height.

Beach profiles vary, of course, according to wave patterns, tide height, currents, and sediment composition and distribution. Above high-tide level, typically, are beach terraces, and above those are dunes. There is usually a shifting series of berms and ridges scored into the sand by recent storms. The frontal beach is a steep slope toward low tide. Below that, many beaches have another steep slope, if the nearby ocean is deep, or a long, flat, low, sandy, and shallow bottom, if the tides are high enough (greater than seven feet). In Sable's case, a third common below-tide formation operates: several parallel, submarine, longshore bars with intervening troughs. Many a mariner has had occasion to rue those bars in rough weather.

The width of Sable's north beach fluctuates dramatically. This, too, is typical. In quiet periods all beaches increase, and the "intertidal beach" acquires a backshore—a flattish, almost-horizontal profile. The sequence varies, but its overall pattern is predictable. In winter, the higher and rougher waves steal sand from the beach and move it offshore, yielding narrower, steeper beaches. Both Sable's east and west spits are shortened in this winter process. In summer, everything reverses. Gerry Forbes remembers the island increasing in length by almost a mile at each end over the course of a single summer.

The slope of a beach also determines the size of the sand that makes it up. Fine sand beaches, like Sable's south beach, are usually flat. Coarser sands are found on steeper beaches.[24]

Tides, winds, currents, and offshore waves operate as sorting mechanisms too, defining accumulations of lighter and of heavy mineral concentrates. Sable's north-beach sand, especially in sunlight, is pale peach, but, if you pick up a handful and leave it to dry before examining it closely, it will resolve into a mix of textures and colors, white, gray, rust-orange, and orange-red. The white is quartz, the most common of beach sands, indeed the most common ingredient of all sands, a crystalline mixture of silicon and oxygen, usually colorless but abraded into appearing white. So common in sand because it is abundant in rocks—from which sand is, of course, derived—it is comparatively hard and thus not readily worn down, and it is virtually insoluble in water. If you look at the sand grains through a microscope, or even a strong magnifying glass, they look like crumbling cubes of pink sugar shot through with veining, and you can begin to see what excites geologists. Here on a microscope's slide is a glimpse of history back to Paleolithic times, the quartz introduced through percolating waters that seeped through fractured rock, itself slow-cooling bedrock from deep underground, deep within a pluton of magma rising from the very basement rocks of the world.

The south beach has a very different profile. It's wider, for one thing—in many places hundreds of yards wide. (This is no doubt why, in modern times, it doubles as the island's landing strip.) It is flatter, and the dunes that line it are smaller, often no more than ten feet tall, and Lake Wallace is exposed along some of its length. The sand is finer than that on the north beach. Sheets of shallow water frequently cover much of it, shifting position as the wind direction changes, further complicating aircraft landings. The intervening sand between Lake Wallace and the ocean can't be much more than eight feet high, though it may have been higher in the past, just as Lake Wallace was larger. (Still, this is a lot of sand. In recent years when the weather was bad and the beach was flooded or too wet to land on, contract workers driven slightly mad by the end of their tobacco supply occasionally started to dig a trench from the lake to the sea, in a futile attempt to drain it and thereby create a safe landing field. Every time, the volume of sand defeated them, requiring far more earthmoving than they had envisaged, and so they retired, gloomy and tobacco-free, to their lodgings.)

The sand on the south beach is not just finer than that on the north beach, but also paler and whiter, being made up almost entirely of finely ground quartz; the predominant color in sunlight is pale yellow. On the western extremity of the beach, the yellow-white quartz blows over bruises of red-tinged violet magnetite-garnet-tourmaline, which in places form layers, some as much as eighteen inches thick, which are being licked away from beneath the dunes. Magnetite is a black iron oxide with distinct north and south poles when magnetized; the ancients called it lodestone and it has been known since at least 500 BC.[25] If the garnet grains had been larger, they would have been a glorious, transparent deep red; here they are ground and abraded, and a dull reddish brown, rather like old paprika. (There aren't enough precious stones here to excite even the most optimistic collector.) Garnet is far from unknown on beaches; in Namibia entire beaches are made up of garnet grains, giving the littoral a startling rose appearance. Tourmaline, for its part, is a semiprecious mineral, appearing in colors that vary from red and pink to green, blue, or even black. At the western extremity of the island, these curious strata are found only on the south beach, but at the eastern tip they're on both beaches. Their color depends on how damp they are. Wet quartz is colorless, and so the strong violet garnet-tourmaline coloring dominates. As it dries, the abrasions on the quartz reappear as white, giving the sand a pepper-and-salt appearance, still darker than the rest of the dunes, but not as violet. In the hand, it is a dark, lustrous purple while wet, but it dries to a paler mauve.

On both sides are lines in the dunes which look oddly like old tarmac, almost like an ancient parking lot chewed away at its edges. It is friable to the touch, made up of ancient vegetation, covered and compacted by the sand. It's only grass and bushes, though. There's no sign that any early forest has ever been turned up by this erosion.

If the "ground" on Sable is sand—if in the precise diction of the geologist, "the earth materials composing the surficial geology of the island are quite homogeneous . . . a sand of particle size that ranges from about 0.003 to 0.07 of an inch in diameter"[26]—is there anything on the island that might legitimately be termed soil? Can it really be soil, at least in the farmer's sense of the word, if the surface of the island has "a deficiency of all the common soil fractions with the exception of sand-sized mineral particles"?[27] Do those friable layers of "tarmac" count?

In the past there have been fleeting references to some peatlike substance. Barbara Christie, the reigning modern expert on Sable's horses, has referred in her writings to the "black and peaty depths of the island."[28] Writing in 1894, the Reverend George Patterson found, "descending into the central valley . . . a soil of black, peaty texture to the depth of fifteen or eighteen inches. . . . it may [further] be mentioned that fresh water is found anywhere in the sand by digging to the depth of about eighteen inches."[29] A few years later, Janet Carnochan discovered that "where the gardens are so productive there is a mingling of earth with sand. At the spott shewn as the site of the old French gardens the soil seemed a dark loam."[30]

Carnochan might be forgiven for having a hazy memory. She never meant to go to Sable Island in the first place and was writing some forty years after the fact. A schoolteacher from Niagara Falls, she had taken it into her head to do a version of the then-fashionable grand tour, and embarked in New York for Europe in 1879. Alas, her ship never passed Sable Island, where it ran aground and stuck fast. Carnochan made it safely to shore, and for the next five weeks, until the survivors were taken off, the young schoolteacher's grand tour was reduced to wanderings along Sable's beaches and poking about in the interior; her notes were later published by the Historical Society of Niagara Falls, to which community she subsequently returned and where she resumed her duties as schoolmarm.

Geographers and geologists were (and still are) skeptical of these peaty, loamy assertions. There are "organic horizons" on the island—those "tarmacs"—but their age and history remain a matter of speculation. There's a general acceptance of localized manufacturing of a quasi soil; many of the human communities that lived on the island, on and off, for several hundred years, started gardens and fertilized them with organic compost, including sea dung (seaweed, on those rare occasions it was washed up on shore) and, of course, animal manure, both from cattle and the horses. No doubt this is the loam that Carnochan found at the "old French gardens," whose site is now lost. A geologic study in 1971 found no organic deposits from the Pleistocene exposed anywhere on Sable; the only such deposit was found through the Mobil test well, at sixty feet, dating back about eleven thousand years.

But other such "horizons," which seems merely to mean layers, are found at sea level and in sections on the slopes of dunes. This is common enough on beaches. Such peat levels often appear in lagoons behind barrier beaches. If a storm pushes water into a flat, low-lying area, plants may grow in the brackish water. Eventually, their roots bind together, and their leaves and stems trap sand, dropping it as silt around the plants. "As the plants go through their annual cycles of birth and death, their carcasses fall to the bay floor. The weight of the water and the sand compresses them into peat. More sand washes onto the peat, and the dune slowly grows backwards and covers it."[31]

The geologist Terry Hennigar, in his study of Sable Island, maintained that the layers he saw on the erosional faces of dunes were two hundred to three hundred years old—well within the periods of human occupation. He speculated that stabilized or heavily vegetated areas (whether natural or introduced through human cultivation) had been suddenly buried by windblown sand. That is, what had been a field of marram grass and blueberry bushes—or a bog—could be overwhelmed by a sudden sandstorm and buried, thereafter turning slowly into a sandy peat.[32] There are plenty of well-documented examples of such burying, many of them indicating that the notion of stabilized surfaces on Sable should be treated with a great deal of caution. In 1963, for example, the Canadian Hydrographic Service established a series of benchmarks and triangulation stations on Sable to map the topography and get a better sense of its dimensions and stability. One of them was set up on a stabilized dune at sixty-two feet above sea level, and well anchored. Eight years later, in 1971, a search for this benchmark by the Hennigar team of the Nova Scotia Department of the Environment found it buried under four feet of sand. They estimated from this that the sand had accumulated at a rate of six inches a year, but it is equally possible—more than probable, in fact—that the whole layer arrived in one or two terrific storms.[33]

Behind the beaches are the dunes. All sand beaches have dunes, except those that are backed by high cliffs; dunes, after all, are really just sand shaped into ridges by the wind under the influence of gravity, not very different from the formations that occur when water moves over a loose bed. Small "dunes" appear as well on the beds of rivers and tidal estuaries, and as sand waves on the continental shelves beneath shallow seas.

There are some differences between beaches and dunes, though. Beaches are ill-sorted sands, what are called bimodal—generally a mix of sand and fine gravel. Dunes, by contrast, being windblown, are finely sorted, and the measurement of sand grains in dunes vary over only a fairly narrow range, from between 0.008 to 0.016 inches.

Sable Island is itself a dune, in its way, as well as a beach, and thus a dune with dunes of its own. And while some of its dunes are anchored by vegetation, others move, just as the island itself stirs and shifts in response to the planetary forces that beset it. On the north beach, as we have seen, the dunes are high, up to eighty-five feet tall, their slipfaces steep, many of them overgrown with grasses and pierced by gaps and blowouts. Along the arc of the south beach the dunes are lower, usually not more than eight feet or so, and not nearly as steep.

There are three main types of dunes: *Seifs* are long ridges of sand, generally aligned in the direction of the prevailing wind; *barchans* are moving U-shaped dunes, with the tips of the arms reaching downwind and the slipface inside the crescent; and *parabolic* dunes are also rough crescents in shape, but with the arms reaching to windward and the steep slipface outside the crescent. There are no seifs on Sable, and only an occasional parabola. The island is made up mostly of compound or coalesced barchans that have flowed together to form a sea of transverse dunes, in which their individual crescent shapes are far from obvious. Sable's barchans are further confused through erosion and because many are blurred by their plant cover. Barchans gradually migrate downwind, through erosion on the windward side and deposition on the leeward side.

The most famous dune on Sable, apart from the island itself, is known simply as the Bald Dune. In fact, there are two other dunes on the island equally bald of vegetation, but *the* Bald Dune is a barchan located on the eastern third of Sable (just southeast of the eastern light). It is moving steadily southeast, crossing the island, driven by northwest gales. From the side, it looks like a squashed dome, about 65 feet tall and perhaps 330 to

500 feet across. The leading edge is steep, and the arms are no more than a couple of hundred feet when they're most prominent at the end of winter. The trailing edge was attached to the north beach in the mid-1970s and is now about one thousand feet to the southeast, which means it has moved at a rate of about thirty-three feet per year. This might seem fast, but it's well within the records set by some of the traveling barchans in the Sahara, which have been clocked at a speedy one hundred feet a year.[34] In a decade or two, the Bald Dune will have marched itself out to sea.

CHAPTER THREE

Its feckless Colonizers

Colonizers, hapless castaways,

stranded ships, curious apparitions,

lurid tales, a mad monk

In time, the Portuguese presence in the North Atlantic diminished as the mother country slipped into its long somnolence. Some far-flung colonies—Angola, Macau—were preserved, but the itch for exploration and conquest faded into the past (Prince Henry the Navigator's lugubrious figure peering out from history books, no longer the animating inspiration he had been in his lifetime). For northern America, and by default for Sable, the seventeenth century belonged to the French, and to a lesser extent to the English, through their New England proxies.

The main purpose of the French adventurers, of course, was to carve colonies from the American landmass to the west, but some of them—either en passant or deliberately—did have brushes with the deadly little island in the Atlantic. Their presence on Sable was sometimes fleeting, occasionally so much so that whether they were there at all has been disputed. One of those was the person variously styled as the "baron de Leri and de St.-Just," the "baron de Levy," or the "baron de Lery," who first appeared in a 1606 account by Marc Lescarbot, a lawyer and historian then living at Port Royal, in Acadia (now Annapolis Royal, in Nova Scotia). In his flowery way, Lescarbot recounted how, in the middle years of the sixteenth century, exact date unspecified, "a nobleman of Champagne, the Baron de Leri and de St.-Just, having a heart inclined to deeds of high emprise, desired to form a settlement in those parts and to lay the foundations of a French colony." Alas, his luck was bad and, during the long voyage, food and water for his pigs and cattle ran out, so he put them ashore on Sable Island. Or did he? Another story says he put the animals ashore on Sable Island and at Canso. But if he could reach Canso, which is on the mainland, why did he have to abandon them there? Others have doubted the whole story. Barbara Christie, for one, sniffs that "there is all but no evidence to support the existence of the Baron's expedition, and by one authority [unspecified] it has been termed utterly improbable."[1]

At least one writer, Terry Hennigar, says the incident happened in 1539, though he cites no sources.[2]

But if you examine the baron's background, his expedition seems not only plausible but probable.

He has been identified as Guillaume III de Miremont, the baron de Lhéry and Gueux, who was known to have married a daughter of François de Salazar, the baron de St.-Just and seigneur de Sauvages, Clages, Baigneaux, and Courson-le-Châtel. Gueux is a small town just west of Reims; Lhéry is another small town, a little farther west. Whether there were any connections with the Protestants of Holland is unclear, but Gueux, for its part, is the French name for Geuzen, which was a Calvinist Dutch guerrilla force that pursued a revolt against Spanish rule. Still, it's the Salazar connection that is most interesting, because the Salazar family were originally Basques from the Spanish Pyrénées, and the Basques of the period most certainly knew about, and were interested in, Newfoundland and the cod fishery, and had the means to do something about it. In addition, three other men with Salazar connections were known to have attempted colonizing forays to North America, some of them with great success: Jean de Biencourt, baron de Poutrincourt, Charles La Tour, and his father, Claude La Tour. They all came from St.-Just in Champagne, a little barony at the junction of the Seine and the Aube rivers, southwest of Paris and twenty-five miles from Troyes. Even more significant, Lhéry's wife was a cousin of Jeanne de Salazar, who was the mother of Poutrincourt—who inherited the St.-Just domain and became moderately famous as the effective founder of Port Royal in Acadia.[3]

Lhéry's Calvinist connection, too, is not without its significance. Other, sometimes political, waves washed up on Sable's remote beaches, and among them were the outer ripples of Europe's Wars of Religion, whose seething animosities created widespread dissatisfaction with the status quo, and a reckless willingness to risk all in foreign adventures. Central to all this was the colorful figure of Henry IV. By the mid–sixteenth century, France was teetering on the brink of ruin, but to its eternal good fortune Henry of Navarre succeeded to the throne, in the nick of time though by fluke and murder, after the War of the Three Henrys. Henry had only been second cousin to the direct line and had never expected to succeed to the throne; the way was opened for him by a series of fortuitous assassinations of the other two Henrys, the duke of Guise and Henry III.

At the height of his reign, in 1598, the marquis de La Roche, a Breton nobleman sometimes styled as Troilus de La Roche de Mesgouez, dreaming his own dreams of grand estates and seeking personal disentanglement from the snare of the religious wars, decided to renew the letters patent he had received from Henry III twenty years earlier, and determined to settle an estate in New France. La Roche was a courtier of note and hovered on the periphery of the courts of Henry III and Charles IX. In the Wars of Religion, he fought against the Catholic League of the

Guises, was deprived of his estates, and had them renewed when Henry IV came to the throne.

Henry the Protestant, and sometimes Catholic, king, himself hailed from Basque lands. He was born in Pau, in the modern French province of Pyrénées-Atlantiques, son of a Bourbon princeling and the queen of what remained of Navarre after Ferdinand and Isabella had dissected it. One can easily believe in his eagerness to have a colony of his very own in the New World, as well as in his determination to reward a Protestant lieutenant, who had spent three years "groaning in the dungeons of Nantes" on his behalf.[4] La Roche, sensibly enough, seemed to be thinking less of his sovereign lord and more of his own ambitions, as his letters patent were styled "Lieutenant-General of the King of Canada, of Hochelaga, of the Newfoundlands, of La Bras d'Or, of the River of the Great Bay of Norumbega and the Isle of Sable and grounds adjacent of the aforesaid provinces and rivers." So many sonorous names for so little known a place! Backed by an assigned monopoly of trade in this vast and untracked region, the marquis set about recruiting his colonists. "Finally, in an enterprise driven more by hope than reason, sixty men and women were taken from the jails of Normandy and sent to establish a settlement on Sable Island, a desolate and barren and storm-swept sandbank in the North Atlantic a hundred miles east of the Nova Scotia Peninsula."[5]

In fact, it was not really a settlement but a military and trade outpost, and this mention of women seems to have been wrong; there was no village with women and children, no attempt at domesticity, only a fort with storehouses and living quarters. The colony was otherwise described as "fifty ex-convicts and beggars, and ten soldiers."[6] La Roche himself never settled there. Some writers have assumed he took one horrified look around and turned for home, leaving his hapless colonists stranded, to make their way as best they could, living partly off the great red cattle of the long-ago "Portugals," a living larder. Others say he had taken 250 prisoners with him, unloading 50 at Sable Island and pushing on with the rest to explore Acadia, looking for someplace more salubrious, and was dashed back to Europe in a great tempest.

More probably, he went back for more people and more supplies, leaving his settlers in good order. He had landed them on the north side of the island, "close to a small river . . . which La Roche named Boncoeur"—a nice imaginative touch, since there are no rivers or even streams on Sable. Before he left, he had overseen the construction of several dwellings and a store. The island had plenty of drinking water and food; not just the "cattel & swyne," but fish, seabirds, and seals. The colonists planted a garden—perhaps Janet Carnochan's "French gardens"—and the marquis had left plenty of clothes and wine. The soldiers were authorized to seize ships that did not have permission from La Roche to fish or trade in furs.

But sometime in the winter of 1602 things started to go wrong. La Roche's patrons at the French court lost their influence, and a rival had him thrown into jail. He lost contact with his colony, and the colonists lost their contact with the outside world.

What happened next is far from clear. Perhaps there was a mutiny, perhaps disease, perhaps a mix of both. The soldiers, under one Querbonyer, were either killed or died without help. The numbers of survivors steadily diminished, and when La Roche's captain, Thomas Chêtodel, arrived in 1603 with a boatload of provisions, he found only eleven wretched, half-starved men clinging to survival. They were taken off and shipped home and displayed as long-haired curiosities at the court of King Henry IV; they resembled, one admiring courtier wrote, the river-gods of old. Before he lost interest, Henry pardoned them all for past crimes and gave each a purse containing fifty écus.[7]

Many legends have accumulated about this sorry tale. La Roche himself was not as charitable as his sovereign, nor was Chêtodel. The captain was said to have tried to cheat the settlers out of the furs they had accumulated on the island, presumably Champlain's "beautiful black foxes." He was sued and had to repay the value of the pelts. La Roche, for his part, was supposed to have wanted the survivors hanged, "since all 48 men who died on the island had been murdered." In any case, the men were left at liberty, and La Roche died three years later in 1606, a ruined man.[8]

Another popular tale was a nice piece of antiroyalist propaganda, and concerned a married woman called Madeleine, otherwise unidentified, who supposedly spurned the advances of the ever-amorous Henry IV (not for nothing was he nicknamed *le vert galant*), and for her refusal was ordered to join the La Roche colonists on their perilous voyage to Sable. There she was struck down by one of the men during a fit of jealous rage at the time of the alleged uprising. It was said that her husband, upon hearing of her death, made the voyage to Sable and, full of anguish and mourning, soon died. His ghost took to roaming the island at night in the mists, and his haunting lamentations for his wife and maledictions against King Henry were heard for years afterward.[9] Mariners' tales about a headless Frenchman seen wandering the island were commonplace, a nice image with a deep provenance in French history.[10] And there is hardly a wrecked French fort in the Americas that didn't have a headless Frenchman of its own.

The most charming of these La Roche legends involves a Franciscan monk, who in this version of events had been part of the colonizing effort. By the time Chêtodel arrived to pick up the survivors, this unnamed monk had fallen gravely ill. "I have no long time to live," he is recorded as saying, "perhaps only a few hours. I shall die here in the little hut which I have constructed, in which I have prayed for five years, as did the hermits of the desert. The winds and the sands will charge themselves with my burial." The good friar had clearly underestimated his toughness of sinew, however, and recovered his health, living for many years afterward as a hermit on Sable. "Prayer and meditation filled his hours and he tended his lit-

tle garden faithfully. He gathered shellfish and berries, and with his vegetables, this made up his daily provision." The numerous shipwrecks on the
island afforded him the opportunity of exercising his charitable instincts,
"and fishermen from Canso, Sambro, La Have and other Acadian ports
visited him to bring news, to see the Ways of the Cross he had erected, and
to receive the sacraments at his holy mass." When he died and where he is
buried are not part of the story, but a hundred years ago his spirit was still
said to hover over the island, and fishermen still caught glimpses of him
marching slowly along the shore, or on the dunes, reciting his rosary, or
"often standing or on his knees on the cliffs, examining the sea tossed with
tempest, watching and praying for the unfortunate mariners in danger of
perishing."[11]

CHAPTER FOUR

Its Serial Shipwrecks

The deadly effect of Sable's secretive

and treacherous nature, as well as its

uniquely strategic location

Sable Island, the land where the horses now run wild, may be a delicate arc of sand hills some twenty-five miles long and less than a mile wide; but Sable Island, the mariner's bane, is quite different in size and scope, at once altogether larger, and more secretive and treacherous.

The central portion of the island, which is where the grasses grow and the horses graze and humans live, on those increasingly rare occasions they are present, includes the east and west sand pits, still above water but washed over too frequently for any vegetation to grow, except for stubborn and ephemeral sandwort. These spits are nevertheless substantial enough, and in recent years have been measured at more than four miles at the east end and almost five on the west. The numbers, though, can be misleading, because the length of each spit can change by up to four or five miles in a single savage storm. Beyond these spits are the east and west bars, submerged extensions of the island, pushing out into the ocean seventeen miles to the east, another eighteen miles to the west—numbers which are also subject to abrupt change. These bars have a depth of water that varies between five and sixteen fathoms, but which, disconcertingly and suddenly, can switch overnight to hardly anything at all, by a complicated series of forces that include tides, winds, currents, and sedimentation. And as though that weren't enough, there are also east and west bar extensions, eleven miles and twenty-three miles respectively. Were they above ground, these bars and their extensions would substantially increase the island's mass. It would be, in fact, six or eight times as wide and at least three times as long—perhaps eight to ten miles wide by a hundred or so long.

Obviously, then, all these numbers should be taken as approximate. Aerial photos of the island in 1981 showed that tip-to-tip in a straight line it was 23 miles, and measured along the arc it was 30.3 miles. The west bar was shorter than the east (about 9.1 miles to 12 miles). The extensions were 13.1 miles (east) and 15.2 miles (west). That would make the island and its extensions somewhere around 75 to 80 miles along the arc.[1]

The west bar's topography is complex—albeit terrifyingly simple for mariners. A few patches that nearly break the surface lie within a mile of the spit, and thereafter the bar is covered by between five and ten fathoms of water, with heavy breakers in bad weather, and even in a mild blow by a great ripple or cross-sea that is deadly to a vessel caught in it. The water then deepens to sixteen fathoms, and then again shoals to ten fathoms, beyond which the water gradually deepens to the west for 7.5 miles. Even then, however, you're not safe: In 1902 the fishing schooner *Maxine Elliot* was anchored in thirty-seven fathoms, out of sight of land, when its dories found a steep shoal 250 feet long covered with a mere two and a half fathoms of water.

In bad weather the east bar is marked by heavy breakers, although it is six to ten fathoms below the surface in a calm sea.

This is not nearly enough for safety. Captain Angus Walters, one of the greatest skippers to sail the Atlantic and commander of the legendary racing schooner *Bluenose*, commenting on the wreck of a sister schooner in three fathoms (eighteen feet) of water, said that fishing vessels like his "never willingly go into 18 feet of water." He added, "[In a blow] it shoals at 15 fathoms, [and] they consider 15 fathoms the limit of safety; they want 25. It is by seas breaking from the bottom that Sable Island destroys the fishermen afar off."[2]

Two other factors compounded the dangers. The first was the simple fact of the island's location in the sailing and transportation universe. At latitude 43.9 degrees north and longitude 60.1 degrees west, Sable was at the center of the Great Circle Route from the New England ports to Europe, not just the most direct route but also, because of the prevailing currents, the easiest. Even skippers who knew its dangers were obliged to take it. Just as freightliner pilots must do today, skippers not only had to watch their supplies of water and fresh food, and therefore the health of their passengers and crew, but were also impelled to worry about the ticking costs of delivery; pursemasters were quick to sack a skipper who didn't pinch his pennies. For all these reasons, the winds and the currents both conspired to convince mariners that the route past Sable was the most efficient.

The other factor was the island's place in the ocean's currents, caught between northeast-bound and southwest-bound water. The currents are partly responsible for preserving and shaping the island itself, but the intricate patterns they create around Sable were endlessly mysterious and therefore perilous to mariners, who often believed they were safely past, then found themselves sucked back into the vortex and trapped on the bars, where they were pounded to pieces by the waves.

A set of sailing directions for the region published for private yachts-
men in 1901 urged extreme caution.

> At each end of the island are dangerous bars, upon which the sea breaks
> in bad weather. These bars are extremely difficult to avoid when at a
> short distance from the north side of the island, and caught with a strong
> northerly wind; and if to this we add the suddenness of the dense fogs
> prevalent at some seasons of the year in the vicinity, a sailing vessel un-
> der such circumstances is placed in great peril, and nothing but the most
> careful navigation can extricate it.[3]

If they were approaching from the south, mariners were advised to make
sure they had "the advantage of a commanding breeze, on account of the
strong and uncertain tides and currents. Vessels seldom anchor off this side
of the island, because of the prevailing southerly swell, and the consequent
difficulty of landing." An 1899 survey by the Canadian authorities dismissed the whole idea of a southerly beaching: "Landing is in general im-
practicable on the south side, excepting after several days of northerly
wind." On the other side of the island, of course, northerlies were the
problem. "Caught within the horns of this crescent in a strong northerly
gale," the *Sailing Directions* say, "the situation of a sailing vessel would be extremely perilous; for the ebb tide sets to southward directly on and over the
bar at a rate of 1.5 or 2 knots, and when accelerated by the wind, much
faster; whilst the flood stream runs at a much less rate in the opposite direction." Outside the north beach are multiple shallow ridges of sand, dangerous to pass in a boat when any sea is running; there can be as many as
twelve of these ridges, or as few as three, depending on the vagaries of the
storms and currents. One can land safely, the 1899 surveyors said, "only in
southerly winds, and after some continuance of fine weather."[4]

Fine weather, however, was hard to come by.

At 9:40 pm I [Joshua Slocum] raised the sheen only of the light on the west end of Sable Island, which may also be called the Island of Tragedies. The fog, which till this moment had held off, now lowered over the sea like a pall. I was in a world of fog, shut off from the universe. I did not see any more of the light. By the lead, which I cast often, I found that a little after midnight I was passing the east point of the island, and should soon be clear of dangers of land and shoals.[5]

How far Sable's bars extend, and with what treachery they can seize hapless vessels, was poignantly confirmed by a newspaper report from Boston in the fall of 1927, a month or two after the great storm later called the Gales of August, during which the glorious schooner *Columbia* vanished, lost with all hands.

WRECKAGE OF THE COLUMBIA
HAS BEEN REPORTED

Boston, Oct. 11—Captain Iver Carlson, of the Boston fishing schooner *Acushla*, reported this afternoon on arrival at the fish pier that he had located the last resting place of the schooner *Columbia,* which was lost in a hurricane on August 24th with her captain and crew. The wreck, Captain Carlson states, is 23 miles northwest of Sable Island. In this location last Saturday he saw a spar sticking out of the water which in type and timber was similar to the *Columbia*'s boom. Carlson steered his vessel as close to the spar as he dared hoping to find a mark on it which would definitely identify it as coming from the lost vessel. But he was unable to get close enough to it to note any such indications. Captain and crew of the *Acushla* watched the spar with feelings of awe as they reflected that beneath it might be the sleek hull of the vessel now a tomb for Captain Wharton and his courageous crew of a score or more of fishermen.

Early Sunday by use of boats and considerable effort this spar, which proved to be that of the ill-fated schooner, was secured. It was brought here by Captain Carlson.

After tying up at the pier, Carlson went to the Government Hydrographic office where he reported the location of the wreck and said it was a menace to navigation. "A government cutter will be sent to the spot and the wreck will be blown up."[6]

CHAPTER FIVE

Its Tides and Complex Currents

Among the forces that sustain and

transform the island are massive

movements of water

The dangerous sandbar called Sable has snared many a sailor, but it has been and is itself beset by planetary forces—some of them of enormous size and very long duration, others as immediate and ferocious as a gale punching a hole in a dune. The longest and most massive of these were the ice ages themselves. If you reckon in geologic time (in which the passing of a million years is an eyewink), the rising and falling of the sea levels caused by the advancing and retreating ice sheets on the continental shelves counts, in its way, as a tide or a wave; ice-age fluctuations are examples of the longest-period waves that we know, fifteen thousand years and more. These immense ice "waves" and their grinding force created the coastline, the Scotia Shelf, and Sable Island in the first place.

Tides represent a tiny speeded-up version of this process. Tides are waves too—waves with a period of approximately half the planet's circumference. Or, looked at another way, tides are the mirror image of waves:

With normal waves, the wave form moves through the sea; with the tides, the wave form is stationary and the sea moves through the wave. The effect of tides on landmasses is generally small and barely noticeable. But at different times, depending on conditions, they erode beaches or add to them, and combined with the other forces at work—winds and currents— have played a role in shaping Sable. By themselves, tides don't carry huge amounts of sediment, unless they're affected in turn by the topography of the coastline, such as inlets or estuaries. (Tides may have had some effect on the silting up of Lake Wallace, for example.) But they do redirect the large quantities of sedimentary sand carried by waves and currents, and they also refocus wave energy by changing the depth of water and therefore the height and position of the shoreline that is assaulted by the waves.

The second effect, the redirection, is the greatest, however; tides change the zone in which waves and longshore currents can do their work. Tides are the gravitational effects of the Moon and the Sun on the Earth's waters. Both pull the water upward when the Earth rotates below them, though the Moon's pull is much greater, it being considerably nearer. The result is two pairs of tidal bulges in the ocean, both behaving—at least to observers on shore, who can't feel themselves whirling along as the Sun and Moon stand still—as long-period waves. The Earth rotates once in twenty-four hours, but the Moon is also orbiting the Earth in the general direction of the Earth's rotation, though slightly slower, so the two lunar-induced wave crests occur about every twelve hours and fifty or so minutes apart. Nor is the tide highest exactly when the Moon is directly overhead; the rotation of the Earth drags the tidal bulge along with it in the direction of rotation, so high tide somewhat precedes the Moon's apogee.[1]

Although it is still impossible, even with sophisticated supercomputers, to predict with accuracy tidal heights and effects on a purely local basis (too many variables, so local tide tables are perforce the result of obser-

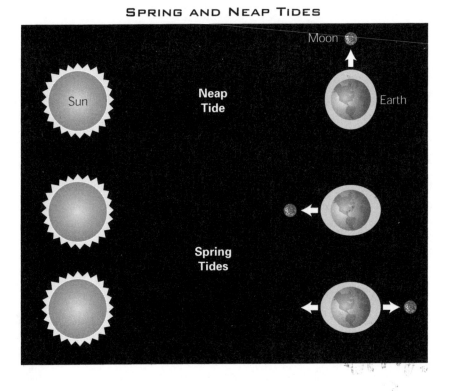

vation, not prediction), the mechanics of broader tidal fluctuations are well known, and mariners have for centuries carried tidal tables in their chart rooms. The highest of high tides occurs, obviously enough, when the solar and lunar tidal bulges are in sequence, lined up with each other. This happens twice each month: once when the Sun and Moon are on opposite sides of the Earth (that is, when the Moon is full), and again roughly two weeks later, when the Sun and the Moon are aligned on the same side of Earth (new Moon). This phenomenon is called *syzygy*. These superimposed solar and lunar tides are called, for no obvious reason, spring tides, while the lowest tides, which occur when the Moon is in quarter or three-quarter phase, are called neap tides. Even during a spring tide, however, the two tidal bulges are usually unequal, which happens because the Moon, most of the time, is not in the geometric plane of the equator. When the Moon's orbit does align with the plane of Earth's equator, two consecutive high tides are more or less equal. This happens twice a year, but on specific days that vary from year to year.[2] A further refinement in the calculus of tides is caused by the fact that the Moon's orbit around the Earth is not quite circular. Every 27.55 days, the Moon makes its nearest approach to the Earth, its *perigee*, which increases the tidal pull, making the tides rise higher and fall lower. The cycles of perigee and syzygy occasionally coincide, accounting for tides that may rise 40 percent above normal.

When the tidal "wave" arrives at a coastline (or, really, when the coast arrives at the wave), the slope of the ocean floor forces the tide upward, and slows it down, until it begins to heap up on itself. When it arrives at the shore, it may raise the water locally by between five and ten feet, occasionally more. Where the tidal flow is narrowed by landmasses, the surge can be much higher. The Gulf of Maine, for example, funnels the rising water into the Bay of Fundy, which narrows from seventy-five miles at its mouth to twenty-eight miles at Cape Chignecto, its narrowest point. More than 110 billion tons of water enter and leave the bay each day, and its narrowing shape forces that water upward, forming the world's highest tides, as much as fifty feet above low water.[3] On the open ocean, tidal bulges are generally much smaller, averaging a foot or so in height, and on small midocean islands, tidal fluctuations are about the same. Tidal effects on the shoreline of such islands is therefore modest.

Sable Island, which is within the confining reach of the continental shelf, has tides greater than this, but still smaller than mainland tides, averaging about four feet or so. On the island's south beach, which is flat and wide but protected by a berm at about the high-water mark, tidal ebbs and flows make little difference to the beachscape. But on the narrower and steeper north beach, exceptionally high tides can reach the dune line. The effect, especially when combined with lateral longshore flows, rips, and storm surges, is that they can and do gnaw away at the undersides of the dunes, tearing at their underpinnings.

The ocean's currents are a force of more direct consequence.

Mariners have known for centuries that the ocean is not still, even in calm waters and gentle breezes—just as they have known what landsmen never really understand: that the Earth is not a series of continents separated by water but a planet of water interrupted by a few landmasses (and that we should be calling it Water and not Earth).[4] The ocean's currents are its rivers, and they have predictable flows within complicated patterns; again, mariners have known of these rivers for almost as long as people have gone down to the sea, although their true intricacy is only recently understood, and there are still many surprises.

This knowledge of currents has not been confined to the intrepid explorers of western Europe. Arab sailors used the Equatorial Current and its countercurrent to make their way from the East African coast to India and back again, as early as the Middle Ages; Chinese junks made the difficult voyage between Asia and the Indonesian islands using an eddy from the South Equatorial Current in the Pacific. And the most eminent king of the West African empire of Mali became king mostly because his predecessor had become transfixed with the notion that there was a river in the middle of the sea.

Mansa Musa, the king in question, recounted the tale to the son of the sultan of Cairo, the gist of which was published by the Cairo encyclopedist Al-Omari in 1340. "If I have become the master of Mali," Musa confided to his host, "it is only because my predecessor refused to believe that the ocean was infinite." The predecessor was Abu Bakari II, the Voyager King. This

restless and energetic monarch spent many hours staring out over the Atlantic, which he came to see as an affront to his ambitions and a barricade to
his more or less endless expansion. Somewhere out there, he believed, must
be other lands for a king to conquer, other sources of wealth to accumulate.
"Therefore," Mansa Musa said, "my predecessor sent a preliminary recon-
naissance fleet of four hundred ships towards the unknown and shadowy
horizon. Only one returned, but that one told stories of a mysterious river
in the middle of the ocean." This was enough for Abu Bakari; he assembled
yet another fleet of pirogues and set off westward, never to be seen again.[5]

In 1593, Sir Richard Hawkins left England on a voyage to the king-
doms of China and the East Indies by way of the Strait of Magellan, at
the tip of South America, and the South Seas. In his observations on the
voyage, published in 1622, he remarked on one of the most famous of
these oceanic rivers, the Gulf Stream:

> The currant that setteth betwixt, New-found-land and Spaine runneth
> also East and West, and long time deceived many, and made some to
> count the way longer, and other shorter, according as the passage was
> speedie or slowe; not knowing that the furtherance or the hinderance of
> the current, was cause of the speeding or slowing of the way.[6]

By the time of Ben Franklin, it no longer "deceived many," or anyone at
all; Franklin recognized it as a powerful stream that could be used to
speed up the delivery of mail and manufactured goods from America to
Europe.[7]

Currents—or at least surface currents down to about 330 feet, which is
what mariners depend on—are wind-reared. Differential heating of the
globe is what gives rise to global wind patterns, and because these patterns
are relatively stable and persistent, they in turn create permanent movement of water, the currents. Moving water is subject to the distortions of

the Coriolis effect, which deflects the moving water through the energy imparted by the globe's spin. In the Northern Hemisphere, water is deflected to the right of the direction of the wind; in the Southern Hemisphere, water is deflected to the left, and surface currents generally move at a more or less forty-five-degree angle to the wind. Each hemisphere of each ocean therefore has its own gyre, a circular movement, clockwise in the Northern Hemisphere and counterclockwise in the Southern.[8]

Currents are critical to the world's climatic stability. They account for fully 40 percent of global heat transport.

The currents that directly affect Sable Island are the Gulf Stream, the Labrador Current, and the cool, shallow, southerly Nova Scotia Current, which flows out of the Gulf of St. Lawrence.

Some of this Nova Scotia Current turns southwestward at Cape Breton to flow along Nova Scotia's Atlantic coast; the rest continues toward the continental shelf break, where it joins the second cool, southwestward-flowing current, the Labrador Current, which moves from the Labrador Sea and around both sides of Newfoundland, but primarily across the Grand Banks.

The Labrador Current is deep, reaching down as far as ten thousand feet, and is, among other things, the conveyor system for "Iceberg Alley," every year carrying a procession of icebergs calved off from the Greenland glaciers down past Labrador and Newfoundland and into the open Atlantic.[9] The current picks up its burden of bergs because it starts out as a northbound current, pushing up from the southern tip of Greenland through Davis Strait into the Arctic waters of Baffin Bay between Greenland and Nunavut's Arctic islands. In Baffin Bay it reverses course and heads south. It splits at the northern tip of Newfoundland, some of it flowing into the Gulf of St. Lawrence through the Strait of Belle Isle, where it joins the

St. Lawrence River's outflow. The remainder of the Labrador Current flows south along the eastern coast of Newfoundland. The Coriolis force pulls it to the right as it flows along the shelf edge, and it continues southwestward between the Gulf Stream and the continental landmass, finally petering out somewhere around Cape Hatteras. Some water is forced downward ("downwelling") to create flows down the slope of the shelf itself.[10]

The third Sable Island current, the Gulf Stream, is not only the best-known oceanic current but the swiftest and most powerful in all the world's oceans. It has been clocked at nearly five miles an hour, or better than one hundred miles in a day; its average width is about forty-three miles, and, like the Labrador Current, it reaches down to ten thousand feet. Scientists at the Woods Hole Oceanographic Institution in Woods Hole, Massachusetts, have estimated it can transport around 5,300 million cubic feet of water a second. For comparison, consider that the sum of all the rivers that flow into the Atlantic, including the world's largest, the Amazon, move only around 21 million cubic feet per second.[11]

Sailors in the Atlantic can easily spot the Gulf Stream. If you head down from, say, Halifax in Nova Scotia toward the Caribbean, you'll cross into Gulf Stream water sometime during the second day. The boundary line is astonishingly sharp; one minute the water is a cool, slate gray, the next a bright turquoise, the color differential a factor of its higher temperature and salinity, and differing biological populations.

The current is formed by water from the Florida Current, which circulates through the Gulf of Mexico and the Straits of Florida, and the North Equatorial Current, which flows westward along the equator. It parallels the coast of North America along a boundary separating the warm and more saline waters of the Sargasso Sea to the east from the colder, slightly fresher continental slope waters to the north and west. It more or less bounces off Cape Cod and is bent eastward, in the general direction of Ireland.

Once past Sable, the Gulf Stream feeds into the North Atlantic Current, which splits in northern and southern directions along the coast of Ireland. The southward flow turns into the Canary Current, named for the Canary Islands off the coast of southwestern Morocco in North Africa, and thence bends westward parallel to the equator, winding up once more off Florida. Water flowing north along the coast of England becomes the Norwegian Current, as it moves along the coast of Norway.

The Gulf Stream is one of the main engines of the conveyor belt that carries water around the globe. When it enters northern latitudes, it cools and sinks, becoming saltier and denser in the process; next it moves south and circulates around Antarctica; it then flows north again to the Indian, Pacific, and finally the Atlantic basins. The Smithsonian Institution estimates that it can take a thousand years for water from the North Atlantic to find its way into the North Pacific.[12] Surface currents move faster. One famous study in the Pacific tracked a consignment of children's bath toys lost overboard in 1992 from a freighter (the so-called rubber ducky study). Scientists enlisted the help of beachcombers everywhere to help them track the landfall of the more than twenty thousand brightly colored toys; lost in the middle of the ocean, they began washing up on Alaskan shores a few weeks later. Scientists from the American Geophysical Union predicted that some would eventually make their way into the North Atlantic, by way of Arctic pack ice and the Bering Sea. They figured such transport would take about five years. In 2004, no sightings had yet been made.

The Gulf Stream passes south of Sable Island in a northeasterly direction; the Labrador Current, for its part, passes to the west of Sable in a southwesterly direction. Sable Island therefore has a "gyre" of its own: The two massive currents set up a counterclockwise

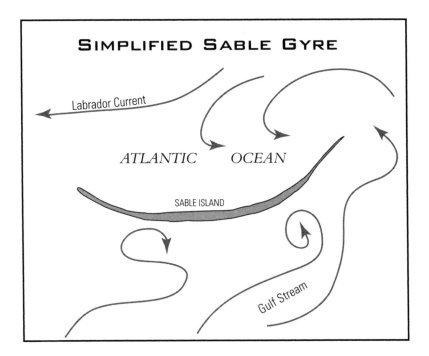

SIMPLIFIED SABLE GYRE

Labrador Current

ATLANTIC   OCEAN

SABLE ISLAND

Gulf Stream

movement of water around the island. But it is not consistent and has some curious characteristics.

Gerry Forbes and his staff some years ago conducted what they called the "drifter experiment," dumping tagged floats off the south side of the island and watching their progress. Contract workers on the island were paid a dollar for every artifact they picked up on the shore. Gerry jokes that one man, who lived a few miles away from the main station and walked to work every morning, made almost the equivalent of his monthly salary in this way—picking up tagged objects—all of them along the north beach. Many others have noticed the same thing: Objects discarded on the south of the island will often wash up on the north, having traveled in a counterclockwise direction past the eastern spit. It is one reason why the north beach is—counterintuitively—usually slightly warmer than the south

beach, if only by an average of one degree, although Gerry Forbes remembers occasions when warm water eddies approached Sable and the
differential was greater, about four degrees.

Some years ago, island resident Zoe Lucas, an artist turned beach-
comber turned autodidact scientist, who has been a fixture on Sable for
decades, spent a couple of days a month surveying the beaches for hazardous materials washed up there as part of the Atlantic Coastal Action
Program (ACAP) study. On the south beach, she found very little. On the
north beach, she turned up almost two thousand pounds of oil, solvents,
tar, and fuels of varying degrees of flammability. (Not all of this can be attributed to the local gyre; some of it could simply have washed down the
St. Lawrence.) More alarmingly, she also found twenty-three military flares
and other devices, many still explosive, and the Canadian Department of
National Defence was obliged to send a team of demolition experts to
blow them up.[13]

Objects to the north, however, seldom make their way to the south.
Driftwood routinely collects on Sable's north beach, its origin the mainland of Cape Breton, brought down by the Labrador Current, somehow
escaping the eddies, but is hardly ever found on the south beach. At the
same time, mariners have noticed for centuries that wreckage and bodies
seldom wash up on Sable's beaches, north or south. The shipwrecked Niagara Falls schoolteacher Janet Carnochan, who had herself made it safely
to shore, noticed that, of the nine people who drowned in the incident,
seven vanished for good. Only two bodies washed up on shore. The others were never seen again. This was a commonplace observation after a
vessel went down. The Reverend George Patterson made the same point,
writing mostly about wrecked ships in the late nineteenth century: "It is
to be observed . . . that the tendency of the currents is not to bring such
wreckage ashore, but rather to carry it to sea. It is seldom, too, that bodies come ashore."[14]

The Sable gyre—and its erratic nature—is another reason mariners have for so long been dangerously baffled in Sable waters. They would never rely on it being there, nor could they ignore it. Sometimes the gyre seemed to be operating at full bore, at other times mysteriously absent. Vessels that crossed without knowing from the Gulf Stream to the Labrador Current found themselves being inexplicably drawn rapidly westward; indeed, many of the ships wrecked on the island supposed themselves to have been well east of it when they ran ashore. The same was true on the other side of the island: "The captain [of the *East Boston*] judged himself well south of the Island, but he found too late that there had been a very strong indraught after passing Cape Race, which carried his vessel to the northward."[15]

Ocean currents have associated with them "structures" (in the oceanographer's jargon) that are essentially rings, or eddies. These rings affect Sable Island in a direct way.

As currents flow along a coastline or in the middle of the ocean, they bump up against landmasses or water with different salinity or temperature, setting up a resistance effect. Some of the flow is forced off course and is pinched into whirlpool-shaped eddies. All flowing water does this; eddies are easy to spot in rivers and streams, circling around upstream of rocks or banks. The process is essentially the same in the ocean, though, of course, much larger and carrying a great deal more energy.

In the year 2000, researchers aboard a Dutch vessel were studying water transport from the Indian Ocean around Africa's Cape of Good Hope into the South Atlantic, one of the critical links in the global conveyor, but one that was ill understood. They found, to their surprise and to the confounding of the nautical atlases, that the Agulhas Current, which flows down the east coast of Africa between Mozambique and the island of Madagascar to the Cape of Good Hope, isn't really a current at all, but a pulsing series of these eddies or rings. There is not, after all, any steady flow of Indian Ocean water, which is warm and salty, into the Atlantic, as had been assumed.

> In fact, flow takes place by large rings being shed from the southwest of the Indian Ocean. We found a whole herd of rings invading the Atlantic, many more than we had thought. . . . We knew that they were 300 kilometers (190 miles) wide, but actually we found that they penetrate all the way to the ocean bottom, five kilometers (3.1 miles) deep.[16]

The Gulf Stream also has rings, which have been photographed from space by NASA in a satellite sea-surface temperature study. These rings are of two sorts, warm-core rings and cold-core rings, and both are caused by the collision of the Gulf Stream with the Labrador Current. As the two converging currents meet, both begin to meander off course. When the meanders intensify, some of them are pinched off from the main flow and become independently rotating rings, whorls, and spirals, some turning clockwise and some counterclockwise.

Those that contain the cold water of the Labrador Current are known, naturally, as cold-core rings. They spin off and are propelled south and then east through the Gulf Stream. They can travel considerable distances and maintain their shape for months at a time. Because they contain cold but nutrient-rich water from the Arctic, a plankton bloom commonly occurs at their centers. Recently, whole oceanographic studies have been devoted to the formation, evolution, and death of these rings and the biological communities they support.[17] The military have been interested too: Cold-core rings act as acoustic lenses and can betray lurking submarines. These cold rings do not, however, directly affect Sable Island.

Some warm Gulf Stream water pinches off too, forming warm-water rings, which spin off north and then east, traveling against the flow of the Labrador Current. These rings do affect Sable. Because the water is warm and nutrient poor, they don't support plankton or attract the attention of feeding fish, but where they intersect with landmasses, or sandbars and banks, they disturb the ocean bottom and its sediments, and transport massive quantities of sand.

And Sable, after all, is nothing but sand.

Sable Island is in the center of this vortex, this complex system of currents, gyres, and rings. They are, plausibly, the reason for Sable's very existence and its continuing presence on the shelf. That is, the reason the island doesn't simply wash away is the circular gyre and its associated eddies set up by those great engines of planetary transport, the ocean's currents. This gyre carries sand and sediment to its center, helping to restore an island torn by storms and wind and waves. "Slight variations in both the current velocity and/or direction, as well as the future impact of atmospheric and tidal effects, could well explain to a large degree the tremendous amount of sand movement on the Sable Island banks, spits, and along the beaches."[18] Glaciation and its aftermath put Sable on its shelf to begin with. The island moves and shrinks and grows, changing with each storm and in each season, but is kept—more or less—in place by the most massive force of all, the ocean's currents.

Some currents are purely local affairs, unattached to the global system. They too are caused by the winds, as the major currents are, but their effects are usually confined to single beaches. Nevertheless, they can have a profound influence in reshaping the landscape, particularly one as malleable as Sable's.

The first of these is a rip current, often wrongly called a riptide, the bane of swimmers everywhere. Not that worrying about swimmers is a preoccupation on Sable, where there are few people to begin with. "Sometimes in summer a visiting worker contemplates a dip," Gerry Forbes says. "And he will ask me if it's safe. I just say, 'See that pack of seals over there? They would just love to have you swim with them. They know that when the sharks come they'll only have to swim faster than you.' Very few take to the water after that."

The mechanism of rip currents is simple enough. When there is either no wind or straight onshore winds, as waves move toward a beach, break, and move backward, more water is carried toward the shore than is pulled back, which results in a slight but significant upward slope of water. In fact, the absolute water level at the shoreline is typically a few inches higher than it is beyond the surf zone. The imbalance is obviously unstable, and water therefore rushes back seaward, through the surf zone, creating a narrow but powerful undertow. How powerful it is depends on a number of factors—how rapid the wave movement is, what the winds are like, and the angle of the beach itself—but rip currents have been tracked at almost a yard a second, thrusting back under the surf, quite enough to drown even a strong swimmer.

In Sable's case, the net effects are on the beach itself, not its denizens. Rip currents can carry substantial amounts of sediment and, in fact, are often spotted by savvy beachcombers as a brown plume of suspended sands carried out beyond the surf zone.

Usually, though, waves approach a shoreline not directly, but at an angle. As they enter shallow water, therefore, they are refracted by the shore, which generates a current along the shore and parallel to it. This is called a longshore current. It will usually extend from the shore itself to beyond the breaking-wave zone. The speed of these currents varies as rip currents do. If conditions are quiet, they can be leisurely things, but in fiercer winds they, too, can move at up to a yard a second.

Because longshore currents are caused by refracting waves, which in turn depend on the wind direction, they can move in either direction along the coast, carrying sand and sediment with them—sometimes large amounts of it, on the order of 3.5 million cubic feet a year. (More precisely, it is the waves that pick up the sand, and the current that transports it.) Where winds are variable, the net effect of longshore currents can be negligible, because they balance out. On Sable the net effects are considerable; but the patterns, typically, are complex.

Sable is kept in place by the currents. But its mass still depends on the winds.

CHAPTER SIX

Its Gales and Killer Waves

Deadly storms and storm-borne

waves form and re-form the island,

tearing at its structure

On Sable, the air is seldom still.

"It is interesting," Terry Hennigar notes laconically, "that winds are calm less than 1 per cent of the time."[1]

The average mean wind speed on Sable Island is around 16 miles an hour, but speeds of 85 miles an hour (hurricane-strength winds) have been routinely recorded from the southwest, and during a storm in October 1974, the wind exceeded the upper limit of the anemometer, which was calibrated to record winds of up to 100 miles an hour (161 kilometers an hour). Staff who were on duty at the time estimated that the speed reached up to 120 miles an hour in gusts, equivalent to a destructive Category-3 hurricane. This went without much comment in the logbook. It was just another gale.

To the staff, business as usual. To the island itself . . . another series of wounds in the dune line. Not a mortal blow, but not trivial either.

The oceans and the atmosphere are linked like Siamese twins.[2] Meteorological and oceanographic processes are twin halves of a single whole, both under the imperial parentage of the Sun and its agent, solar energy. Oceans govern the heat transfer provided by the Sun. The winds, in turn, are the fundamental engines that drive the world's weather.

Global weather patterns are notoriously complex and difficult to predict; shifts in microclimates and local weather patterns depend on an array of factors, including ocean currents, the temperature of the seas, the Earth's orbit, and the extent of ice and snow cover. But winds are a key player in the unfolding of life in every region on Earth.[3] Winds are critical to climate, among the main components of weather, and one of the agents that change the contours of Sable.

In the conventional taxonomy of climate, weather occurs in the troposphere, a layer of air ranging from the Earth's surface, where it is densest, to somewhere between 3.7 to 5 miles (at the poles) and 10 miles (at the equator) in thickness. Within the troposphere, the air gets colder the farther away from the Earth it is, which is why airplanes flying at around twenty thousand feet usually push through air whose temperature is well below zero Fahrenheit, even at equatorial latitudes. Despite the commonsensical observation that winds are largely horizontal, which is how we perceive them, the prevailing movement of air within the troposphere is vertical. The next layer up is the stratosphere, which extends approximately thirty miles from the Earth's surface; temperatures within the stratosphere rise with altitude, and air circulates within the layer almost entirely horizontally. Beyond thirty miles is the mesosphere, where the air is too thin to circulate much at all, and beyond that the thermosphere, which is the outer limits of Earth's thermal reach. Just to complete the set, however, atmospheric scientists generally include one more layer, the exosphere, which, as its name implies, is simply that part of space beyond any influence from Earth; the exosphere, therefore, includes pretty much all the remaining universe. The human species is a parochial one, measuring influence by its own small corner of its own small galaxy.[4]

Winds begin with the Sun, and so the key to understanding global wind patterns is to start where solar radiation is most intense, at the equator. The air warmed by the radiation rises sharply, causing a quasi vacuum that draws air toward the equator from semitropical latitudes. The winds so created head directly for the equator but are turned by the same Coriolis force that twists the currents, becoming the steadiest, most reliable winds on Earth, the so-called trade winds. Eventually, these reliable trade winds, because they are paralleling the equator, also warm, rise, and drift toward the poles.

The new high-altitude air begins to cool and sink again, at around thirty degrees of latitude—the latitude of the northern rim of Africa and the Gulf of Mexico in America. Some of this sinking air heads back to the equator, completing what is known as the Hadley cell. But some of it moves toward the middle latitudes. It, too, is deflected by the Earth's spin and the resulting Coriolis effect, turning clockwise in the Northern Hemisphere and counterclockwise in the Southern. As it does so, it meets cold air, drifting in from the poles, and warm cells, coiling their way as low-pressure systems from equatorial regions. There, it mixes and dips and swirls in an apparently patternless turbulence. This is the weather that affects the temperate zones—and Sable Island.

In the upper troposphere the mixing air generates atmospheric waves that drift around the Earth from west to east. We know these from our weather reports as jet streams,[5] long, narrow air currents with a strong vertical shearing action—an effect that creates the clear-air turbulence so hazardous for aircraft. At their centers, jet streams have been tracked at

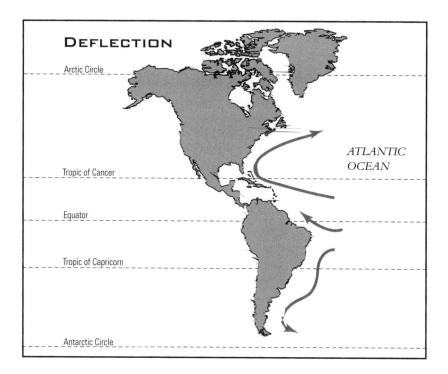

DEFLECTION

Arctic Circle

ATLANTIC
OCEAN

Tropic of Cancer

Equator

Tropic of Capricorn

Antarctic Circle

speeds of up to three hundred miles an hour, more intense even than tornadoes. Fortunately, these speeds are only in narrow bands and are seldom found outside the troposphere. There are often two or even three jet-stream systems in each hemisphere; the most active is a discontinuous polar front, lying in varying places in midlatitudes. This boundary is the locus of squalls, cyclones, and storms.[6]

North Atlantic weather is complicated further by more or less permanent zones of low pressure around the sixty-degree mark (Greenland), and zones of high pressure, in the so-called horse latitudes, around the arid zones of the Middle East and the deserts of the American Southwest. The actual flow depends on a number of incalculables, including seasonality and jet-stream positioning. The circulating air tends to skirt the highs and get funneled into the lows, a tendency that is complicated by topography

Trade Winds

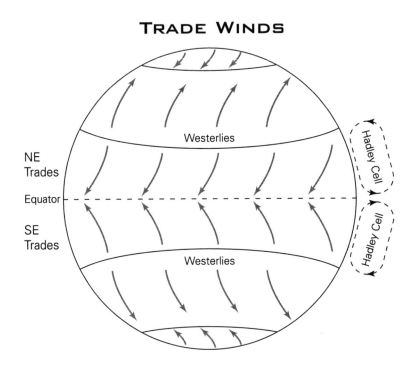

(air flows more smoothly over water than over land, and less smoothly over mountains than plains), and, to an even greater extent, by the smoothly flowing stratospheric winds, which sometimes have the benign effect of sawing the tops off massive cyclones before they can coalesce into hurricanes. Over continents, winds must weave their way between pressure cores and over land features such as mountains, valleys, even cities, which muddy their flow and retard their passage. But out to sea, the patterns are simpler and much more direct: "The northeasters set seas chopping at shorelines like ravening beasts."[7] Those are the gales that batter Sable.

And a formidable force they are. At higher velocities, winds exert occasionally irresistible forces on vulnerable features, whether buildings or beaches. The rule of thumb for calculating the inertial force—that is, the force exerted when a not-yet-movable object meets the wind—is that it increases geometrically with wind speed. A flat object one foot square will experience roughly one pound of inertial force in a twenty-mile-an-hour wind. Therefore, a wall, say, forty feet long and ten feet high will experience four hundred pounds of inertial force in a twenty-mile-an-hour wind. But because force increases geometrically, doubling the wind quadruples the inertial force—and so that same wall in a forty-mile-an-hour wind will be pushed not by eight hundred pounds of force, but by sixteen hundred. A hundred-mile-an-hour gust, therefore, by these same calculations, will exert ten thousand pounds of push—five tons pressing against a wall. A building that survives an eighty-mile-per-hour gale would need to be more than twice as strong to survive a 120-mile-per-hour hurricane.

The effect is exaggerated by the so-called blast effect of a gust. In the case of a building, if a window or door suddenly breaks open in a gust, wind can explode into the building and destroy it from the inside. "No realistic amount of structural engineering can safeguard a building against the blast effect. It makes much more sense to take every possible precaution to ensure that windows and doors will not break or fly open during high winds."[8]

On beaches, the same thing happens. High winds and sudden gusts can blast large holes in the dune line.

Winds form the dunes in the first place. Beaches are exposed to onshore winds, and sand is carried off to the back parts of the beach, where it forms small hummocks or foredunes. If the beach has lots of sand, several rows of dunes will be formed, and, when they reach a certain height, the sand will bypass them to the countryside beyond—or, in Sable's case, to the ocean beyond.[9] Winds can also be channeled around dunes, developing patterns of secondary flow that modify the shapes of the dunes themselves.[10]

Winds can affect even the so-called stabilized or vegetated dunes on Sable. The heavily grassed dune ridge on the east end of the island is about sixty-five feet high. In the same Canadian Hydrographic Service study that found sand accumulating on the dunes at the rate of six inches a year, a benchmark was set up about five hundred feet south, near the edge of the dune system. During the winter of 1973–74, the benchmark was undercut by erosion of the face and later found at the bottom of the slope. In other words, the wind was increasing the dune system's height but decreasing its width. In a study by Terry Hennigar for the Nova Scotia Department of the Environment, the Bald Dune was monitored for a twelve-month period from April 1974 to April 1975. A profile was established along the center line of the dune and was monitored at four-month intervals. During the study, the whole dune steadily migrated eastward. At the same time, a profile of the beach itself was taken near the center of the island and monitored for the same period. In those twelve months, both the profile and the width of the beach underwent marked changes: The beach widened by over 150 feet, primarily in intense storm conditions.[11]

Like many natural phenomena, wind velocities have what the scientists call a log-normal distribution, which is to say that there are a large number of breezes, few winds, and many fewer gales. Obviously, the largest amount of sand is moved by the stronger winds. The calculation is also exponential—that is, if a six-mile-an-hour wind carries 0.45 ounces of sand, a twelve-mile-an-hour wind won't carry 0.9 ounces, but 9.6 ounces per hour, and an eighteen-mile-an-hour wind as much as 41.5 ounces.[12]

The prevailing winds around Sable are westerlies, blowing from the southwest in summer and from the northwest in winter. The winds and the longshore currents they produce therefore tend to drive the island's sand eastward, apparently propelling the whole island in an easterly direction. On the other hand, the same winds and their associated currents are driving sand from the relatively shallow area to the southwest of Sable onto the island itself, adding to its westerly mass.

The worst storm winds in the region, though, are not westerlies but easterlies—the northeaster for the most savage storms, the southeaster for your average run-of-the-mill gale. One would logically think that the sand driven by these powerful winds, and their equally explosive waves, would move in a westward direction, but historic observations on the island are that "normal winds accrete sand, gales remove it"—gales can blast large chunks from the island and drive them out to sea. However, there have been powerful blows from the northwest that have shifted masses of surface sand toward the southeast.

All these trends are complicated by the counterclockwise gyre around the island, which, if it does anything at all to sediment, would tend to move it from the west to the east along the island's south beach, and from the east to the west along the north shore.

The shape—and movement—of Sable therefore depends to a considerable degree on wind patterns over the short and medium term. Stronger winds move much more sand, but they are fewer, and on Sable Island, generally come from northerly directions. Gales and storms blast holes in the island and remove sections of it, mostly from the east, which has the net effect of seeming to move the island westward. Lighter winds carry less sand, but they are much more constant—and come, in Sable's case, generally from southerly or southwesterly directions, tending to push the island eastward; but they can also accrete mass to the western side, rebuilding it there. Some years these forces will be in balance, and the island will stay where it is. In other years one or another of the forces will predominate, and the island will grow or shrink or "move" accordingly.

Powerful short-term trend versus less powerful long-term trend; like the currents, the winds maintain Sable Island in an uneasy balance.

The other obvious way winds affect Sable Island is by the waves they generate.

Even without a gale, when a "breeze o' wint" is blowing, as the fishermen from Nova Scotia's LaHave Islands often put it, the swells around Sable Island can be immense. Men who make their living on the sea are watching constantly for changes that might affect their safety, for signs that a storm is coming. When the holds are full and they're running for home in front of an imminent nor'easter, they'll listen carefully to the sounds of the sea: the reassuring rumble of the diesels, the creak and groan of the hull as it lifts and settles under the groundswell, the slap and gurgle of the waves as they run along the waterline, the hissing white fan flying off the cutwater, the spattering dance of spray, diamonds of beaded water on the cuddy. . . . They are used to the massive rollers of the open ocean, but such swells are still awesome. They slide up the swell and get to the crest before tipping back into the trough, and all they see are more giant rollers, green glass mountains with white water running down their sides or blown off their crests like a sea creature's spittle, an endless succession of them in a world without horizons.[13]

This is when you do not want to see Sable Island. You most definitely do not want to be in the vicinity of Sable Island in any kind of a blow. And if you can see white water breaking, you are almost certainly too late to worry about it.

Often, the ocean swells restlessly even before the wind arrives; a storm whose low-pressure cell is moving slowly can generate large waves hundreds, and even thousands, of miles in advance of its center. Among the signs fishermen look for: unnaturally clear air and a calm sea with an uneasy, slightly feverish swell, for then the sea can change from a flat calm to cat's-paw ripples to chop to heaving green mountains in an unnervingly short time.

Those swells are waves, wind-born and wind-borne, as the currents are. The ocean is not deadly—until the gales get hold of it.

A wave is described by three measurements, and its characteristics by three factors.

The height of the wave is measured from crest to trough bottom; its length is measured by the distance between successive crests; and its period is the length of time between the passage of two successive crests. Little ripples have periods of just a few seconds. The tides—which are, after all, just waves—have a period of better than twelve hours.

Waves grow as they absorb energy from the wind. In a stiff breeze, small waves can't contain all the wind energy, and chop ("white horses") results. These short, steep waves are unstable and tumble over themselves, "breaking" in the surfer's jargon. It looks utterly chaotic, but it is not. A wave breaks in the open ocean when its height is more than one-seventh of its length, and so a three-foot wave must be at least seven yards long, or it will tumble over in a chaos of white foam. As the waves grow in height, they can absorb ever more energy; but they also grow longer and longer, and therefore cease to break—swells are just waves with substantial lengths and therefore no compulsion to topple over. Sometimes swells might appear to break when they really do not. The white-water "spittle" is caused by smaller but unstable parasitic waves that grow on their backs.[14]

The factors that govern the behavior of waves, in the absence of land or shoals, are these: the strength of the wind, the length of time it blows, and the distance over which it blows, which is called the "fetch" of the wind. A fully developed sea is the largest wave that can be raised by a particular wind speed, regardless of duration and fetch. A twenty-knot

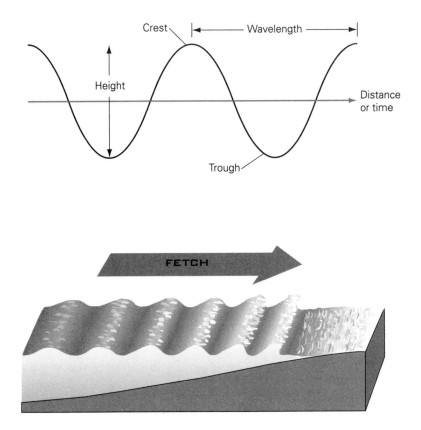

wind (a wind of twenty nautical miles an hour, or thirty statute miles an hour) blowing for ten hours will raise seas with an average wave height of five feet, and the highest 10 percent of the waves will reach ten feet.[15]

The energy stored in a wave increases in proportion to the square of the wind. So, if the wind increases from twenty to forty knots over a sufficiently long fetch, the seas will have a wave height of twenty-eight feet, nearly six times greater, and the highest 10 percent will now reach fifty-seven feet. A fifty-knot wind blowing steadily for an improbable sixty-nine hours over a fourteen-hundred-mile fetch will raise maximum seas approaching one hundred feet in height.

In real life—on the real sea traversed by real sailors—waves are seldom as neat as this. The sea in a windstorm has no apparent coherence but resembles a random series of turbulences. Complex waves like these are waves riding on other waves, crossing still other waves, forming deeper troughs and higher peaks than any of their individual components.

Is there a theoretical maximum for waves? It is—at least in theory—possible for waves of 220 feet to be generated in the deep ocean, about the height of a twenty-story building. That no one has ever reported such a wave doesn't mean they haven't occasionally occurred; after all, hundreds of thousands of ships have vanished since men began venturing onto the sea five thousand or so years ago. Slightly smaller but still gigantic waves, however, are experienced too often for comfort. In September 1995, for example, the luxury liner *Queen Elizabeth II* was en route from Cherbourg to New York, and had to change course to avoid Hurricane Luis. Nevertheless, the vessel encountered a series of seas sixty feet tall, with occasional taller crests. At four in the morning—mercifully after even the most persistent revelers had retired for the night—the Grand Lounge windows, seventy-two feet above the water, were smashed by a breaking wave. Ten minutes later, the bridge crew saw a wave dead ahead that looked, they reported later—before the publicity-spooked owners told them to *hush up*—as though they were heading "straight for the white cliffs of Dover." The wave seemed to take ages to arrive, but it was probably less than a minute before it broke over the bow. A second wave, immediately behind the first, crashed over the foredeck, carrying away the forward whistle mast. The captain, R. W. Warwick, admitted that it can be difficult to gauge the height of a wave from a vessel, but declared that the crest was more or less level with the line of sight for those on the bridge, about ninety-five feet above the surface. The officers declared that it was not a swell but a true wave. Canadian weather buoy number 44141, moored in the area, recorded a maximum wave height of ninety-eight feet (thirty meters).[16]

Sometimes tankers can be caught, hoisted on two successive swells, their centers essentially raised into the open air. No vessel is constructed to bear such forces, especially not when full, and such vessels can break abruptly in two and sink within minutes.

Oceanographers have predicted that a storm capable of producing forty-foot waves in the relatively shallow waters of the continental shelf will occur less frequently than once a century, but in 1991 the Hallowe'en Storm, a nor'easter that blew for a depressing 114 hours, produced storm waves that hit the coast at high tide, riding a storm surge. (A low-pressure system exerts less push on the ocean's surface, allowing the sea to swell upward beneath it.) The resultant fifty-foot waves destroyed property from North Carolina to the St. Lawrence.

A hundred years earlier, another storm had produced much the same results. West Ironbound Island is on the outer fringe of the cluster of islets at the mouth of the LaHave River on Nova Scotia's south shore.

> The bank near the lighthouse is forty-seven feet above sea level, and the waves have often gone over it in boisterous weather. On the 15th of April, 1881, there was a heavy gale with rain during the day, and about 9 p.m., the wind blowing violently, a tremendous sea, which the keeper thought was about fifty feet high, broke over that part of the island where the lighthouse then stood, and in which he and his family lived. When he first saw it coming it looked like an immense white cloud. Miss Maude Wolfe was in the kitchen, and her screams, caused by the sudden bursting in of the water, were heard by her father, who rescued her with some difficulty from her perilous position. The waves, which covered the cooking stove, took in a quantity of sand and stones. A large portion

of the foundation wall was torn out, and part of it carried twenty feet away. The oil store was struck on the gable end and shifted five feet, ten feet of the shingling being removed. The wood and lumber lying about were carried as with a flood, about an eighth of a mile. This was the wildest storm Mr. Wolfe ever witnessed there. In 1892, for greater security, the lighthouse was moved sixty feet further from the sea.[17]

Wind-driven waves have a steep face and a long, sloping back. They become swells (long, low, rounded waves, almost symmetrical in shape) when they leave the wind's influence. The writer Silver Donald Cameron quotes the oceanographer Wallace Kaufman as saying that swells "move through the ocean like a shiver through the skin," a nice metaphor, because the water itself doesn't travel much, only the pulse of energy. You can feel this for yourself if you stand beyond the breaker line in the ocean swells, which will lift you up, move you forward, then gently shift you back again, almost to the point at which the cycle started. The process is very much like sand dunes moving in the vast ergs of the Sahara Desert; the dunes move, but the sand seas, the ocean-equivalents, stay where they are. In the open ocean, swells, no matter how large, are not dangerous; vessels simply ride them to the top, acquire a magnificent view of millions of other such swells, and then gently ride them down again, until the boat is surrounded by hills of water.

At sea as on shore, the dangerous waves are the breakers. In a forty-knot sea, where the average wave height is twenty-eight feet, one wave in twelve hundred may be three times that height, and one in three hundred thousand may be more than four times higher—more than one hundred feet.[18] Such a wave is inherently unstable; the winds will knock over its peak, pouring thousands of tons of water down its slipface. These are the waves that roll yachts over, tear containers off supertankers, break the spines of lesser vessels, and swallow ships whole. Rogue waves.

Rogue waves—freakishly large, isolated, and destructive waves—can appear in ostensibly calm conditions. There are a number of factors that create them, and a number of more or less plausible theories to account for them. The stock theory involves the chance accretion of two smaller waves from intersecting wave trains produced by different storms widely spaced on the ocean. If these two waves were to collide peak-to-trough, they would cancel each other out, but when they collide peak-to-peak, they build on each other, producing a wave form much higher than either storm would have produced on its own.[19] Another theory is that ocean currents or large fields of random eddies and vortices can concentrate a steady ocean swell to create unusually large waves, the current or eddy field acting like an optical lens to focus the wave action.[20] Yet another theory is that the abrupt release of vast quantities of sedimentary gases trapped underwater could create blowouts large enough to set off a rogue wave.[21]

These gigantic waves are often referred to, without any particular reason, as tidal waves, though they have nothing to do with the tides. They are more accurately known as *tsunamis* and are sometimes produced by underwater volcanoes or by subsurface landslides or earthquakes.

Of course, all waves, including tsunamis and storm waves, are superimposed upon the natural rise and fall of the tides. A huge wave that makes landfall during a high tide will therefore do more damage than one that arrives when the tide is low. In themselves, the tides are benign and relatively predictable, but they can significantly elevate the effects of other waves that ride upon them.[22]

A tsunami moving across the open sea will be barely noticed, except that a vessel will ride up higher than usual, then ride down again. If, say, the waves were set off by an undersea earthquake, the waves on the water's surface can have no more total energy than the energy released by the source, and because a circular wave front expands in all directions away from its source, its energy is spread over an increasingly large region, and the wave height diminishes. Sometimes, though, landforms and the configuration of the seafloor can cause nasty surprises, focusing the wave energy in an unexpected fashion. In just this way, relatively modest waves of about twelve or thirteen feet, with periods ranging from twenty to thirty seconds, knocked away stones weighing up to twenty tons from a breakwater in Long Beach, California. No damage was done anywhere to nearby shores or structures. It took seventeen years before an explanation was found: "An underwater hump less than 4 miles away acted as a lens to focus waves coming from a particular direction, and when such waves happened to have a 20–30 second period, the focal point of this lens coincided precisely with the location of the breakwater."[23]

It is only when tsunamis get close to shore, in shallow water, that they "trip," and their full destructive force is unleashed.

Swells in the open ocean don't move much water, as we have seen. The energy is contained in the height gradient, and the angle of slope is quite shallow. But something dramatic happens as the waves approach shore: In the area of the surf, the waves become ever steeper, and the water itself begins to move forward at the speed of the waves. When they crash down they can gouge massive amounts of sand from the beach itself, either punching it inland to the backshore or, if breaking during high tides or storm surges, tearing away at the backshore itself. On Sable Island, where this frequently happens, much of the damage is done on and to the north beach, because the worst storms are northerlies, and because of the beach's steep slope. A gently sloping beach disperses the energy of rolling waves. But the steeper the slope, the deeper the cut of the waves and the more a beach is eaten away.[24] There have been occasions on Sable Island when giant waves were breaking on both beaches at once, the spray clearly visible above even the large north beach dunes, causing a thunderous roar.[25]

These waves and their associated longshore currents are constantly reshaping the island's topography. Waves dredge up vast quantities of sediment, which they then turn over to the longshore currents. Large waves, conventionally, remove shoreline, smaller ones contribute sand to it, but the real mechanics on Sable are still only guessed at. What is known for sure is that the quantities moved by the wave-longshore combination are considerable. In one well-documented case, a study at the Mobil-Tetco well Cohasset, located in a trough about five miles south of Sable, showed that about thirty feet of sand had accumulated over a mere two years.[26]

In the general course of events, though, Sable's treacherous sandbars, such a hazard to mariners, are paradoxically a protective device for the island itself. Waves, even massive waves, trip on the outer bars and release their pent-up energy a long way from the beaches of the island proper. If you stand on the beach, you can clearly see the white spray from such waves breaking a mile or more from shore. Sometimes, when the winds are particularly brisk, the waves will re-form, albeit into smaller and less destructive waves, breaking yet again at another shallow bar. The bars themselves shift and adjust to the onslaught. Sometimes they're dismembered altogether; at others they become extended crescents, often pierced with erosional gullies. "From the top of the dunes I've sometimes seen up to twelve lines of breakers during a storm," Gerry Forbes says. "I remember one instance, when a tropical storm passed, then stalled south of Newfoundland, and led to fully developed seas with spectacular surf. I'm certain I've seen twenty-foot breakers, but I wouldn't want to venture a guess for how much higher they might have been."

Fine for the island, and its onshore staffers. But a ghastly sight for trapped mariners, with scant chance of making dry land safely through the roiling seas.

Its Human Drama

Several times owned and abandoned,

Sable's once thriving "beeves" vanish

from ken

The next explorer to pass Sable's way was Pierre du Gua, Sieur de Monts, but his was an expedition of a different stripe. For one thing, he didn't intend to go to Sable—he only brushed by, in an unnerving and nearly fatal fog—but was planning to settle the mainland, armed with another of those sweeping royal warrants granting him wide powers and domains. He was a serious player, a man of influence at court, with good connections and extensive resources. He would have considerable impact on the founding of the French colony at Quebec.

De Monts was born in 1558 into a merchant family in the province of Saintonge, just north of the Gironde estuary in the southwest of France—not, for once, in the Basque country, or within the borders of Navarre, but within reach of the influence of the cities of Bordeaux and the Protestant stronghold of La Rochelle. He, too, was sponsored by Henry IV.

Some sources say de Monts made only one trip to the New World, in

1604, but there is evidence he had made a fleeting trip to Acadia in 1600, with an expedition headed by Pierre Chauvin de Tonnetuit.

His royal charter from Henry was granted in 1603. It gave him, for a period of ten years, the exclusive rights to colonize New France, a monopoly over the trade in furs with the Amerindians, and the title of governor of Acadia. In return, de Monts promised the royal house considerable profits and undertook to import sixty new colonists a year to the new lands.

The expedition, in two ships, left France in the spring of 1604. On the *Bonne Renommée*, de Monts's own ship, was that nobleman of distinction and influence in the court of Henry IV, seigneur de Poutrincourt; Samuel de Champlain went along as chief adviser and cartographer. Also on board was a priest, Nicolas Aubry, though some sources indicate that two clerics accompanied the expedition, one Protestant and one Catholic, which seems plausible since Saintonge had a substantial Protestant population. The total complement was somewhere between 100 and 120 men: workmen, artisans, mercenaries—and some convicts from French prisons, taking the easier of two tough choices.[1]

The de Monts expedition had little influence on Sable Island, except in two peripheral ways: Its vessels narrowly escaped running aground on the Sable bars in thick fog, thereby acquainting Champlain with the treachery of the island; and de Monts himself, by locating his colony on the Fundy shores, played a significant role in locating the future Acadian settlements, which in turn influenced what Sable was to become.

His first colony was not a success. The narrow escape from being stranded on Sable aside, the first winter at Ste. Croix Island was brutal, and those that survived moved to Port Royal in the more protected Bay of Fundy in 1605. There they prospered, after a fashion; but the colony's profits were meager, and in 1607 the king had had enough—he ordered de Monts to pack up and come home, revoking his charter.

De Monts never went back to the Americas, but his importuning did gain him another charter, this time to trade in furs with the natives of the St. Lawrence Valley. In the flowery language of the time, de Monts's parchment was "given at Paris the seventh day of January, in the year of grace sixteen hundred and eight, and the nineteenth of our reign." It was apparently aimed at everybody the king or his minions could think of ("our beloved and faithful counselors, the officers of our admiralty in Normandy, Brittany, and Guienne, bailiffs, marshals, provosts, judges, or their lieutenants, and to each one of them, according to his authority, throughout the extent of their powers, jurisdictions, and precincts"), and went on to declare:

> Acting upon the information which has been given us by those who have returned from New France, respecting the good quality and fertility of the lands of that country, and the disposition of the people to accept the knowledge of God, We have resolved to continue the settlement previously undertaken there, in order that our subjects may trade without hindrance. And in view of the proposition to us of Sieur de Monts, gentleman in ordinary of our chamber, and our lieutenant-general in that country, to make a settlement, on condition of our giving him means and supplies for sustaining the expense of it, it has pleased us to promise and assure him that none of our subjects but himself shall be permitted to trade in pelts and other merchandise, for the period of one year only, in the lands, regions, harbors, rivers, and highways throughout the extent of his jurisdiction. . . .

Armed with this sweeping permission, de Monts dispatched Champlain and the sea captain Pont Gravé to open a commercial station at Quebec in 1608, thus playing his major role in the foundation of a permanent French colony in North America. De Monts maintained his commercial interests until 1617, when he retired to the Ardennes. He died in 1628.[2]

All of which left Acadia vacant, so to speak, apart from the aboriginals, about whom no one cared, and the English, who were sniffing about in a worrying way. To fill this vacuum, the Company of New France was formed in 1627, aimed at increasing royal profits through the fur trade and bringing some coherence to this notion of permanent settlement. Isaac de Razilly, cousin to Cardinal Richelieu, then the real power behind the throne of Henry IV's son, was designated lieutenant general of "all parts of New France called Canada, and governor of Acadia." The grant explicitly included the Fundy shores—and Sable Island.

The Razillys took their name from the Château de Razilly, near Chinon on the Loire, which had once been the residence of Charles VII and then Louis XI. Isaac was born in 1587, one of eight children, and rose rapidly in prominence. In 1605 he was made a knight of Malta and in 1623 a captain of the French navy. He distinguished himself in several campaigns in Morocco and participated in the siege against the Protestant forces at St.-Martin, Île de Ré, near La Rochelle. (He narrowly averted drowning when his ship, the *Virgin*, was sunk, and he apparently lost an eye in the campaign.)

Razilly declined the title of lieutenant governor of New France in favor of Champlain, whom he declared was more competent in the affairs of the colonies. But he gladly accepted the position as governor of Acadia. The cardinal put at his disposal the ships *l'Espérance-en-Dieu* and the *Saint-Jean*, and two other vessels, unnamed, along with three hundred souls (among whom were three priests), farm livestock, seeds, tools, and agricultural implements. The first continuing agricultural development in

Acadia stemmed from this expedition and later shipments. Included with these were two other important arrivals: the first female colonists, peasant women all, and some horses—along with admixtures from New England, the progenitors of all Acadian horses.

In 1632, Razilly's little flotilla arrived at La Have, Acadia, now on Nova Scotia's south shore near Lunenburg, and built a small fort there, which they called Ste.-Marie-de-Grâce.

Two years later, in a nice piece of profit-taking, the Company of New France gave Razilly the island of Ste. Croix and its environs for his personal domain, and at his urging gave to his brother Claude Port Royal, La Have, and Sable Island, a grant Razilly defended on the grounds that Claude, the "Parisian Jean Condonnier," and he himself had "advanced 50,000 écus to facilitate the settlement, without having retrieved therefrom any profit at all."[3]

Claude lost no time in cashing in on his new grant. That he did so, we know from the testimony of a curious visitor to La Have from Boston, John Rose, the same Rose who made a cameo appearance in Governor Winthrop's history of New England. Rose had sailed out of Boston in 1633, and a short time later, his vessel, the *Mary and Jane*, was wrecked on Sable Island. An enterprising and energetic man, Rose lived on the island for several months, cobbling together a small yawl from the wreckage of his larger vessel, after which he managed to set sail for the mainland, arriving first at the La Have colony and its fort, Ste.-Marie-de-Grâce. There he made the mistake of recounting to the governor and his brother Claude tales of the eight hundred head of cattle he'd seen grazing on the island— the still-extant red cattle of the Portuguese. (Another version of this story is that Rose and his men "were received very kindly by the French on Sable Island and with help they constructed a small vessel . . . and at La Have, Commander de Razilli was most generous and provided Rose and his men with a shallop . . . and they returned to Boston." But there is scant evidence for French living on Sable at the time, so this account is almost certainly wrong).[4] In fact, Claude seems to have bullied Rose into leading an expedition back to Sable, where they built temporary houses and began rounding up the cattle, not so much for food, which they didn't need and in any case would have had difficulty transporting to the mainland before it spoiled, but for their hides. Leather was a prized commodity in the new colony.

So thorough were they that, by the time Rose finally reached Boston with news of his discovery, a hastily formed New England expedition to Sable found only 140 head left, hardly worth the chase over forty miles of loose sand. A few years after that, not a single animal remained.[5] A contemporary, Nicholas Denys, in his survey, *Description and Natural History of the Coast of North America*, wrote of Sable Island that there was no longer anything upon it except the pond and some grass, "there being no cattle left, these having been killed solely to obtain their skins."[6]

As for Razilly, he died in 1635 at La Have, and Champlain was moved to pen a nice little tribute: A "bon et parfait capitaine de mer," he called Razilly, "prudent, sage, laborieux."[7] He left all his rights and property in Acadia to his brother Claude, who in 1642 passed on the whole inheritance to Charles de Menou d'Aulnay. After that, the Acadian colony deteriorated into squabbles between d'Aulnay and his rival Charles La Tour, who spent more time scoring points off each other than watching out for the English. Sable Island, stripped of its cattle, was of no further importance to either man and was abandoned.[8]

To this point, records existed of 120 vessels that had foundered and been lost on the island, and no doubt many more went unrecorded.[9]

CHAPTER EIGHT

Its Boston Connection

The Reverend Andrew Le Mercier

and his eminent network, the Faneuils

and the Hancocks

The next time Sable Island made its way into the greater public consciousness was almost a hundred years later, early in the eighteenth century, a period of high tension between France and England, and between France's colonies and those of England. Razilly's Acadians had long settled into the Fundy shores of Nova Scotia, and the French had a formidable base at Louisbourg, farther up the coast, where in 1713 they began to construct a European-style fortified town that came to be called, in an early version of Chamber of Commerce boosterism, "the Dunkirk of the Americas." (The expense was so great that Louis XIV complained from Versailles that he expected to see its turrets rising above the horizon.) The English, and their surrogates, the New Englanders, were a threatening presence to the south. There was a good deal of trade going on up and down the coast, much of it illicit.

The connection with Sable started a few years earlier with a wealthy

Boston merchant and his most interesting and far-reaching connections in New England and British colonial society.

André (Andrew) Faneuil, a generation older than the others, was born in France sometime before 1670. In 1685, when Louis XIV of France revoked the Edict of Nantes, which had officially tolerated Protestantism, he set off a great exodus of people who came to be called Huguenots, many of them from the strongly Protestant southwest, centered on La Rochelle, the same port from which de Monts had launched his colonizing efforts at the turn of the seventeenth century. The Huguenots were almost all "Reformed Protestants," followers of John Calvin. The Huguenot scattering sent thousands of people to Holland, to the new Dutch settlement at the southern tip of Africa, at the Cape of Good Hope, and to England. The first American Huguenots, Andrew Faneuil among them, arrived in the British American colonies as early as 1686. Partly because of a native shrewdness and partly because he was soon able to tap into what one historian has called the Protestant International, a vast network of French, Dutch, and English Protestant merchants whose connections he exploited in America, he prospered.[1]

He also, it seems quite clear in retrospect, made a good deal of money trading with the Acadians around the Bay of Fundy. This was not exactly illegal, but it was certainly disapproved of, at least in England and by the French colony's governors. Faneuil was no doubt popular in Acadia as a fellow Frenchman and would have downplayed his religious convictions in the interests of commerce. That his ships did trade in Acadian waters has been amply proven. Among the evidence is an invoice with his name on it, found at Port Royal and dated 1691. The scribbled document noted that "I, André Faneuil and brother, have given to Mr. Boudrot to sell for us at Port Royal plus our profits as follows . . . ," a promise supplemented by lists of commodities such as fabric, ribbon, silk lace, stockings, beads, nutmeg, and cloves.[2]

The garrison at Louisbourg was ambiguous about trade with the New Englanders and occasionally urged the authorities in France to legitimize the traffic more directly. Matthieu Des Goutins, a French officer stationed at the fort who sent regular dispatches to his superiors in Paris at the Ministry of the Marine, wrote on December 23, 1707:

> We would be very happy sir, if at present our enemies [the English] would bring us the necessary items in exchange for beaver pelts which we have in abundance. Without the goods they brought us last time, we would not even have had soup. We would have no pots, no ovens, no scythes, no knives, no iron, no axes, no kettles for the Indians and no salt for the inhabitants.[3]

But what was fair for the garrison and the Louisbourg officials was not, apparently, appropriate for the farmers of Acadie, and the Acadians were obliged to indulge in a considerable amount of prevarication about what they were up to. French merchants complained constantly about the Acadians' apparent hoarding of the "specie" they were paid in exchange for meat and grain. They weren't behaving, in the French view, as proper consumers, and spending the money on manufactured goods. But the specie wasn't being hoarded; it was being spent in Boston on luxury items like glass and lace and meerschaum pipes. And when a French bishop, Jean-Baptiste de Saint Vallier, visited Acadia in 1686, he described a bucolic scene in which the happy colonists were

> in more easy circumstances, and there is an abundance of pasturage in the vicinity, they have let loose a number of cows and other animals, which they brought from Sable Island, where the late Commandant de Razilly formerly left them. They had become almost wild, and could only be approached with difficulty but they are becoming tame little by

little, and are of great advantage to each family, who can have a good number of them.

Since the Razillys had removed all the cattle from Sable, and since in any case the Portuguese cattle there had been red, and the Acadians' cattle were black, it seems clear that they were really obtained in an illegal barter with New England, and that the bishop had been fed a little white lie.[4]

In 1715 or thereabouts, on a trip to Europe, Andrew Faneuil met André Le Mercier, who was then twenty-three, a graduate of the Protestant academies in Geneva and a fellow French speaker, and invited him to come to Boston to succeed the Reverend Pierre Daillé as pastor of the French Protestant church there. Le Mercier, who like his mentor was soon called Andrew in the English fashion, took up his post before the year ended.

Clearly, he did well. A decade or so later, in 1729, Le Mercier, probably with the encouragement and possibly the financial backing of Faneuil, petitioned the governor at Annapolis Royal (the former Port Royal, by now British-controlled) for a grant of land, enough for a township and five thousand or more acres. He intended, he said, to settle on this land a group of a hundred Huguenot families, at the time refugees in London. Though everyone seemed to agree that it was a well-prepared presentation, he was turned down.

A year later, in 1730, his mentor, Andrew Faneuil, died, and Faneuil's commercial empire, then considerable (he was regarded as the wealthiest man in Boston) passed to his nephew, Peter. His estate included a substantial house, the largest in the city, constructed in 1710 across from King's Chapel in the heart of Boston.[5]

At about this time, a young man named John Gorham was working the boats trading up the Fundy shore, for Peter Faneuil and then for Thomas Hancock, coproprietor of the wealthy trading firm of Apthorp

& Hancock. This firm and its proprietors soon became even wealthier than the Faneuils themselves, for Charles Apthorp was paymaster and commissary for the British troops quartered at Boston, a position guaranteed to make him vulgar sums of money, and Hancock's vessels were trading wherever there were the British settlements—he was, for example, to be instrumental in the founding of Halifax in 1749.

All these people—the Faneuils, who bequeathed to Boston its beloved Faneuil Hall, Le Mercier himself, later the Gorhams, the Apthorps, Thomas Hancock, and his more famous nephew John, a signer of the Declaration of Independence—were intricately connected, an early version of the Old Boys' Network. The linkages were financial, political, and military. Huguenots were prominent among this tightly knit circle, but the circle wasn't exclusively French in origin; army service, money, and politics remained the keys. The Gorhams, for example, were descendants of the Plymouth Colony, and Gorham's Rangers were to become notorious in the Indian campaigns. John Gorham was a protégé of Governor William Shirley of Massachusetts, who was connected to General Sam Waldo and to the Wentworths, cousins to a British prime minister and serially governors of New Hampshire and Nova Scotia. Among this cozy little group was Paul Mascarene, another Huguenot émigré, who was appointed lieutenant governor of Annapolis Royal in 1744 (a post that specifically included authority over Sable Island). Mascarene, in turn, knew Gorham and Shirley, and through them Waldo and the Hancocks.

Sam Waldo, for his part, not only was a general but also owned a tidy five hundred thousand acres of Maine, and was connected through politics to the Wentworths, and through trade to the Hancocks and Apthorps.[6] (For a few years in the 1730s, Waldo actually claimed proprietorship over much of Nova Scotia, and modern New Brunswick as far as the St. Lawrence River.)

Governor Shirley, for his part, had Gorham sign a contract in 1748 with the Massachusetts government to supply land and sea forces "to clear out French troublemakers" at the St. John River and the Minas Basin in Acadia, which connected him directly to Hancock and Apthorp, whose ships he used. . . . And so it went.

On July 7, 1737, a crucial date in Sable's history, the *Catherine,* 110 tons, from Ireland bound for Boston with 202 persons on board, went aground on the island and was wrecked. This was the story that the *Boston Weekly News-Letter* later reported with such gloomy relish (how ninety-eight had perished, and how the master, mate, freighters, and five more of the "sorrowful company" had made it safely to Canso in the ship's longboat). When the survivors reached Boston, the story was the sensation of the season—and for good reason, because it was "a journalist's dream, containing poor immigrants, women and children saved in a dramatic rescue, and lost treasure." Reported the *Weekly News-Letter,* "It is said the *Catherine* was accounted the richest vessel that ever sailed from the north of Ireland"; on board had been two wealthy cloth merchants bound for Boston to establish a manufactory, and several families had with them their entire estates. Silver and gold in plate and specie were said to amount to more than three thousand pounds, a considerable sum.[7]

Le Mercier saw in this famous wreckage another chance at establishing an estate, no matter how small, and lost no time in petitioning Governor Armstrong at Annapolis Royal for a grant of Sable Island, claiming he and his partners (Thomas Hancock, perhaps Apthorp, and possibly even Gorham) had already sent people and animals to the island to help rescue any future victims of wrecks. There is no reason to doubt this story, for while Le Mercier and all his well-connected cronies seem to have had a very good nose for a dollar, Le Mercier himself seems to have been mainly well-intentioned. It would be wise to be skeptical, however, of his concurrent claim that he himself had been shipwrecked on the island, which was no doubt an equally well-intentioned embellishment.

The grant was not forthcoming, but because he already had men and material on the island, he was given de jure control, and the governor agreed to issue a proclamation prohibiting interference there by others. Whether this halfway measure satisfied Le Mercier is not known, but he seems to have taken it in good spirit. His men stayed busy, he wrote later:

> The Care of Gardens and Cattle take up of our People's Time in Summer, in Winter they go and kill Seils and boil their Fat into Oyl, as well as that of Whales, which now and then are cast away dead upon the Beach. The island finds them in Turf, and the sea brings them Wood; so they are not deprived of Necessaries of Life, nor without Profits of several sorts; besides their having the Pleasure of saving often many Men's Lives, according to the Motto of the Island, viz. *Destruo est Salvo*.[8]

The governor's proclamation didn't seem to have the desired effect, however, of keeping away malefactors. In 1738 Le Mercier wrote to Armstrong in Port Royal, complaining that "evil-disposed fishermen" kept stealing his cattle and goods, and in 1744 he advertised in the Boston papers offering a reward of forty pounds for the "discovery of the depredators."[9]

The partners kept trying for greater control of Sable. John Gorham, who was by then in military service, was sent in 1744 to Nova Scotia with Captain Edward Tying to relieve the siege of Annapolis Royal. (The fort and its settlement had previously been liberated from the indignant French, who were now trying to get it back.) This was the first appearance in history of Gorham's Rangers, a mostly Mohawk mobile force that was later to terrorize the region and became notorious for its bounty scalpings of the local Micmac, as the Mi'kmaq name was then rendered. The expedition was successful, and Gorham took the opportunity to petition Paul Mascarene, who was by now de facto governor, for an outright grant of Sable Island, on behalf of "himself and his partners" (that is, Hancock and Le Mercier). The petition should have been well received, because Mascarene was a part of the Boston connection: One of Le Mercier's sons, Bartholomew, was in service with Mascarene a few years later, and another, Andrew Junior, went along on the British punitive expedition in which Gorham's Rangers helped seize Louisbourg, under the command of Waldo. Still, there is no record that such a grant was ever made.

In 1746, Sable Island played a small, though typically aggressive, role in that great debacle of maritime history, the doomed French expedition to retake New France from the *maudites anglaises*. The commission given the expedition's commander, Admiral Jean-Baptiste de Roye de la Rochefoucauld, duc d'Anville, was no small one: "To retake and dismantle Louisbourg, effect a junction with the army of Bay Verte and expel the British from Nova Scotia, consign Boston to flames, ravage New England, and waste the British West Indies." That he did none of these things was a fault of the storms that plagued the Atlantic, and partly—though only partly—due to Sable Island.

D'Anville's fleet consisted of twenty warships, including eleven ships of the line, thirty-two transports, and twenty-one smaller auxiliary vessels, containing in all thirteen thousand men, the largest flotilla ever to venture into American waters to that time.

The first setback was a storm in the Bay of Biscay that damaged several of the ships and upset the carefully prepared timetable. The second and more serious was a disastrous gale off Sable Island that irrevocably scattered the fleet. In addition to a fire ship and a transport, no fewer than three ships of the line—two-thousand-tonners carrying upwards of six hundred men each[10]—were lost near the island on the same day, presumed cast onto the bars and smashed to pieces. As though that weren't enough, the corvette *Légère*, commanded by Charles François Guillimin, was wrecked too; the captain had believed he was safely past Sable "until the sand-choked waves crashed over his bow."[11] Of the great armada that left France, only three ships of the line and a few transports made the safe haven of Chebucto, later Halifax. There d'Anville perished of fever, and his second-in-command, Vice Admiral Constantin-Louis d'Estournelle, in a fit of despondency, threw himself on his sword in his cabin. Some reports say he bled to death there, others that he survived a few more years. All accounts agree that he no longer exerted any influence on what little remained of the expedition.

There were sixteen survivors from the *Légère*, all of whom scrambled ashore and found shelter in the lee of the dunes. They were discovered there by Le Mercier's men, who shared with them food and warm huts, doing their duty as the good reverend had promised. The castaways passed a comfortable winter before being picked up in the spring by a New England schooner.

Three years later, Louisbourg reverted to the French anyway, in the Treaty of Aix-la-Chapelle; Apthorp and Hancock, of course, provided the transports to bring away the British troops. The firm "ha[d] always been so employed" on the part of the government, Nova Scotia governor Charles Cornwallis wrote at the time to the duke of Bedford.[12] The company also supplied "all the frames, timbers, etc for barracks and officers' quarters" in the new settlement of Halifax, which was being constructed as a countervailing presence to Louisbourg. "The difficulty of procuring provisions was very great," the quartermasters wrote later.

"The Government appears to have been altogether dependent on the contracts of Apthorp and Hancock of Boston and Delaney and Watts of New York, for the necessary supplies for the settlement [of Halifax]."[13]

In 1751 John Gorham went to England, partly, as his papers admit, to seek redress for debts, and perhaps once more to press for an outright grant of Sable to himself and his partners. He died of smallpox before he could accomplish either of these missions.

Then, in 1753, something puzzling happened: Andrew Le Mercier put his interest in Sable Island up for sale. In the *Boston Weekly News-Letter* of February 8, he gave a comprehensive account of his holdings and their ability to produce a profit.

> When I took Possession of the Island, there were no four-footed Creatures upon it but a few Foxes, some red and some black, now there are I suppose about 90 Sheep, between 20 or 30 Horses, including Colts, Stallions and breeding Mares, about 30 or 40 Cows, tame and wild and 40 Hogs.[14]

But if he only had de jure control, what was he selling? And why was there no mention of partners? There are some hints in Boston French church documents that Le Mercier had a falling out with the Faneuils (they had supported him and complained of his ingratitude), but what about the others? Why, when he died in 1764, leaving his entire estate to Thomas Hancock, was there no mention of Sable Island among either his possessions or his entitlements? And why, by extension, when Thomas Hancock himself died the same year and left everything to his nephew John, was Sable Island still conspicuous by its absence, although it is clear on later evidence that Hancock retained an interest in it, and perhaps considered it "his"? Who owned it or controlled it, and where were the animals?

Whatever happened, Le Mercier never sold the island, but he did abandon it. There was no one living there in 1756, and there were no animals left. All the livestock had been rounded up and taken away, perhaps by passing fishermen, perhaps by those "depredators" of whom Le Mercier had complained, but by whom and to where remains a mystery.

CHAPTER NINE

Its Acadian Roots

The horses finally appear on Sable,

payoff for Hancock's help in expelling

the Acadians

A few years after Le Mercier's men left and the island was stripped of livestock, horses reappeared on Sable, this time to stay. These were the progenitors of the animals that can still be seen galloping across the grasses and flying along the edge of the Great Pond, manes tossing. Hardly anyone remembers the details of their crossing from the mainland; they're now mostly just romantic symbols, in their own improbable survival an inspiration, to be cherished but left alone, protected but not coddled.

But how did they get there? And why were they taken, and from where, and by whom?

The answers are rooted in politics, and not very pretty politics at that.

In 1755, in a lamentable episode which was widely criticized even at the time, and which resulted among other things in Longfellow's famous tear-jerker *Evangeline*, Razilly's Acadian descendants were rounded up and summarily deported from the colony. The modern conventional wisdom is that the mass deportations were an early example of the ethnic cleansing more recently attributed to the Balkans, but—as usual in these matters— events at the time were more confused than clear, and what seems now like an act of brutal *realpolitik* was more a result of insecurity, uncertainty, and preemptive revenge. Reports of British brutality served to bolster the Acadians' cause and gave Longfellow a nice narrative line, but seem to have been greatly exaggerated.

Still, the hapless farmers were deported. That main fact remains.

The political context was complicated. After years of sporadic skirmishing, the 1632 Treaty of St. Germain-en-Laye between England and France had fully restored Acadia to France. But in the interim, the commercial power of New England—and especially Boston—had been growing steadily, and by the time the city reached a population of twelve thousand in the early eighteenth century, it was a major outpost of the British mercantile system, its merchants dominating the triangular trade between New England, the West Indies, and Europe. Boston therefore had been deeply drawn into Britain's century of warfare with France, which lasted from 1689 to 1763, and was a staging ground for attacks on French Canada, a source of soldiers to fight the Indians, and a provider of badly needed tax revenue, much of it only grudgingly yielded up.

In 1710 Port Royal, the tiny fortified French capital on the Bay of Fundy, had been captured by an expedition from New England and its name changed to Annapolis Royal. Three years later, in the Treaty of Utrecht, France had ceded to Britain its claim to "all Nova Scotia or Acadia according to its ancient boundaries," while retaining for itself the islands of Cape Breton and St. Jean (now Prince Edward Island). For the next thirty-six years a British governor or his lieutenant had maintained himself precariously at Annapolis Royal, with a gradually deteriorating fort and an aging and neglected little garrison, while the French had the brooding presence of the newly constructed fortress at Louisbourg.

In British colonial policy, control of Acadia and Fort Beauséjour (at the border between the present Nova Scotia and New Brunswick) was to be one of the four cornerstones of security. (The other three were Niagara on the Great Lakes, Duquesne in the Ohio Valley, and Crown Point on the north shores of Lake Champlain.) But security remained elusive. Even after they acquired de jure control of the Acadian lands, their on-the-ground influence over the affairs of the province had been minimal. The population remained entirely French, and the authorities in Louisbourg had made it clear enough that, one day, they would be called on to help with the reconquest. Curiously, priests operating in Acadia remained French subjects, were paid by the bishop of Quebec, and were expected to act as agents of France, duties that some of them carried out with unseemly enthusiasm. To an astonishing degree, therefore, in practice Acadia was being run by the French settlers and their Indian allies. Indeed, British authority in Nova Scotia scarcely extended beyond the picket lines of the few places where they maintained garrisons. Indians and Acadians roamed it at will, and anyone venturing beyond the British blockhouses risked his life. The Indian bands were small in numbers, but enthusiastically on the side of the French. Even so, they didn't always accept French orders and had their own views of when punitive or plundering raids were necessary. "With their ability to slip mysteriously through the country, and their occasional ferocious barbarities [they were] a bafflement and source of terror to the English, far beyond anything justified by their mere numbers."[1]

The 1713 Utrecht treaty had given the Acadians a year of grace to declare their allegiance to the British Crown, or to leave the province. When the year expired, few of them had accepted either of the alternatives, and they remained defiantly in place.[2] Even those who had declared their intention to move had not done so; there really wasn't any place for them to go, and Louisbourg didn't have the resources to accept them.

Many of them then had the gall to demand that they be accepted as neutrals in any future conflict between France and Britain.

With this escalating tension as background, on June 11, 1755, Britain's Admiral Edward Boscawen captured a French fleet in the fogs off Newfoundland and, in an early instance of disinformation propaganda, conveniently discovered among the French admiral's papers a document detailing how French troops planned to precipitate an uprising among the Acadians, with the intention of assaulting and burning Halifax. This document was alarming enough, but the admiral also found a "smoking gun," guaranteed to set off a hysterical reaction: the discovery, packed into the ships' holds, of thousands of scalping knives. This stash of knives was even more convenient than the document, and it had the no-doubt-intended effect: A ripple of revulsion and melodramatic horror passed rapidly through the British colonies, prompting the lieutenant governor of Massachusetts, Spencer Phips, to demand of Nova Scotia's governor, Charles Lawrence, that he "effect the prompt removal of the French neutrals, as they are termed" in order to secure the British defenses. Lawrence's council was prodded into action in July, when delegations of Acadians showed up at Halifax, as ordered, but defiantly refused to sign any oaths. They were all locked up, and the council's minute book recorded the momentous decision "to send them to be distributed amongst the various colonies on the Continent; and that a sufficient Number of Vessels be hired with all possible Expedition for that purpose."

Early in August, Colonel John Winslow and a force of New England troops arrived at the Acadian town of Grand Pré. Winslow was from an old Massachusetts family (his great-grandfather had been governor of Plymouth Colony in 1633) and, judging from his phrasing, seems to have resented the orders he was obliged to carry out. He ordered all the Acadian males to assemble in the church and read them the following:

Gentlemen,

I have received from his Excellency Governor Lawrence the King's Commission which I hold in my hand and by whose orders you are convened together to manifest to you his Majesty's final resolution to the French inhabitants of this his Province of Nova Scotia who for almost half a century have had more indulgences granted them, than any of his subjects in any part of his dominions. What use you have made of them you yourself best know.

The part of duty that I am now upon is what though necessary is very disagreeable to my natural make and temper as I know it must be grevious to you who are of the same specia.

But it is not my business to annimedvert, but to obey such orders as I receive and therefore without hesitation shall deliver you His Majesty's orders and instructions, viz.

That your lands and tenements, cattle of all kinds and livestock of all sorts are forfitted to the Crown with all your other effects saving your money and household goods and you yourselves be removed from his province.

Thus it is preemptorily His Majesty's orders that the whole French inhabitants of these districts be removed, and I am through his Majesty's goodness directed to allow you liberty to carry of your money and household goods as many as you can without discommoding the Vessels that you go in. I shall do everything in my power that all those goods be secured to you and that you are not molested in carrying them, and also that whole families shall go in the same vessel and make this remove which I am sensible must give you a great deal of trouble as easy as his Majesty's service will admit and hope that in what every part of the world you may fall you may be faithful subjects, a peaceable and happy people.

I must also inform you that it is his Majesty's pleasure that you remain in security under the inspection and Direction of the troops that I have the Honour to command.

The actual rounding up of the colonists was entrusted to Major John Handfield of Annapolis, who also bitterly resented his duty, writing to Winslow, "I heartily join with you in wishing that we were both of us got over this most disagreeable and troublesome part of the service." Handfield's wife was herself Acadian on her mother's side, and the major found himself obliged to deport his sister-in-law, nephews and nieces, aunts and cousins. Winslow himself confided to a friend, "It hurts me to hear their weeping and wailing and gnashing of teeth. I am in hopes our affairs will soon put on another face, and we get transports, and I get rid of the worst piece of service that ever I was in."

Nevertheless, he did his duty, and within a short time all residents had been confined in town, and their homes and barns destroyed by fire. Following orders to burn and lay waste, soldiers moved from village to village, torching everything in sight.[3]

The transports that Winslow wanted arrived soon enough, courtesy of that most eminent of Boston shipping firms, Apthorp & Hancock.

By the end of the year, about 6,000 Acadians had been shipped out of the colony, 2,200 of them from Grand Pré. By the end of 1758, the year of the final fall of Louisbourg, the expulsions were pretty well complete, and transports were ordered to Île St. Jean to carry off the Acadians there as well, and take them to England. That part of the forced exodus was a disaster, for two of the transports, the *Violet* and the *Duke William*, were wrecked in a violent storm and more than seven hundred people drowned; only twenty-seven survived and made it to Penzance in a longboat. Others, taken to the West Indies, mostly died of smallpox.[4] Even on the transports from the Acadian shores to New England, a good many of the deported settlers perished, and the survivors were distributed up and down the coast, from Massachusetts to South Carolina. A few were imprisoned for a while in Halifax, then shipped back to France. Virginia refused to accept its quota of "French neutrals," and they were instead shipped to England as prisoners of war; after the Treaty of Paris in 1763 the survivors were taken to France, mostly to the port cities of Morlaix and St.-Malo.

In the end, only a few of the deportees stayed where they were put. The overwhelming majority of the survivors made their way, in small groups, families, and as individuals, back up the coast to their former homes in Nova Scotia; a few others traveled south to Louisiana, where they settled down and evolved into the Cajuns.

The majority of the expelled were back within a few years. Others, who had stayed behind hidden in forests and isolated communities, soon emerged to join them. For some of the Acadians, however, the deportation turned into years and years of wandering.

The English called the deportations the Expulsion. In French, however, they called it the *Grand Dérangement*, the Great Upheaval.[5]

Some of the justifications for the expulsion were so thin they were widely criticized. (For example, the chief justice, Jonathan Belcher, attempted to rationalize it by maintaining that one of the treasonous activities of the Acadians was their attempt to induce the newly arrived Germans at Lunenburg to desert to the French, which no one much believed. The German settlers were Protestants, brought in specifically as a countervailing presence to the Catholic French, and few had any fondness for France, its people, or its religion.) It's also interesting that, from the middle of 1755, the official records suddenly become suspiciously thin, as though a cover-up was attempted, leading the historian Winthrop Bell to assert that "one consequence [of this putative cover-up] is that our information is very scrappy."[6]

Within a few months after the deportations were complete, Lawrence suggested to Governor Shirley in Boston that it was time to replenish the vacant Acadian lands with English-speaking (and Protestant) settlers. Shirley was skeptical. He pointed out that New Englanders "were fond not only of being governed by general assemblies consisting of a Governor, Council and House of Representatives but likewise of Charters" and that Nova Scotia, which was still controlled directly by Lawrence himself, was therefore not at all to their political taste. Nevertheless, in the three-year period from 1760 to 1763, some 4,500 New Englanders, the so-called Planters, settled along the Fundy shores in the ancient lands of the Acadians, giving the colony a distinctly New England air.[7] They were brought there, of course, by ships supplied by Apthorp & Hancock, acting as Nova Scotia's Boston agent.[8]

There was one more piece of unfinished business. The Acadians had been obliged to abandon their livestock, and many thousands of cattle, horses, and other animals were wandering at large on the farms and in the surrounding woods. No count was made at the time, but estimates derived from 1748 to 1750 at Annapolis Royal, Minas, Psiquid, Cobequid, Chignecto, and other Acadian villages accounted for 17,750 cattle, 26,650 sheep, 12,750 swine, and 1,600 horses. The numbers were presumably somewhat higher by 1755.[9] A great many of the cattle were rounded up and driven to Halifax by army units, there to be slaughtered, salted, and added to commissary stores. But that much wealth on the loose attracted the attention of more than the army. Farmers from elsewhere in the colony, especially the new settlers across the peninsula on the Atlantic shore, Germans from Lunenburg, made forays to see what they could get. They were given some animals, because Lawrence wanted at least to keep the beasts alive, but others they simply took. Colonel John

Winslow, in a letter to John Gorham's brother Joseph, then in Lunenburg with a party of Gorham's Rangers, referred in a matter-of-fact way to "the return of the next party" coming up for cattle. Lawrence wrote to Winslow to order the Germans to desist for some time from their efforts to round up the animals, "since they Fright them all into the woods." Early on, before the deportations were over, Winslow actually blamed the remaining Acadian women and children for themselves driving the animals "back into the country; and as soon as we are rid of the People Make no Question but their Beasts may be Found." The surveyor general, Charles Morris, on the other hand, asserted that the Lunenburgers had simply removed and kept as many cattle as they possibly could. Lawrence himself came under fire later for giving animals away to his cronies. An accuser in 1760, in a letter to the Board of Trade, mentioned a cattle drive of over one thousand head to Halifax, some of which were sold there, others given in charity, but many "given to persons in Halifax."[10]

Almost all of these assertions, accusations, and counteraccusations involved cattle. Horses were seldom mentioned. So what happened to the 1,600 Acadian horses?

To answer this question, we need to provide some background and a small digression.

Until recently Sable's horses were referred to as ponies, even in the technical literature, because they're small in size, seldom standing more than 14 hands (54 inches) to the withers, and the conventional measure of a pony is 14.2 hands.[11] But they're true horses, even if small—the stallions weigh up to nine hundred pounds, mares to eight hundred.

They're chunky in shape, with narrow but deep chests, heavy shoulders and necks, and short heavy legs. They have small, rounded wide-set ears slightly tipped inward, and many have fine muzzles and thin, curved nostrils. Roman noses are common, although they generally have finely dished faces. Their hooves are small and round, but often become overgrown in the soft sand. The stallions have exceptionally long forelocks, manes and tails and, in extreme cases, mane and tail may even reach the ground. Manes and forelocks of mares are relatively short.[12]

Those curiously convex Roman noses, low-set tails, and muscular shoulders give away their ancestry, for these are also characteristics of the North African Barb horse that originated along the Barbary Coast (Morocco, Tunisia, Algeria, Libya) and came to Europe when the forces of Islam swept into Spain in the eighth century.

It's generally accepted that the first domesticated horses were bred in the steppes of central Asia. In time, two broad groups emerged: the northerly so-called cold-blooded types, and the Arab horse to the south, of which the Barb is a variant. (The Barb is slightly larger, with a lower-placed tail, and has hair at the fetlocks. It is noted for speed and endurance.) It is possible the horses got to North Africa with the Berbers of the Barbary Coast, the indigenes of the North African coast, whose origins have remained obscure but who plausibly originated in what is now Afghanistan.

Over the centuries, Arab-Barb genes have been downloaded, in the jargon of our times, into a variety of subbreeds. The true Arabian, a light horse prized for its intelligence, was already widespread in Arabia by the seventh century; one of its genetic markers is that it has only twenty-three vertebrae instead of the usual twenty-four. The so-called Thoroughbred is an English variant developed after a stock of Arab and Barb horses was introduced into England as early as the third century by Roman legions. The breed was further refined when forty-three more Arab mares (the *soi-disant* Royal Mares) were imported into England during the reigns of James I and Charles I, and the *General Stud Book,* the family tree of all Thoroughbreds, was begun. In this holy document of breeders you'll find only those horses that may be traced back to the Royal Mares in direct line—or to only three other horses: the Byerly Turk (imported 1689), the Darley Arabian (after 1700), and the Godolphin Barb (aka the Godolphin Arabian, about 1730). The English Thoroughbred has since been introduced to most countries. It's what you'll be gambling on if you lay down money at the betting windows of tracks all across the world, from Macao through Dubai to Kentucky.

Since humans have always shown an aptitude for tinkering with the genes of other species, it is not surprising that by now there are a baker's dozen of other breeds listed in the stud books, among them some of the world's biggest farm animals (the Percheron, the Shire, the Clydesdale, and the Pinzgauer), descended from the ancient warhorses of the Middle Ages. The Arab-Barb stock has yielded up many subbreeds, including the Asian (a blending of Arab and Persian breeds, such as the Tartar, the Kirghiz, the Mongol, and the Cossack), and the Anglo-Arab, whose origins are obvious enough from the name. There are also various American breeds, including the Standardbred, developed during the first half of the nineteenth century from a Thoroughbred imported from Britain in 1788; the quarter horse, said to descend from a small Thoroughbred stallion imported into Virginia in the eighteenth century; the Morgan, which originated from a stallion given to Justin Morgan of Vermont around 1795; and the Appaloosa, which developed in the Nez Percé Indian territory from wild mustangs, which in turn descended from Spanish horses brought to the New World by explorers, which in turn, of course, descended from the Barb.[13]

These tightly identified breeds are relevant when it comes to untangling the origins of Sable's horses. It is their genetic makeup that argued, in the end, against the rather romantic notion that the island's horses are the sole survivors of a Spanish or Portuguese shipwreck in the early days of exploration. Many early writers on Sable made much of this lovely idea: horses as the only survivors of a ship dashed to pieces in the breakers, the horses snorting and gasping their way to safety while their owners perished. . . . a poetic beginning to the wild freedom the horses enjoy today. But had that been so, they would have been more purely Barb in their physical characteristics. As Barbara Christie points out, their genes also argue against yet another romantic notion, that the horses were in the direct line from the Royal Stud begun by Colbert under the reign of Louis XIV, whose offspring were shipped out to Quebec and other places from 1665 to improve the stock there, resulting in what is known today as the Canada horse. Colbert was well informed on Acadian affairs (and a great admirer of their sheep), but there is no record that he ever shipped them horses.[14]

In truth, the Acadians were an independent-minded crowd and freely traded with the New Englanders, in defiance of French policy, as we have seen. By the late 1600s, Acadia's governor, Joseph Robineau de Villbon, was mildly regretting that such traffic was obliged to exist, and at the same time recognizing his community's "need to obtain from them stallions and mares for breeding purposes, so that the stock may be completely changed." The horses Villbon coveted were themselves already very mixed, being the descendants of earlier horses brought to the New World by Spanish, English, Dutch, Finnish, and Swedish colonists. Several shipments of Irish horses had also arrived in Virginia during the 1620s. Degrees of Spanish, Barb, or Arabian blood could be found in all these imports. Typical was the Chickasaw, bred by the Choctaw, Cherokee, Seminole, and Cree Indians, which were naturalized Andalusians. The Virginians, in turn, bred them to their own stock and made of them the forerunner of the modern quarter horse.[15]

Nor was there any shortage of horses for the Virginians and New Englanders to export. By the 1660s horses were already a nuisance in Virginia, rampaging through village streets at night and damaging crops. "The irate and sleepless Virginians thinned their ranks by sale and export."[16]

The genetic markers of Sable Island's modern horses closely match those from Acadia—a blend of Barb, Canada horses, and animals from the early American colonies. The evidence, both circumstantial and genetic, is therefore persuasive that they are Acadian in origin, descendants of stock commonly used along the Fundy shores of Nova Scotia by the French-speaking farmers and traders there, and abandoned in the deportations.

There is no mention in the records that Thomas Hancock was among the "persons in Halifax" to whom Lawrence gave livestock, but it is known that Hancock's ships were available for British use, that he had interests in the West Indies eager for stock, and that he landed animals of all kinds on Sable Island a year later. Hancock's own records never admitted owning Acadian animals or shipping any of them offshore, but that he did so was asserted some years later by Governor John Wentworth of Nova Scotia, who wrote that Hancock had "before 1760 fitted out a schooner and sent to Sable Island horses, cows, sheep, goats, and hogs."[17] He was in a position to know, because he was yet another part of their close-knit circle; a female cousin of his had married a son of Charles Apthorp, and it is therefore entirely reasonable that he would have known this firsthand. We don't know why Hancock took them to the island, however, for Wentworth never said. Was it used as a way station before shipping them to the West Indies plantations, as some have claimed? Or was he simply following up Andrew Le Mercier's notion of having men and livestock on the island as a benevolent lifesaving resource (and thus indirectly asserting his own right to the island itself)?

The notion of leaving horses and other livestock on islands was a commonplace in British colonial history; in 1834, for example, it was recorded that seven thousand head of cattle and five hundred wild horses roamed the Falkland Islands.[18]

The circumstantial evidence is convincing: The Boston merchant Thomas Hancock benefited not only directly from the expulsion of the Acadians (his transport ships were hired for the chore), but also indirectly, by somehow acquiring animals for his own use, either as payment or by simply confiscating them. Some of these animals, most notably sixty of the horses he acquired, he took to Sable Island. He died before he could take them off. Their descendants are still there.

The horses would have embarked in October 1756 from Grand Pré in a dumpy little two-masted schooner.[19] It would have beat out into the Bay of Fundy, tacking its way down the coast, rounding the tip of peninsular Nova Scotia at what was later to become Yarmouth and heading into the open ocean. It would have taken another day to get to Sable. October is near the end of the hurricane season, and the wildest gales would have been winding down, but it was always prudent to be suspicious of wind changes. June or July would have been better as far as the wind was concerned, but in summer Sable seemed always shrouded in fog, as great a hazard to sailors as the gales in these parts. In any case, if you're a commercial skipper, you go when the cargo takes you.

Overnight the schooner would have stood out a cautious distance away to the north, too far away to see the surf, and at daybreak, after making sure that the wind hadn't shifted, edged cautiously toward the dunes, sounding constantly. If the weather was good, vessels could approach the beach and even the channel to the body of water called Lake Wallace that then had eight feet of water at high tide, about enough to "admit vessels of perhaps 30 tons or more if not sharp," as the Reverend Le Mercier claimed a few years earlier, in 1750, attributing this opening to the divine will of

Providence, which was, of course, on his side. This lake was then fifteen miles or so long and a few hundred yards wide; the sea had breached the dunes sometime earlier, and it was open to the ocean to the north and southwest. The schooner from Grand Pré would not have tried to enter the lake, however; the vessel drew a good fifteen feet, the keel far too "sharp" to carry the vessel over the bar and into lake waters.

The animals—there were "beeves" too, and sheep and goats—would have been slung overboard in canvas slings rigged to gaff and boom cranes, and left to swim to shore. But only the horses stay in memory. No one remembers the cattle, for their fate was to have no fate, and the hogs and sheep and goats were of no account anyhow, being only food. The horses were small and sturdy, with long tails and shaggy manes, powerful in the withers and strongly muscled, with long-lashed eyes and heavy teeth. These were not romantic castaways. They were there for hard business reasons, a product of politics gone astray. They were also farm horses, bred for work in harsh places, and tough in the fiber. They'd need to be tough, on this desolate shore.

CHAPTER TEN

Its Curious Ecosystem

*A surprisingly moderate climate which
allows the abundant presence of fresh
water and horse fodder*

Sable is desolate, yes, and deadly to careless
sailors, prone to sudden storms and dense fogs, but how harsh is the climate? After all, those horses have survived, without human protection,
feeding themselves and finding their own population balance, for more
than two hundred years. And at times other creatures lived there too. Not
just foxes, but cattle, sheep, goats, swine. How did they make it through?

In another October, 247 years after the landing
from Grand Pré, the wind was fresh from the south-southwest, the temperature in the high teens, the water as cold as always, its color a furious
emerald. On the south beach, the surf was pounding at the berm, waves
with a fetch of a thousand miles or more. A fresh trail of hoofprints along
the high-tide line of the north beach stretched from some infinity to the
east. Thirty feet or so to the right, a blowout in the dunes, overgrown with

tangled grasses and storm flotsam, sheltered a small freshwater pond where horses had paused to drink; the sand was scuffed by their hoofs, and horse dung, some of it still steaming, lay everywhere. A broken spar from a long-dead vessel was propped up in the sand, almost as tall as a flagpole.

Some distance to the left, a hundred yards or so on, a group of gray seals lay on the wet sand; from a distance they looked like beach rocks, but if anyone approached they lumbered quickly into the sea and slid away to a vantage point where they could keep an eye on what was up. They would parallel walkers up the shoreline, effortlessly keeping pace. Seabirds—gulls, mostly, but also the occasional tern—wheeled overhead. There were few shells on the beach, and those few, almost always broken, were from prehistoric creatures; there are no shellfish on the banks now, of course, none of the rock-clingers like mussels and periwinkles, nor are there clams or scallops. No weeds either; nothing grows in the restless surf. Bits of broken Styrofoam and torn netting littered the beach.

On the north beach, small waves rolled in, endless, restless, coming in from deeper water beyond. Up there, somewhere beyond the horizon, was Cape Breton and then, across the gulf, Newfoundland and the frigid Arctic. The water temperature off the beach was about forty-three degrees Fahrenheit (six degrees Celsius). It would get a few degrees colder before the winter was over, and in summer would go up, but not by very much, unless a Gulf Stream eddy coiled its way past the island. Typical summer temperatures are around fifty-four degrees Fahrenheit (twelve degrees Celsius). Cold, but regular. The ocean maintains Sable's homeostasis.

Sable Island's climate is in fact mild by the standards of its latitude, despite its position as a locus of winter frontal storms and summer tropical cyclones. Climatologists call it temperate oceanic, which makes it considerably milder than places at the same latitude on the continent to its west. In capsule, the climate is stormy, but mild in winter, cool in summer, humid and windy year-round. Ocean waters maintain winter air near freezing and keep summer temperatures below what would be considered room temperature in other parts. Winter air temperatures are normally between 41 degrees Fahrenheit (5 degrees Celsius) and 14 degrees Fahrenheit (−10 degrees Celsius), and summer temperatures peak in August at 77 degrees Fahrenheit (25 degrees Celsius),[1] and the average annual range is only 33.5 degrees (or 18.6 degrees on the Celsius scale), compared to 44 degrees (or 24.3 degrees on the Celsius scale) at Halifax International Airport, and 70 degrees (38.9 degrees on the Celsius scale) on the prairies. The island experiences frost on average only 102 days a year, and there is scant snowfall. It hardly ever gets hot; the highest temperature ever recorded is 82.04 degrees Fahrenheit (27.8 degrees Celsius), on August 27, 1951.

But although Sable's winters are milder than the mainland's, the weather does get cold. The lowest temperature ever recorded on the island, on January 31, 1920, was −19.4 degrees Celsius, a shade below zero on the Fahrenheit scale then used on the island; and since records were first kept there have been many years of extended cold spells, with pack ice to the north, massive icebergs drifting past, and "slob ice" accreting to the beaches.

In 1833, "from the 14th Jan to the 10th Mar; ducks, rabbits and horses . . . perished from the severity of the weather."[2] On July 7, 1836, the packet *Express,* on the southern edge of the Sable Bank about seventy-five miles southwest of Sable Island, reported two bergs, one 180 feet high and the other 150 feet high. On April 27, 1862, Captain Morrison of the bark *Gillilema* bound from London for Halifax "report[ed] having fallen in with great quantities of ice. . . . When between Sable Island and Cape Breton saw as many as twelve at once of the large size bergs, some of them much higher than ship's trucks."

It has been cold enough, at any rate, to threaten the existence of Sable's livestock, including the horses, which at times were reduced from an average of three hundred or so to a mere few dozen. On May 29, 1823, for example, the schooner *Two Brothers* arrived at Halifax from Sable Island, bringing news "that the last winter was extremely severe, so much so that all the wild hogs on the island are said to have perished."[3]

Sable Island is also wet. It rains often and hard. Since the island is in the path of traveling frontal storms year-round, most of its precipitation comes from large-scale storms. Thunderstorms are infrequent (only about eleven thunderstorm days a year), but hurricanes and tropical storms are a dime a dozen. The yearly precipitation averages just short of fifty-five inches, of which only 9 percent is snowfall. The number of wet days almost equals the number of dry days. Even the driest months, July and September, receive an average 3.6 inches of precipitation each, while the wettest, December and January, both receive an average 5.7 inches.[4]

Adding to this cheerful picture is Sable's reputation as the foggiest place in Maritime Canada. Alas, the most cloudless and driest time—the summer—is also the time with the most fog. July has a depressing average of twenty-two fog days, and in 1967 it got even worse: Fog was present on thirty of thirty-one days. June of the same year recorded the longest duration of fog, 126 hours—more than five whole days of the stuff.[5] A survivor of the wrecked steamer *State of Virginia,* which ran around on Sable in July 1879, recounted afterward that

> the thick grey mist [had] seemed to envelop us like a shroud. . . . The only danger we feared was collision with another steamer, but with as close a watch as ours, and the incessant fog signals, an accident did not seem possible. An inspection of the day's record, however, showed the somewhat ominous words "not accurate" following the latitude and longitude, since the fog had of course prevented any correct observation at noon.[6]

Norman Campbell, who later became famous as a theatrical producer, but who spent some time on Sable working as a meteorologist, is sardonic about the weather he encountered there. "Fog? Weather? Rain? Yes, indeed, even in fine weather there could be a banana-shaped cloud hanging directly over the island."

Whatever the climate, of course, a supply of fresh water is critical for the survival of terrestrial life. Of this most precious commodity, Sable has more than enough. At least for a modest population.

There seems, at casual glance, to be water everywhere on Sable. For such a small island, there are a surprising number of small lakes and ponds scattered throughout, and fresh water can be collected, even where there are no ponds, with a simple shovel and fifteen minutes' work. Sheets of salt water cover large areas of the flat south beach, particularly at high tide, and occasionally along the shores there are patches of supersaturated sand treacherous to the footing. Sable's quicksand is seldom hazardous to humans or animals, though humans have been known to get mired up to their thighs and have had to be helped out, and there's occasional evidence that a horse has struggled to extricate itself. The horses, clearly, have learned to be wary of quicksand; hoofprints skirting an apparently hard piece of wet sand should be taken as a reliable indicator that there is instability underfoot. And, indeed, the sand might look solid, with a hard crust, but if it feels a little unstable, then suddenly a foot will break through, tripping you up, and you go down on your hands and knees, water springing up as though squeezed from a sponge. It means small airplanes must land on the beach with great care; the sand is tricky enough to trap untracked vehicles.

But nothing on Sable, not even water, is stable or predictable, any more than the island itself is. If you now stand on the western dunes and look along the arching curve of Sable to the distant eastern dunes, just visible as a low stain on the horizon across the lines of breakers, you would be able to see the waters of Lake Wallace ahead and to your right, past Dead Horse Pass, if the dunes didn't intervene. But the same body of water, into which Andrew Le Mercier had observed one might send a small vessel to shelter, was once also behind you—much of it was west of what is now the island's westernmost point. The island has shifted east in the interim, taking the lake with it.

Of the dozens of freshwater ponds on the island, some are small and almost empty between rains, their carrying capacity fluctuating with the weather and the seasons. Because they're shallow, and have a high organic content (code for natural contamination, mostly by the horses) at their bottoms and along their shores, they're useless for human purposes, whether for domestic or industrial uses. Only a few of these ponds are of any significant size and contain water of reasonably good quality. In these few, whose overall depth is only about five to ten feet and whose water level fluctuates in the order of three to four feet a year, there is a dependable small supply during dry summer periods.

All the other freshwater bodies on the island are small depressions in the sand that have been scoured below the high-water-table mark. These ponds, therefore, have a useful reservoir only during periods of high water. During the summer months, when the water table falls, most of the ponds become dry. These ponds are quite small in area and are used as occasional watering holes by the horses.

"There are neither River nor Brooks of fresh Water on the Isle," Le Mercier wrote in a treatise devoted to justifying his colonizing efforts, "but everywhere, even on the beach, you may come to fresh clear Water by digging about three feet."[7] The Sable horses know this basic fact and in dry seasons can commonly be seen energetically burrowing into the sand up to their withers to get at the water.[8] There are no streams, because the island is just sand, and the water seeps into the ground faster than it can run off. Scientists have measured the infiltration rate of water through Sable sand in a range from seventy to ninety inches per hour, much faster than even the greatest hurricane-caused rainfall intensity recorded on the island. Rain and melting snow and dew, therefore, directly recharge the underground aquifer, the island's groundwater.[9] The ponds are just the surface manifestation of the underlying aquifer. Life on Sable is made possible and sustained by this aquifer, which is one of the great curiosities of the island.

In shape, the freshwater aquifer is like a low dome, highest in the center of the island and sloping down to the beaches. Hydrologists have described it as a shallow lens, located only slightly above sea level,[10] varying in depth from less than a foot to about one hundred and twenty feet, deeper on the north part of the island than on the south. The gradient from the center of the island to the beaches is small—only one or two feet. But, of course, it is not as neat as that sounds. Like everything else on the island, the freshwater resource is far from stable and shifts in response to a number of external factors. Although the aquifer is continuous from the west end of the island to the east, the freshwater reservoir is not; smaller discontinuous reservoirs occur wherever the conditions are right, which essentially means under any significant land area surrounded by a dune system. In addition, the groundwater fluctuates in resonance with the tide, its peaks and troughs coinciding exactly with those of the tidal stages. In consequence, several low-lying areas of the island are periodically flooded with salt water, which occasionally breaches the freshwater lens, infecting it with slugs of vertically infiltrating salt water. Also, the storms and high seas flooding the south beach create sheets of salt water that seep through to the aquifer and contaminate it, however temporarily.[11]

What, then, sustains the aquifer? Why doesn't it become permanently contaminated with salt water from the surrounding ocean? If there is salt water on every side in such volumes, and in many places salt water on the

surface, and frequent vertical intrusions of salt into the freshwater—why
and how does the fresh water stay fresh? Are the rains sufficient to keep
it so?

The answer is yes, but not by much. The aquifer is kept intact by two
other factors: by its head, which is the pressure caused by the height that
the peak of its dome is above sea level, and by the simple fact that seawater and freshwater don't mix easily. Seawater is denser, and freshwater
tends to float on its surface, even where there is an unconfined aquifer in
the sand such as the one that makes up and underlies Sable. Hydrologists
define the boundaries between saline and nonsaline waters by something
they call the Ghyben-Herzberg relation, which predicts the position of
the seawater by measuring the head of the freshwater aquifer. It has become obvious through many studies (the Ghyben-Herzberg relation was
generated in studies off the Netherlands and in the North Sea) that the
key to preventing seawater intrusions into coastal aquifers is to keep some
pressure in the freshwater aquifer above sea level, and consequently that
measuring the freshwater elevations can yield accurate predictions about
saline infection of an aquifer.

Ominously for Sable Island, the predictions are that lowering the water table by one foot would mean a seawater infiltration of forty feet. That
is, for every foot the water table is drawn down by pumping, the aquifer
will in fact get shallower by forty feet.[12] And since the aquifer is only one
hundred and twenty feet at its deepest point, careful conservation of fresh
water on Sable is more than just good practice; it is the key to keeping
the aquifer fresh and therefore available to the island's human and animal
population. Overpumping, or drilling too deep, won't just suck air; it will
suck in seawater, and the damage could be permanent, or at best last a
very long time.[13]

The same factor makes disposal of wastes on the island difficult. Because
the aquifer is shallow and exists entirely in permeable soils, liquid waste

readily seeps into the aquifer and spreads through the upper levels, threatening the station's wells. Solid wastes, for their part, break down easily thanks to an abundance of low-pH precipitation, and the resulting sludge will also move easily through the aquifer, at first vertically and then horizontally.[14]

Among other things, this means that the human population on the island will always have to be small. Not for Sable a resort hotel, however ecologically conscious; there would be no use for gray-water recycling, and no way to deal with the large amounts of sewage such a place would inevitably produce—unless humans did as the horses do, and randomly scattered their sewage over the island's surface to decompose there. It is hard to see anyone really thinking this a good idea.

W̲ater is critical, but the horses need plant life for their survival too, and plants have a precarious existence on the island.

There is one solitary tree on Sable, hard by the helipad, a scrawny pine, dozens of years old but a mere three feet tall, not exactly an example of the forest primeval. In any case, it is not native here but was planted by the staff, dragged over to its fate on a supply boat many years ago. It's true that, in a botanist's more generous view, the prevalent bayberry and juniper plants on the island are "trees" too, but they're even shorter than the pathetic thing at the helipad, and in common-sense definition are really nothing but small bushes. Real trees can't survive Sable's ferocious winds; not even those gnarled spruces that cling to ocean-side cliffs on the mainland could make it through Sable Island gales. Besides, there is no real soil into which a proper tree can put down roots.

Plants that thrive on Sable are those that cling close to the ground. Small shrubs, bushes, gorse, grasses. Particularly grasses.

Less than half the island's 8,400 acres has plant cover—about 40 percent of the whole. But in that 40 percent are more than two hundred species, including some real curiosities, and including six species of positively tropical-looking orchids, mostly *Calopogon pulchellu*. Now there's an astonishing sight amid the beiges and duns and greens of Sable: In the warmth of July, in the moist depressions between the inland dunes, dense carpets of brilliant pink and rose and coral blossoms suddenly appear like little novae, glowing like small suns in the hollows.[15]

The most fragile plant ecology is on the spits at either end of the crescent. These are sometimes called the sea beaches, and sometimes even the bars, although a bar is more properly awash, except perhaps at low tide. The only plants that establish a toehold in these shifting, ever-changing environments, often flooded in storms and subject to being washed away altogether, are highly salt-resistant types such as sandworts, which derive as much of their nourishment from the water itself as from any rooting. Not surprisingly, these are called colonizing plants, or sometimes pioneer plants.

On the high dunes, which are constantly being eroded from the ocean side and built up on the landward side, and where the moisture content of the sand is vanishingly low, only highly adaptable plants can survive. The most common are seaside goldenrod, beach pea, lime grass, and marram grass, though toward the west end of Lake Wallace, a small colony of native bluegrass has taken root. In a few less windy areas sheltered by dunes, mats of beach pea blanket the sand. Uniquely, the beach pea derives its nitrogen not from soil or water but via bacteria in its root nodules, which convert airborne nitrogen into usable nitrates. Marram, a beach-binding grass, also called beach grass or sand reed, grows in many coastal areas of North America, Europe, and North Africa. It has evolved to thrive in accumulating sand; it is salt-resistant, strong enough to avoid the sand-blasting effect of high winds, can withstand periods of being buried alive, and has long underground roots or stems called rhizomes. As a tuft of marram gets overtaken by piles of sand, it sends up another shoot at some distance away on the underground stem system, sometimes as far as thirty or forty feet distant, and new shoots emerge through the dune. This network of undersand stems has two important roles on Sable: It helps to stabilize the dunes, and it provides the fodder on which Sable's horses survive.

In the low dunes in the middle of the island are thick carpets of beach grasses, at least three kinds of juniper, centaury, and primroses. If you examine a patch of this fragrant ground cover, you are likely to see wild strawberries, cranberries as large as grapes, blueberries, a columbine, pearly everlastings, a flower called blue-eyed grass, blue flag, wild roses and rosa rugosa gone wild, leather-leaved bayberry and many others. On the low, flat areas around ponds are the bog mosses and orchids, marsh arrow grass, and sago pond weed. Eelgrass grows in Lake Wallace. The insect-trapping sundew thrives in the boggy, nitrogen-poor earth around the ponds; occasional water lilies grow in the water itself.[16]

More than forty of the total number of plant species on the island were introduced here by humans—probably. Some may have hitched a ride, seeds carried on another seed's back, or been dropped here by overflying birds. Or been carried by the winds. Or even, though less likely, been washed up onshore and driven into the dunes by the wind.

CHAPTER ELEVEN

Its Lurid Rumors

More shipwrecks, reports of wreckers,

the sad tale of Mrs. Copeland's ring,

the establishment of Sable Station

For fifty years or so after they splashed ashore, the horses were left to run free, and only the wrecked ships and the occasional miserable castaway were there as witness, and few of the castaways lived to tell any tales. The horses grazed on the marram and gorse and the berries that grew wild, mated and bred and lived and died, and the surf thundered on the beaches and the sand drifted across the island, but there was no one there to see. Within a few years of their arrival in 1756, the men left on the island by Hancock's schooner were withdrawn or died—no one mentioned which, or seemed to care. The fog rolled in, and if a stallion galloped at full stride down a beach, its hoofs muffled in the sand and its snorting breath stifled by the mist, no one saw it happen. A shipwrecked sailor, one of the lucky ones rescued by a passing vessel, raved of gales howling up and down the beach, the blowing sand exposing forty wrecks in a row and, when the sand was blown back, uncovering forty more, but of the horses he made no mention.[1] If a foal was

dropped in the grass in spring, only the gulls were there to see it totter to
its feet. Men stayed away, and most of the cattle and sheep and hogs died
or were killed. Fishermen, though, of course, not all of them, had learned
to keep clear. At that time the west point of the island stretched north-
westerly in a mile-and-a-half bar that was dry in good weather, then another mile partly dry, then another nine miles over which the sea broke
at all times, then seven miles farther in which it broke in foul weather and
always showed an eerie ripple and strong cross seas, about seventeen miles
total from dry land, and at the eastern end the same, more or less. That
means that there were fifty miles of terrific breakers in a storm, and besides these, shoals and ridges in parallel, all of them white water when a
sea was running.[2] In the center of the island, the horses multiplied, and
foals no doubt skittered and jumped for the sheer joy of living, as foals
do, and soon there were a hundred or more, but no one counted them
or cared. Offshore, the current pulled and sucked and swallowed in the
fog. And sometimes, even in clear weather, ships sailed unknowing
straight for the bars, for the island was low to the horizon and perfectly
treeless and in color presented little contrast to the surrounding sea, and
too often there followed cries of dismay and then terror as the ships began to break up. The horses that cantered up and down the beaches
would have passed the remains of ships sticking out from the sand in
spikes and jagged ends and broken spars, from one end of the island to
the other, on both shores. They would have paid little attention to the
stranded sailors, most of whom died in the deadly winters without the
wooly coats the horses grew, and even the horses died when the cold got
too intense. Sometimes those who were shipwrecked made crude shelters and, if there were enough of them, even rudimentary huts and other
buildings.

On April 22, 1757, the *Buchanan* under Captain Lawrence, bound for
Maryland from Gibraltar, went aground with no survivors.

In April 1758, a French privateer foundered. No survivors.

On November 15, 1759, a schooner under the command of one Major Robert Elliott, on his way back to Boston after the capture of Quebec from the French, was pulled onto the island by unexpectedly strong currents and stranded deep in the sands of the northwest bar. The survivors' lamentations added more substance to Sable's already colorful legends: "They could see land but it was too far away. The midshipman cried for a boat to be launched but the seas were too dangerous. Suddenly the wind rose higher. With increased horror, the poor travelers felt the ship move under them. . . . They were released, free of the sandbar. . . . They were floating [but only to be] lodged in the sand again, this time just off the south beach. Disembarkation was still impossible." Two sailors, both able swimmers, tied lines around themselves and without hesitation leaped into the sea. Within seconds the surf took them under, and they were drowned. A third seaman made it to shore and fastened the line to the beach. Elliott and his wife then tied their two daughters securely to their own backs and struggled, hand over hand, to shore. Amazingly, everyone else made it safely to the beach.

A little bit inland, in the lee of the dunes, they cobbled together rudimentary shelters from the ripped sails that had washed up on the beach. Elliott was obviously a capable and enterprising man, and within a few weeks he had supervised the construction of a storehouse and barracks from lumber salvaged from their vessel.

In December 1759, before they were rescued, yet another ship went aground on the north beach, an unnamed fishing schooner from Ipswich, Massachusetts, and was broken up in the surf. The survivors joined the Elliott party, inflating the island's temporary population to almost seventy people.[3]

Elliott built exceptionally well, for in 1842, close to a hundred years after his vessel ran aground and his little community was founded, an old landmark in the form of a pyramid, said to be one hundred feet high, would be completely blown away during a severe gale, exposing a few small huts built of the timbers and planks of a vessel. Inside were pieces of furniture, stores put in boxes, bales of blankets, a quantity of military shoes, and, among other articles, Elliott's brass tag identifying him as an officer of the forty-third regiment.[4] About the same time as this discovery someone noticed a blackened line on the face of a dune, which was found to be the site of an even older encampment, date and provenance unknown. Scattered about were rusty guns and bayonets, knives made from iron hoops, broken glass, a tattered English ensign, human bones mingled with those of cattle and seals, and an English shilling from the reign of Queen Elizabeth, "as sharp as when it came from the die."[5]

The Elliott party found no one living on the island. At least some of Hancock's "beeves" were still there, however, because years later cattle bones were found at the Elliott encampment. The castaways apparently lived on beef, and on provisions they had succeeded in dragging ashore, hauled onto the beach in boxes from the disintegrating vessel. No horse bones were found. Either they didn't need them for food, or couldn't catch them if they did—they had salvaged no firearms. The horses were left alone, to live and to multiply, unmolested.

In 1761 an unidentified French ship apparently went aground. Its very existence is disputed, since its presence on Sable has been deduced only from the fact that in 1777 a vessel named *Aurora* went down, and the "survivors found [living on the island] seven negro women from a French ship that had been wrecked there 16 years before." These women were presumably taken off and have disappeared from history.

In 1766, an unidentified vessel of seven hundred tons, bound from Bristol to Boston, was broken up in high seas. Fourteen of twenty-eight crew died.

In 1769, an unidentified vessel bound for Philadelphia. No survivors.

In 1773 (or 1776?), the *Sophia*, under Captain Hastington, from Philadelphia for Quebec. No survivors.

In 1777, the aforementioned *Aurora*.

In 1779, the *Fame*, under Captain Murphy, or possibly the *Fame Murphy*, captain unknown, went down. No survivors.

In 1780, the *Jane*, under Captain Wilson, from London for Halifax. No survivors.

In 1781, the *Potowack*, under Captain Mitchell, from London for Quebec. No survivors.

In 1786, the *Telemachus*, under Captain Sargeant, from Georgia for Amsterdam. No survivors.

And so it went.

In 1774, records of the Nova Scotia colony show a permission granted by the then-governor, the always irascible and quarrelsome Francis Legge, and "approved by the King," to Michael Flannigan and his associates to live on Sable Island. Nothing is known of the purpose for which they went there or how long they remained.[6]

And according to the *Nova Scotia Gazette* of February 10, 1789, one Jesse Lawrence was living on Sable Island, helping shipwrecked sailors while earning his living at seal fishing. This unlikely hero came to light only in the aftermath of the American Revolution because "one day he was attacked by people from Massachusetts, who landed there and wantonly pillaged and destroyed his house and effects, and then compelled him to leave the island." There was a great deal of Nova Scotian indignation about this sordid event. It was later recorded that he did receive "a small compensation from Governor Hancock and the Council of Massachusetts, [but] it was not nearly enough to cover his losses."[7] Thereafter, the chronicles of the day make no mention of Lawrence; perhaps the need for anti-Yankee propaganda was sated. Presumably also the Hancock family had nothing to do with the wreckers.

In 1792, the *Rambler*, under Captain Kaquet, from Philadelphia for Boston. No survivors. Also in 1792, *La Feliz*, "a fine Spanish vessel," origin and destination unknown. No survivors.

In 1795, the *Orb*, under Captain Brigs, from Liverpool for Halifax. No survivors.

In 1797, the *Tribune*. No survivors. Also in 1797, the *Harriet*. (But there were *Harriets* recorded wrecked also in 1801 and 1804, which might be the same vessel.) Its skipper, its destination, its purposes, and whether or not anyone survived the wreck are unknown.

To say, then, that Sable Island was a hazard to shipping and imposed a huge cost on trade would be a gross understatement. Vessels were going down every year, sometimes four or five of them in a twelve-month span, and valuable cargoes were routinely lost, as well as dozens, even hundreds, of lives. When the French lost three ships of the line on the island, up to eighteen hundred men might have perished in a single day. There was considerable grumbling in Massachusetts and Nova Scotia about the ongoing costs of these shipwrecks, and a feeling that something had to be done about it. But nothing was, until, late in the century, the loss of two particular vessels drove indignation to the point where it precipitated political action.

The first was the wreck of the brig *Princess Amelia*, which ran aground on Sable Island's south beach in late November 1797. The vessel had been under the command of one Captain Wyatt, first name unknown, origin unknown, number of passengers unknown—for a vessel that was a media sensation at the time, an astonishing amount remains unrecorded. Nevertheless, we know that at least thirty people survived the wreck, because, on December 4, 1797, a Massachusetts schooner, the *Hero*, under Thomas Cunningham, was passing by Sable on a fishing trip when the skipper spotted a crowd of about thirty men signaling from the shore. Tempestuous weather, he reported, drove him off, and he could do nothing about it. Instead, he made for the mainland and, at Cole Harbor, left a written note of what he had seen "respecting the wrecked people." This leisurely communiqué was passed in time to the colony's council, whence it made its way to the governor, John Wentworth—the same Wentworth who was connected to the Apthorp family of Boston, and whose own wife, Frances (or Fannie as she was known in the demimonde) had become notorious for her amorous dalliances and quasi-political intrigues, some of them actually on behalf of her husband. Sir John was an energetic governor, who, some said, was as much at home in the deep woods with the Indians as he was in the drawing rooms of what passed for Halifax society; he had, after all, once been His Majesty's surveyor general of forests and had personally tramped the woods marking the best trees for the Royal Navy's ships. He immediately publicized the *Princess Amelia*'s plight around town and through public subscription collected blankets and provisions to help succor the castaways. Then he hired a vessel from the port of Liverpool on Nova Scotia's south shore to take all this provender to the island. This Captain Thomas Parker and his schooner *Black Snake* duly did.

Meanwhile, on Sable itself, the survivors, no doubt believing they had been abandoned by the departing Thomas Cunningham and his *Hero*, set about trying to save themselves. The captain, Wyatt, with the help of the passengers, wrestled his ship's longboat over to the island's north beach, a distance of a mile or more, loaded it with water and hardtack, and embarked with four of his crew and a Lieutenant Cochrane of the Fusiliers, one of the passengers. Off they rowed, like their 1737 predecessors from the *Catherine*, and a few days later made landfall in a cove east of Halifax, from which they made their way to the capital to spread the belated alarm. Perhaps they felt better when they were reassured in the capital that a rescue operation was already under way (or perhaps they were merely irritated by its dilatory nature and leisurely progress). In any case, by the middle of December, Parker's *Black Snake* reached Sable Island safely and returned on January 28 with the rest of the crew and passengers. He left a number of men on the island for the winter, "to save property and assist vessels,"[8] an initiative widely praised at the time.

At the end of the winter, that is, sometime in April or May 1798, Governor Wentworth, this time at the colony's expense, sent Andrew and William Miller to the island and commissioned them "keepers" of Sable Island. Clearly they didn't last, because by the next winter they were gone. Accounts from Barrington Township, a community on Nova Scotia's south shore, show that, in the spring of 1799, Captain John Reynolds left two more men—Coleman Crowell and Ziba Hunt—on Sable Island to hunt seals and look for wrecks during the summer. Later in the year Captain Reynolds returned in his schooner to take them back to Barrington, but foul weather drove him off. The unfortunate seal hunters were therefore left to fend for themselves for the winter, during which they reportedly survived on horsemeat and berries. In December, when the *Frances* (sometimes rendered *Francis*) went down, their diet was supplemented by barrels of ship's biscuits washed ashore. Alas, no people washed ashore, at least not alive. The sealers found the swollen corpses of animals and humans, as well as several casks of liquor.[9]

The plight of the *Princess Amelia* heightened emotions, but it was the wreck of the *Frances* that directly precipitated the establishment of a lifesaving station on Sable. This was mainly because of its interesting royal connections: Among the lost were the surgeon of the Royal Army's Seventh Fusiliers, who had been charged with delivering to Halifax the personal furnishings of Prince Edward, duke of Kent, commander in chief of His Majesty's forces in North America, such as they still were. (The prince was one of Fannie Wentworth's infatuations.) The surgeon was a Dr. Copeland, and with him were his wife and children. The unfortunate

Mrs. Copeland and her ring were later to become the subject of many romantic and occasionally lurid rumors. Also on board, His Royal Highness's coachman and gardener, several regimental officers, and a crew of nineteen.[10]

In a subsequent inquiry, the two sealers recounted how they had spotted the *Frances* off the northeast bar on December 2. By nightfall, they said, the island was in the grip of a storm, and they believed the vessel had been driven on the sands and broken up, for there was no sign of it in the morning. After the storm abated, the sealers added this piquant detail: Lying on the beach was the body of a woman with a ring on her finger, and with her a number of articles, unspecified, that were later carried to Barrington. They claimed to have buried the woman, ring and all.

Stories of these two sealers and their discoveries soon made their way back to the mainland, swelling in the telling. Rumors circulated that all the men on the *Frances* had been murdered for their booty, perhaps by the sealers, perhaps by imagined wreckers lurking elsewhere on the island. The story of Mrs. Copeland's ring, particularly, was engorged in the retelling. No longer was it discovered on her body, but instead the body of a fingerless woman had been found; ring and finger had been removed by some dastardly work. In short order, Mrs. Copeland herself was resurrected—or at least her ghost was.

One Captain Torrens, in the brig *Hariot*, sent to rescue what royal baggage he could find but instead wrecked on the island, made himself at home in a miserable hut he found in the dunes. Returning to it one night, the story went, he found a dog barking at the door, and inside a woman sitting by his fire, with long, lank hair and a gown much the worse for wear. She didn't say a word but held up a bloodied hand that was missing a finger. When Torrens turned to find bandages, she got up and left. He followed her to the lake, into which she stepped and disappeared. When he returned to his hut, he found her again seated before his fire. He addressed her as Mrs. Copeland and promised her he would do everything he could to return her ring to her family. She then disappeared and was not seen again. On his rescue and return to Halifax he tracked the stolen ring to a family living on the south shore and thence to a jeweler in Halifax. He purchased the ring and did indeed return it to her family.[11]

Unsurprisingly, in the world of rumor, within a few years Marie Antoinette's jewels had also made it onto the *Frances*, courtesy of Corporal Bonaparte and parties unspecified.

Partly because these rumors were so lurid, and partly because of the royal connection, Governor Wentworth set up a commission of inquiry to see if treachery had been at work in the sinking of the *Frances*. He sent Lieutenant Joseph Scrambler to Sable to see what he could find out about the *Frances* or any other ship that had been wrecked there in the interim. Scrambler took with him a consignment of farm animals, which he loosed on the island for the use of future castaways.

When he got there, Sable was deserted, but a schooner was riding at anchor at the northeast spit. He couldn't reach it; the currents prevented his attempt to "beat up where she lay." Later in the afternoon, he noticed the schooner had hauled anchor and was under sail, and took off after it. It was the *Dolphin* of Barrington, laden with fish, sealskins, and seal oil— and also several trunks, very much damaged, one of which was labeled with the name of Prince Edward, and the other directed to Captain Sterling of the Seventh Regiment of Foot. Both were empty. A third trunk contained two greatcoats marked with Prince Edward's insignia.

Scrambler's reports only fueled the rumor mill. Dozens of stories made the rounds about murderers and wreckers at work; goods from the *Frances* were said to have turned up in dozens of homes on the south shore. Not all were false. Barrington's Captain Reynolds went back to Sable again to remove Coleman Crowell and Ziba Hunt, left on the island a year earlier, and while he was there thought he might as well add some of the *Frances's* booty to his own ship "without notifying any authority," as an official report said later in entirely justified dudgeon. When he returned home, Reynolds peddled these appropriated goods all over town. Soldier's caps, officer's apparel, silk stockings, and red coats soon appeared on the townsfolk. The red coats were the most popular, and the locals took to wearing them to meetings and town functions. Some were patched into quilts.

Reynolds was subsequently ordered to Halifax by military authorities for questioning but in the end escaped punishment. Nevertheless, the duke of Kent, whose chattels Reynolds had been selling, later met him by chance in the street, an irresistible opportunity to be haughty: "Your conduct, Sir, might do very well for Americans, but it is certainly not suitable for British subjects!" he proclaimed. With that, the duke spun on his heel and marched off.[12]

The city of Halifax swirled anew with rumors of wreckers and pirates on Sable Island. Yes, it was a hazard to navigation, and yes, the storms were frequent and the currents erratic, and yes, it was on the Great Circle Route from Boston and New England to European ports, but still . . . more would be saved if criminals and ne'er-do-wells didn't lurk—murderers and thieves and looters. There were reports vessels had been lured onto the bar, by means unspecified, their crews and passengers tossed into the sea and the boats stripped.

So vivid were these stories, and so feverish the indignation, that the colonial legislature in 1800 passed the Act of Assembly, which prohibited residence on the island without a license; the penalty was up to six years in prison. The following year the legislature added to its Sable repertoire by passing an act for the protection of shipwrecked property, a bill aimed directly at the evil persons said to be still lurking on Sable. The governor was authorized to appoint "a person from time to time, to inspect the island, who should have the power to remove from it any person who may have gone there voluntarily, without a license under the hand and seal of the governor, lieutenant-governor, or commander in chief, together with all goods found in his possession."[13] If such a person were apprehended, justices were empowered and instructed to order him to be imprisoned for a period of not less than six months, the goods found in his possession to be sold, and the surplus, if any, paid over to the rightful owner if known, or, if not, into the treasury to be held for said owner's benefit.

Immediately afterward, reports circulated that "a man and a woman of bad character had taken up their abode on the island for evil purposes," and one Seth Coleman was dispatched with the legal power—and with any luck the ability—to remove them.

The rumored wicked characters, he reported on his return, were conspicuous by their absence. Instead, he did discover the remains of a wrecked ship, a young cabin boy who had survived the wrecking, and a man named Patrick King with his wife and three children, origins unknown or at least unreported. Whether this family had also survived the wreck or had come ashore from the mainland Coleman failed to note. They were there, however, on legitimate business. They were living in a small hut and were employed by the master of the wrecked vessel to collect and dry the cargo of cotton that had washed ashore, and to wait for the owner, who would return with another schooner to pick them up.[14]

One of Coleman's lesser tasks had been to report on the possibility of permanent residence on the island for a lifesaving crew. His report was noncommittal.

Early in 1801, Governor Wentworth acquired an eloquent ally in his efforts to persuade the legislature to vote the money for a permanent station on Sable Island. This was John Howe, who is most famous in Canada as the father of Joseph Howe, trenchant newspaperman, flamboyant politician, and "father of confederation" in 1867 (he was the skeptical voice of Nova Scotia in the confederation debates that created Canada). John Howe is remembered in history mostly as a relative—rather like Thomas Hancock is to his more famous nephew, John.

John Howe was born in Massachusetts of sound Puritan stock. (One of his ancestors was named Thoughtful Howe, a nice Puritan conceit.) John, however, chose the losing side in the American Revolution and remained loyal to the Crown. Just after it became obvious that the American revolutionaries were to have their way, he and his family joined the exodus of other loyalists who flooded out of the new United States. He was clearly well connected, for shortly after he settled in Halifax he was given a very decent sinecure, being assigned the job of king's printer, and postmaster general of a wide range of territories, including Nova Scotia, Cape Breton, Prince Edward Island, New Brunswick, and the Bermudas. In 1781 he founded his own newspaper, the *Halifax Journal*.[15]

Sometime in 1801, whether at Wentworth's instigation or not, he put together a report titled *Statements of Fact Relating to the Isle of Sable*, whose main thrust was the necessity of establishing a lifesaving station on Sable Island. It was a grand report in a great newspaperman's tradition. Written shortly after the wreck of the *Frances*, it contained all the right popular ingredients: accounts of the actions of wreckers, the sad tale of Mrs. Copeland and her ring, and a reckoning of the large number of ships lost at Sable Island. Put-up job or not, the governor used it to bolster his contention that a "Humane Establishment" be created and permanently installed on Sable. In the spring, Wentworth decided on his own to endeavor to "get two pieces of cannon, one on each end of the island to answer signals in dark weather, also some rockets to distinguish the island."[16]

That same spring, two more ships went aground on Sable and were wrecked, with all hands perishing: the *Packet*, from Boston, and the schooner *Industry*, from Liverpool, Nova Scotia. Wentworth added these to his growing dossier, and by October he had built a sufficient case to persuade the burghers of Halifax to vote the money for his Establishment. The first superintendent was to be a former navy man, James Rainstorpe Morris, the son of the first surveyor general of Nova Scotia and the grandson-in-law of the attorney general of Massachusetts, a man of eminent family but otherwise unknown to the public—at least until his appointment.[17] He would live on the island until his death in 1809.

Morris's father, Charles, had been commissioned as a captain of the army by Governor Shirley and had fought in the battle of Grand Pré in 1747. As a Massachusetts citizen and a "Protestant interested in stamping out the influence of Popery so close to British shores," Charles had been recruited to report on the French presence in Nova Scotia.[18] His son Charles Junior, James Morris's elder brother, was surveyor general for Nova Scotia in his turn, succeeding his father, and was an eminent-enough citizen that, when the Nova Scotia legislature appointed five commissioners to hire a superintendent for the Sable Station, Charles was one of them.

It was not to be a grand establishment. The Nova Scotia legislature was never a free-spending one, and it voted a mere six hundred pounds for the enterprise. Faced with this meager budget, the commissioners at first tried to get families to settle permanently on the island without government aid, but not surprisingly, they found no takers and had to agree to pay a reasonable wage and cover expenses. Under those circumstances, James applied for the job and got it. He was not a young man—he'd been baptized in Hopkinton, Massachusetts, fifty-one years earlier, in May 1750, and had moved to Nova Scotia with his family as a young boy—but his credentials, according to the commissioners' report, were considerable, and included fourteen years of naval service that had provided him with considerable practical experience. He was, they said, "much noted for his enterprise and uncommon mechanical genius," especially in "nautical affairs." Active, resolute, resourceful—Morris was to need all of the characteristics attributed to him.

Wentworth had been thinking about this job for years and was able to provide Morris with full instructions. He was to be responsible for the behavior of everyone on the island, and responsible also for the enforcement of all the rules and regulations of the humane service. No person other than those who worked for him was permitted to settle there. He was to take command of all shipwrecked persons and was given careful instructions about disposing of salvaged goods. He was even ordered to keep a journal of all events, a duty that he faithfully carried out; the original now resides in the archives of the Massachusetts Historical Society.

The plan had been that three families would proceed to Sable under Morris's authority, but there was not enough money. In the end, all he could afford were himself, his wife, and two children, plus three men and a boy in his employ. He added to this small complement later. When he arrived at Sable, he found a man and his family already living there, in a hut they had constructed from debris. These were the Kings—Patrick, his wife, and their three children—the same family Seth Coleman had found going about their legitimate business on the island. In any case, Morris seized the opportunity. Instead of sending them off, he conscripted them, and they became a part of his station.

CHAPTER TWELVE

Its Eccentric Governors

The governors of the Humane Establishment,

sequestered lunatics, and the boundless

goodwill of Dorothea Dix

Morris sailed from Halifax with his small crew, a prefabricated dwelling, and his farm animals, in a little convoy of two, the brigantine *Earl of Moira* and the schooner *Hannah*. They stood out past Cape Sambro in what Morris recorded was a fresh breeze. That was on October 6, 1801. "In the morn," he scribbled later in his journal, "wind westerly with rain." There were heavy seas on shore—"fresh gale at WSW." They couldn't land that day, nor the next—"heavy gale" that day. On October 9, he reported "all well tho' some Sea Sick."

And so it went. It wasn't until October 11 that the party was able to send the sheep ashore, but it was still blowing too heavily to risk humans or the larger livestock. Two days later, on October 13, seven days out of Halifax, all finally landed safely, "and at 6 p.m. all gave three cheers at the flagstaff."

It was the superintendent's first taste of Sable's notorious weather—but far from his last. Fully a month later, on November 11, he was at last able to record, clearly with some relief:

Calm morn and continued until 7 p.m. the first calm day I ever saw on this isle—8 a.m. took two men with me in the boat in order to try the Coast for fish—made a trial for cod and mackerel 4 leagues off in from 8 to 16 fathoms, all along from our first landing to the NW bar, and caught none, took onboard the boat on return, from the bar, several pieces timber—The other men raked up all the hay that was left, 22 cocks—Our water growing rank, I began two other wells, in hopes to obtain better—day ends cloudy wind SE and likely for a storm.

He was, unsurprisingly, right—it was again "likely for a storm," and his journal for the next day recorded a "strong gale from the SE with heavy rains—a terrible sea on the South beach—11 a.m. wind shifted to SE and foggy."

The party's early chores were obvious enough: to build homes for themselves, to build barns and sheds for the livestock, to erect picket fences for their new gardens, to make nails for the buildings, and to gather shipwreck debris for use as building material and for warmth in winter. All this without neglecting the main purpose of the station, the erection of warning flagstaffs on island prominences, and the creation of a roster to patrol the beaches for shipwrecked sailors. His men also had to build boats for their own use, which they employed mostly for hauling wood and supplies, and occasionally for fishing. These boats, seaworthy as they were, were never used for actual rescues at sea; Morris very sensibly understood real rescue work to be beyond his capabilities, and took as his role the succoring of those who managed to get ashore by themselves, and the salvaging of what cargo he could.

The wild creatures on the island he treated as his larder—seals for their flesh and their oil, used for lighting and cooking, terns and gulls for their eggs. But two species of animals consumed much of his attention and made frequent appearances in his journals, the horses—and rats.

He never questioned how the rats had got to the island, assuming, probably correctly, that they had made their way into the dunes after being driven ashore in a shipwreck. Of course, they multiplied rapidly, for they had no predators and plenty of birds' eggs to eat. They were a constant plague for the new station, and their predations drove Morris to distraction, and to the closest he ever came to profanity in his writing. During one excursion to visit a wreck for salvage, he was obliged to turn back early; as he explained, "We had Bread sufficient for our intended Journey, but the boy had neglected to secure the bag, and in the night the d———nd rats had taken all away, even the dust."[1]

Morris had been uncertain from the start how difficult it would be to tame the wild horses for transport and labor, and had taken his own riding animal, Jolly, to the island for his personal transportation. At first, Jolly's importation had seemed sensible. Patrick King, the squatter Morris co-opted into the Establishment's service, was full of tales of the wild horses' ferocity, regaling the still-credulous superintendent with anecdotes to illustrate how intractable they were, how impossible to approach safely. Consequently, Morris dealt with them cautiously.

The first time he spotted them was two days after his first landing: "8 a.m. Saw eight wild horses to westward, all in fear of the reports by Mr. King—that they run after people—I took advantage of the banks with a Glass and arrived, within 10 yards of them, but they soon ran off." A week later, riding on Jolly toward the eastern end of the island, he frequently saw groups of wild horses:

> About 400 yards from the beginning of the bar . . . I was met by a wild Stallion, which appeared determined to attack me or the Horse[;] he came on a fierce trot, in front, I stopped the horse, and he passed me to the right, and soon disappeared. [On my return] I again saw 4 Stallions which at first sight, ran, and again halted on a sand cliff—one of

those horses more bold than the rest, came for me full speed, blowing his nostrils and making a direful appearance, I was not great alarmed for my own safety, but the horse, I expected, would be destroyed or terribly mangled—I had it in my power to make my retreat and leave the horses—I had no fire arms to my sorrow—the Animal came up within about 4 Yards and made a stand—he was a dark bay, about 15 hands, stamping his foot like a Sheep at a dog—I raised my hand and gave a loud huzza—the wild brute, to my agreeable surprise turned off the way he came.

As time went on, he came to understand the horses better—just as he began to understand his Mr. King and his generally feckless nature.

Morris made no careful census of the horses, only noting that they gathered in several herds. At one sighting he counted sixty-one horses of all sizes,

> in general Bay colored—a few black, only two Iron greys, and 2 pied, white, and dark bay—I kept undiscovered to them—until I was satisfied viewing them, when I made a push down the hill towards them, which gave a general alarm—and they flew off in all directions—some padded very close to me, but with no appearance hostile—I saw them five times, the same number, the last time they appeared fatigued.

A month later he was once again attacked by a wild stallion, and this time fired his "musquet" to "turn off [his] Adversary," but that evening his own horse, Jolly, disappeared to be with the wild bunch: "I returned in the eve to the cabin and found my horse had made his elopement," he recorded laconically. (Jolly came back a few days later and promptly fell sick, "lying on his back as if dying," though he later recovered.)

Once he got over his initial fear of the feral horses, Morris set about trying to domesticate them. He intended them no real harm, although later he occasionally had one killed for food; he needed them for their labor and for transportation. But catching them was a tricky business, and the horses led him on a merry chase. Morris's drawings showed horses being captured by mounted men with lassoes—but how to get mounts from which to use the lassoes? Jolly wasn't enough on his own. And in any case, the men had little expertise with ropes, aside from the usual mariners' skills with knots and so forth. Morris tried snares, but the horses broke free; he tried digging a pit, but the horses scrambled out. "These Horses, when they are first caught, are exceeding fierce and strain every nerve to extricate themselves, but soon after the first struggle they are easily handled, but with much caution." It was the catching of them that was tricky. They seemed to be able to knock down picket fences at will, and to scramble up apparently unclimbable dunes, and, of course, they were fleet of foot and easily outdistanced the panting men.

"Tuesday, 3rd," he noted in May 1803,

was a dark rainy morn—wind S.E.—9 a.m.—The wind shifted to the northward and fair weather—All hands, eight in number, set off for a wild Horse chase, four being stationed from the works to the north Beach in order to prevent their flight on that side of the Isle, as our trap lay in the south Side—The other four turned the horses from the eastern part of the island—At 1 p.m. about 40 of the horses appeared in the three divisions at full gallop, in a direction fair to be caught, but one of the Sentinels firing his musket too soon, turned off the whole of the troop except twelve, which stood on until they came within 100 yards of the works, and there made a stand, being opposite where I was stationed—Made the alarm, but they observing some of the heads of the Pickets, turned off towards a sand hill to the right of the works, which we supposed impossible for a horse to ascend—And thus [we were] disappointed—A horse at the same time caught in a snare, made his escape.

Total for the day: zero horses.[2]

Early in the new year, 1803, Morris was nearly faced with a revolt by his discontented hands, who were complaining of overwork and under-payment. He wanted to dispatch one of his men with a gun to kill a wild horse "for its beef," but the man balked, leading to a minor rebellion "in which dissatisfaction was expressed with [the conduct of] their superior." Morris suppressed it with the help of the crew of the newly stranded *Hannah & Eliza*, who had been rescued, and by making an example of the unfortunate Patrick King, already in his bad books and an easy target for discipline.

The savage weather also much occupied the superintendent's mind, not just because it made the lifesaving tasks much harder, but because it affected everything they did, and at times threatened their survival. In September 1803, he confided to his journal:

> Our garden before the last storm appeared all exceeding well, but now has melancholy appearance, the division of Indian corn and beans is ruined, the blades are all in strings, the pease are all dead, the other beans, cucumbers, seed cabbage, lettuce and pumpkins are dying—the beets, carrots, cabbages and Turnips stood the blast very well—the whole of the potatoes are damaged, the whole of the garden appears as scorched by fire, and the Island in general has changed its colour from a dark green to a yellowish tinge."[3]

Of course, in between keeping themselves alive, the staff did the jobs for which they were recruited. In 1802, four vessels were wrecked on the island: the barque *Packet*, the brigantine *Sylvia*, the brig *Union*, and an unidentified ship from Malaya, bound for Boston. The following year another three went down: the ship *Hannah & Eliza*, bound for Boston from Lisbon via Amsterdam; the schooner *Charlotte*, bound for Sydney from Halifax, and the topsail fishing schooner *Martha*, bound for New York. The same thing happened the next year, another three vessels were driven ashore: a Lunenburg schooner, the brig *Harriot,* and the ship *Stark Odder,* bound for Copenhagen from St. Croix. In the last, nine of fourteen crewmen perished, but the overall total was satisfactory for the new Establishment, for the Committee of the Nova Scotia Assembly reported in 1804 that in three years, forty-one persons had been saved. Two more vessels went down in 1805, another two in 1806, two each in 1807, 1808, and 1809.

In one way, the timing of the Establishment was perfect, for it anticipated a sudden upswing in the number of vessels setting out for America from Europe. "Greater speed, greater comfort and cheaper prices went hand in hand" to drive up the numbers; by 1829 there were packets sailing from London to New York twice a month, and fares fell steadily, at one point dropping below a pound to fifteen shillings.

> In the years 1815–1840 alone, over a million [people] left the British Isles . . . joined by hundreds of thousands more from north and central Europe. . . . 1816 was the year without a summer in Europe . . . torrential rain and even sleet and snow during the summer months wrecked harvests, [causing] distress and starvation in the countryside, while the post-war industrial recession was hitting the towns. In central Europe the roads were crowded with ragged wanderers.[4]

Early in his tenure, Morris submitted plans for building two lights on Sable Island, one at each end. John Gorham had come up with the same idea years before, but it had gone nowhere when his bid to claim the island failed. The notion was then taken up in Halifax by Benjamin Lincoln of Boston, who recommended that "a wooden pyramid built with good white pine timber, without sap, covered with seasoned feather-edged boards and these covered with shingles well painted, with three coats of paint, will last for more than fifty years."[5] Nothing was done about it, and so a few years later, in 1808, a Lieutenant Burton suggested to Sir George Prevost, then governor of Nova Scotia, that the British government might provide funds.[6]

This funding never happened, but it wasn't an implausible suggestion. The British, and the French, were just embarking on a revolution in navigation safety. In the early eighteenth century, only about a hundred places on the globe had been accurately fixed as to latitude and longitude, but the accumulation of records swelled this number to over six thousand by 1817. A decade later, the Admiralty hydrographers began the accurate series of charts covering the entire globe and known as Admiralty Pilots; and in the same decade both compasses and chronometers were improved, if not perfected. As late as 1807 the key Eddystone lighthouse in the English Channel was still lit by a mere twenty-four candles; only a decade later Augustine Fresnel designed a modern lighthouse lens and burner for the French Ministry of Marine and devised a system of identifying flashes. In the mid-1820s both the British and the French authorities embarked on major lighthouse programs, much assisted by the invention, in 1824, of Portland cement (which made building in concrete possible). In 1824—two decades after the Sable Island Humane Establishment was set up—the British founded the Royal National Institute of the Preservation of Life from Shipwreck, and then started work on Lloyd's Register of British and Foreign Shipping (1834), which supplied the data and impetus for scientific safety measures. The Americans began to take safety at sea seriously from 1820 on, raising the number of lighthouses on their coasts from 55 to 256 and adding thirty lightboats and over one thousand buoys. Although travel on water remained hazardous, the number of those lost at sea, as a proportion of those traveling, began to fall steadily after 1815.[7] Not so on Sable.

In 1833, a commissioner was sent to the island to once again report on the feasibility of lighthouses there. He reported himself in favor, and even selected a site, but after four years, during which time nothing was done, yet another commissioner visited Sable and found that the selected site, near the west end, had been washed away by the sea. This was not in itself too surprising; in the thirty years prior to 1833, eleven miles of the western end had disappeared.[8] By 1850, there was still no action, and Joseph Howe, who had taken over his father John's businesses and interests, reported that lighthouses were a subject that had been anxiously discussed in Nova Scotia, and "opinions were divided as to the propriety of such erection."[9] The following year a Lieutenant Orlebar, who conducted an Admiralty survey of the island, reported that he considered a lighthouse at the west end unnecessary, because the west bar could be safely approached from any direction by taking careful soundings. He thought a lighthouse on the east end would be more advantageous, for the northeast bar extended fourteen miles, with a very steep drop on the north side.

Another two decades went by before a lighthouse finally made its appearance on Sable—two decades, and no fewer than fifty-two lost vessels later. The new Dominion government of Canada set up two lights, one at the east end, the other at the western, both fueled by vegetable oil, which by then was much cheaper than the conventional sperm oil. The eastern light, which could be seen eighteen miles out at sea, shone from a wooden octagonal lighthouse 123 feet high. It lasted until 1917, after which it was replaced by a steel skeleton.[10]

The superintendent was also the lighthouse keeper. Each lantern weighed almost three tons and had to be kept in perfect working order. Made of brass and glass, these huge lights floated in a vat of mercury. As the atmosphere changed, mercury had to be added or drained off to keep the light balanced. Every four hours the keeper wound up heavy weights situated at the bottom of the lighthouse. They were geared so that a man could wind them without too much trouble, and the gear system kept the light revolving.[11]

In 1809 Morris died, and Edward Hodgson took over as superintendent of the Humane Establishment. He would be in charge for the next twenty-one years, during which time no fewer than thirty-five vessels were wrecked on the island, and 1,050 lives saved. One of the wrecks was a French frigate, *L'Africaine*, bound from Martinique for Brest with 248 troops and officers on board. Hodgson and his men managed to pull all of them safely to shore, and the next year Louis XVII sent a silver cup filled with gold coins and medals to the superintendent and his crew. So important was the work they were doing that, in 1812, despite once again being at war with Britain, the American authorities issued an order forbidding their armed vessels "to injure or intercept vessels bound to or from Sable Island."[12]

For the rest, Hodgson was silent; he was no journal keeper in the Morris mode, and the only time we hear his voice is when he frets about the appalling weather. He retired in 1830 and was succeeded by Joseph Darby, who relinquished the lucrative supply contract to his son. Darby was in charge for another eighteen years.

The rescue work went on. In 1839 Darby received his second French medal for his role in the rescue of the crewmen of the barque *Maria*, bound from Le Havre to New York. This one was issued by Louis Philippe, who also sent three hundred francs to one Martin Clye for his apparently exceptional duty. In 1845 the American ship *Eagle*, headed south from St. John's, was stranded on the south side of the island, half a mile from the eastern station. On board were a hundred tons of bar copper, probably from a mine at Twillingate, on the northern side of the Avalon Peninsula in Newfoundland, which soon closed because of the losses. The vessel was a write-off. James Farquhar, whose father was an assistant superintendent on the island and who himself grew up there, remembered the wreck filled with sand and water. All the superstructure had broken off, and the hull had settled down into the sand. Four years later the timber heads of the vessel could still be seen at low tide, just awash. Sometime later the hull disappeared entirely. "In the month of March, 1860, a severe southeast gale uncovered the ship, and a large part of the hull was washed up on the beach, along with some of the linen goods which had composed the rest of her cargo. They were uninjured, after fifteen years."[13]

Farquhar's journals are silent on the nature and character of Joseph Darby himself. Others weren't so reticent, and rumors reached the mainland of cruelties and mistreatments, and of fiscal and other improprieties. The rumors were strong enough that the government dispatched a one-man commission of inquiry, Captain W. T. Townshend, to find out what on earth was happening. His report was sufficiently alarming that a more formal inquiry was established as a committee of the executive council, whose mandate was to investigate thoroughly "the whole condition of the Establishment."

They found a pretty mess. None of the commissioners had ever bothered to visit Sable Island, yet their relationship with their superintendent was such that they were barely on speaking terms. Darby's subordinates seemed to hate and fear him. The committee checked out Townshend's more sensational allegations, found them to be true, and promptly fired Darby, who left the island in disgrace.

The superintendent, it was discovered, had for years been making a little extra money operating the island as a sort of unofficial lunatic asylum, as such places were then called. At the time there was no home in Nova Scotia for the insane, and families perforce had to look after the unfortunates themselves. This wasn't so unusual. Institutions for the insane were only beginning to be built elsewhere in the British Empire; and even in London such places as did exist treated inmates with a casual brutality that makes hard reading today. Moneyed families sometimes paid people to take mad relatives off their hands; rumors that this was happening at Sable precipitated Townshend's mission of inquiry.

The island wasn't exactly teeming with the insane, but he did find two instances in which insane people had been incarcerated there for some years before being removed. A third man, however, was still on Sable when Townshend showed up. This was one William Etter, "a man of respectable family, heir to some property, and his guardians of the highest standing in the community," who had been on Sable for seventeen years.[14] Darby told Townshend that, for his first ten years, Etter had been extremely violent and endlessly troublesome, "so that very harsh measures had to be adopted toward him," but subsequently had been docile enough, "quiet and inoffensive, and was now employed carrying wood and water, and otherwise doing the drudgery of the kitchen." Townshend asked Etter whether he was being kept against his will, but, "being in such a state of helpless and hopeless idiocy," he was unable to give a coherent answer. Through an accounting fiddle, he was listed in the records of the Establishment as "schoolmaster, or any other capacity that might be agreed on," and paid a government salary, which Darby presumably pocketed. When they fired Darby, the committee of the executive council strongly condemned the treatment Etter had received, "left unvisited and uncared for seventeen years, the drudge and butt of the establishment, squalid and half clad, beaten and taunted till every attribute of manhood was crushed."[15] Etter's family was apparently left unmoved.

Sable was also used occasionally as a remote and draconian cure for alcoholics. As Janet Carnochan put it, the island is "utilized sometimes as an Inebriate Asylum by those who have unfortunate friends of this class. As no liquor is allowed and no opportunity to acquire it can generally occur for months, there is a good chance of having the madness cleared from brain and blood without the necessity of bolts, bars, enclosures, or physicians."[16] At times this wouldn't have been so efficient, for island staff frequently fermented liquors from honey and wild berries. On a few occasions barrels of rum or "canary wine" (Madeira) fortuitously washed up on the beaches. One castaway came across such a barrel, cracked it open, and crawled into the dunes to drink it; he was later found frozen to death, the barrel half-empty beside him, presumably embracing a better end than the terrified and lonely starvation he might have envisaged.

One by one, the wrecks accumulated in the Sable Island journals. Matthew McKenna took over as superintendent in 1848, and in the seven years he remained on post, there were twenty-three wrecks—two of them on the same day in August 1851, the vessels having collided with each other in dense fog. Young James Farquhar, who spent fourteen years on Sable, himself saw thirty-six vessels wrecked.[17]

The stories start to blur together. In July 1849 the schooner *Brothers,* laden with birch timber, went aground, then remained on the beach for years before it was covered with sand; finally, a gale came, lifted it up, and broke it into pieces. The following August the barque *Blonde,* with timber destined for England, was beached and broken up. Three months later the brig *Growler,* with a cargo of provisions, including tobacco and pork, broke up in a storm, but not until its cargo had been safely landed. In April 1850 the schooner *Transit,* which had in error been routed for Newfoundland instead of Boston with its cargo of wine, oil, raisins, and hides, was stranded on the south side of the island. Three months later the *Adonis,* 538 tons from Portugal, on its maiden voyage without a cargo, broke up, but its timbers were salvaged. Another three months went by, and the *Margaret Walker,* with yet another cargo of timber, broke on the west bar, its cargo later used to make new barns. And so it went: the brig *Science* with a cargo of molasses, the brig *Gustave* with sugar, honey, tobacco, and cigars; the schooner *Vampire* and the barque *Margaret Dewar* on the same day, the latter laden with wine, whiskey, and scrap iron. One of the vessels had a cargo of live canaries, but they were in cages and none survived.

On September 13, 1851, the sailing ship *Hargrave,* bound from Newport in Britain for New York with a cargo of railroad iron and a contingent of rats as stowaways, went aground in a dense fog in calm seas on the north side of the island, two miles from the eastern station. The rats left the sinking ship in just the way the folktales say they should, by hurling themselves into lifeboats and scuttling under the baggage; officers later recounted that "they had kicked up a terrible racket when the ship struck." They made their way to shore, too, but were eventually all killed by a rat terrier kept at the station for just that purpose. During the night the wind changed, and within a few hours the ship was in pieces.[18]

Not everyone on every ship was saved. The station by now had surf boats of their own construction, but no sturdy lifeboats, and mostly had to wait until the crews and passengers made it ashore before being able to offer any help. The schooner *Marie Anne,* which struck in a northerly gale hard by the station, saw one of its crew caught in a backwash and drowned; two others swam to safety. "One of the crew had his feet so badly frozen that he had to be carried to our house; and yet another man was still on board with a broken leg. It was with great difficulty that this man was brought ashore. . . . The day after she stranded, the *Marie Anne* was broken up; vessel and cargo were a total loss."[19]

The superintendent, McKenna, had further set-tos with the *Marie Anne* and its rather unruly crew, who resented the three months they were cooped up on the bleak little island. He wrote afterward to his employers in Halifax about "a pair of Villans" who gave him trouble merely because "[he] ordered all the Cards on the island to be burned when . . . informed by [his] foreman that those Villans were playing them on Sundays."[20]

There were other sorts of "villans" at work as well. When the *Amazon* was stranded on the west bar in June 1853, the crew made their way to shore on their own. "Some of the wrecked men found their way to our house shortly after dark. That was our first knowledge of the wreck. . . . the Superintendent arrived early the next morning with some of his men. When the crew went off in the surf-boat to the wreck, they found two Nova Scotia schooners busy stripping the sails and removing other gear. They were told to proceed to the East Station and land all the material they had taken from the *Amazon*. One did as she was told. . . . The other flatly refused to give up any of her loot. . . . When the delinquent vessel reached her home port she was seized by the wreck commissioner."[21]

Shortly afterward the formidable Dorothea Lynde Dix made her first foray into Nova Scotia.

She came to Nova Scotia on the track of lunatics, her life's work. She was, according to contemporary accounts, a "wealthy and philanthropic New York lady," but her own opinion has a more hardheaded tinge: "I have no particular love for my species," she said once, "but own to an exhaustless fund of compassion." She had taken on as her life's work the founding of institutions for the insane, and eventually ended up in St. John's, Newfoundland. There is no evidence that she founded an asylum there, but she did become familiar with the ferocity of Atlantic storms, and the battered vessels and haggard survivors who made their way into that city's cozy harbor evidently made a deep impression on her. She subsequently traveled to Halifax, where her sponsor and chief supporter for the founding of an institution for the insane, Hugh Bell, then mayor of Halifax, also happened to have Sable Island under his jurisdiction, for he was chairman of the Board of Works, which had replaced the Sable Island commissioners as overseers of the island. Bell was a brewer of Irish descent who had prospered in Halifax. He had put in his time as a commissioner for the Halifax Poor House, also as it happened occupied by "lunatics and idiots," and had been appalled at the conditions he found there: In one ward he found forty-seven patients forced to share eighteen beds; many of them were naked, and chained to the floor, their treatment frequent bloodletting, induced vomiting, and constant restraint. He met Dix on a fact-finding mission to the MacLean's Asylum, in Massachusetts, which had pioneered humane treatment for the insane, and she happily joined Bell's crusade for a similar approach in Halifax. In 1849, after a tour of Canada's institutions (she was affronted in turn at the conditions in Toronto, Montreal, and Quebec, impressed by those in Saint John, New Brunswick), she bent her formidable energy to fixing Nova Scotia. She succeeded, too, for in 1856 the cornerstone was laid for the new Provincial Hospital for the Insane, built to plans donated by Dix. She even donated two peacocks to grace its grounds.[22]

It was the irresistible combination of rumors of lunatics incarcerated at Sable Island, and Bell's stories of the work of the Humane Establishment, that drew Dix to the island in 1853. She traveled on the regular supply ship, the *Darling*, and landed on Sable in the middle of July. Fortuitously, less than a week later the schooner *Guide*, under its master Henry Millichamp out of New York for Labrador, ran aground on the south side of the island in a dense fog, whose hazard was compounded by heavy seas and southwest winds. The schooner was, by Farquhar's account, under full sail when it struck. Dorothea Dix was on hand to see it, riding on horseback down to the beach to witness the drama herself—not for her the inadequacy of a secondhand account.

After a long struggle, the crew and much of the cargo were brought to safety, but the captain remained on deck and refused to leave. What followed has entered Sable's lore, though it has the smell of vigorous embellishment:

> The captain . . . had become a raving maniac and would not leave. Miss Dix arrived at the beach as the last boat landed from the ill-fated vessel, and learned the sad fate of her commander, who, the sailors said, was a kind-hearted man. She pled with them to return to the wreck and bring him on shore, and to bind him if it was necessary for his safety. They obeyed her summons, and soon were again on the beach, with their captain bound hand and foot. She loosened the cords, took him by the arm and led him to a boathouse built for the shipwrecked, and there by kind words calmed his mind and persuaded him to thank the sailors for saving his life. She trusted that rest and nourishing food would restore him to reason.[23]

Though we'll never be sure about what actually occurred, what is certain is that Dix was not impressed with the Humane Establishment's equipment, which lacked the essential means for rescue: good-quality lifeboats and modern lifesaving apparatus. When she returned to the mainland, she contacted her formidable network in Philadelphia, New York, and Boston and appealed for help. As usual when she had set her mind on something, it began to happen. Within months, the chairman of the

Boston Humane Society made arrangements for four Francis-class metal lifeboats to be constructed, sturdy double-hulled boats with large one-way scupper drains that emptied the boat rapidly if a wave broke over its gunwales. By the end of the year the lifeboats *Victoria, Grace Darling, Reliance,* and *Samaritan,* plus a rescue car, a mortar for throwing lines to stranded ships, cables, trucks, and harnesses were all put on public display on Wall Street. There they remained, mysteriously, for almost a year, during which time two more vessels foundered on Sable Island, and the stern portion of another drifted ashore in thick ice. (Another version of this tale says the boats weren't on display in New York at all; rather, the ship carrying them to Sable had itself been wrecked on the Nova Scotia mainland, and the boats were returned to New York for repair. There is scant evidence for this tale, though the detail—lifeboats being themselves wrecked—is nice.) But by November 1854, two of the boats, the *Victoria* and the *Reliance,* reached Sable.

Less than two weeks later, the *Reliance* was pressed into service when the barque *Arcadia,* a 715-ton vessel from Antwerp for New York, was wrecked on the east bar during a dense fog. It carried a cargo of glass, iron, and silk, and 147 German passengers.

The wreck was spotted at daybreak by Farquhar, who sent a messenger to the main station. The *Reliance* was deployed immediately, but it was sixteen miles from the wreck and had to be rowed in heavy seas, and it wasn't until three in the afternoon that the wreck came into sight. The *Arcadia* was lying on the east bar, about two hundred and fifty yards from the beach, with a slight list to seaward. The passengers and crew huddled in the forecastle, as huge waves broke over the stern.

The *Reliance*'s first pass at the ship failed. It was swept to leeward by the strong current and heavy sea, and forced to land on the beach. The crew dragged it up the beach to windward and launched it again. This time it got alongside and took on board several of the *Arcadia*'s crew to help with handling the passengers. Perhaps misunderstanding, and thinking they were being abandoned, some of the passengers leaped overboard into the lifeboat, and the coxswain ordered his men to shove off for fear of being swamped. When the lifeboat made the beach with the first load, one of its crew was so terrified by the experience that he refused to return to the wreck, and he was replaced by an *Arcadia* crewman.

The passengers seemed generally ill prepared for the rescue. One woman came ashore dressed only in a tablecloth, which fell off as she jumped from the boat to the beach, and she had to be covered up by her fellows.

The exhausted rescuers made a total of six trips to the stranded ship, bringing about eighty people to shore. Two more attempts were made, but failed to reach the ship when oars and tholepins were broken by the sea's violence. An attempt to run a warp line from the ship to the shore was frustrated by the strong currents. Night then fell, and the rescuers had perforce to draw the boat up on the sand and wait for dawn. The superintendent, McKenna, poignantly described the scene:

> When night came on and we had to haul up our boat, the cries of those left on the wreck were truly heart rending. In the hurry of work families had been separated and when those on shore heard the cries of those on the wreck at seeing the boat hauled, a scene was witnessed that may be better imagined but cannot be described. I walked slowly from the place leading my horse till, by the roaring of the sea, the whistling of the winds and the distance I had traveled, their doleful cries could not be heard, and then I took my seat in the saddle.[24]

During the night the wind and sea moderated, and at dawn the rescue work began anew. By noon the last of the passengers were safe ashore and taken to the Sailor's Home, a large two-story house attached to the main station.

McKenna added to his journal: "The ship was broken in a thousand pieces [by a second storm] on the night of the 29th."

In the aftermath, England's Mariners' Royal Benevolent Society, impressed by the "gallant conduct and courage of Captain McKenna and his men," rewarded the superintendent with a gold medal and each of the crew one of silver.[25]

But the work went on. The following month, a brig from New York, the *Nisibus,* went aground on the south side of the east bar; another vessel went missing around Sable in the same storm, its existence and fate only acknowledged by the lonely bits of wreckage that washed up on the shore. All hands were lost.[26]

Superintendents came and went, the population of Sable Island swelled and shrank, wrecks appeared, broke up, and disappeared. Ernest Baker, who fished in the early part of the twentieth century with the schooner *Sylvia Mosher* and lived, on those rare occasions he was home, on the picturesque islands at the mouth of the LaHave River close to Razilly's Fort Ste.-Marie-de-Grâce, once reminisced about his time working near Sable:

> We used to fish right close to the island, half a mile, maybe, the vessel was anchored off. There was no fishin' on Sundays, not in them times. You wasn't dare to do anythin', so we'd get in the dories and row ashore. . . . What we used to look at was the stuff that come ashore from them ships . . . cases and piles of cases, and the fishnets and buoys what the shore fishermen had lost. You could have filled a dory again and again. They had the stuff all piled back on the beach where the storms couldn't get it. And the wrecks. You couldn't hardly walk for the wrecks, especially at the northeast end. There was storms when some old ships that had been

buried years and years came up through the sand. Then the next week it would all be covered up again, that bad the sand was shifting.[27]

The superintendents were men who lasted. McKenna was followed by Philip Dodd, who was eighteen years on Sable. Duncan McDonald followed Dodd and lasted eleven years, to 1884. He was followed briefly by J. H. Garroway as acting superintendent, who yielded to Robert Jarvis Boutillier, who was there until he died in 1912, a total of twenty-eight years. He was followed by Captain V. W. Blakeney (seven years to 1919), John Campbell (twenty years to 1939), and finally Donald S. "Deep Sea" Johnson, the station's last manager, who was there until 1948, just nine years. They were also hard men. Morris faced revolts against his sometimes harsh regime. Darby, as we have seen, was a skimmer, who cheated his own people and left in disgrace. McKenna ran the island like a prison camp. Though not a preacher, he held a church service every Sunday morning at his residence, insisting that everyone attend. He summoned his "parishioners" with an old ship's bell, and when after a year or so they simply stopped coming he smashed the bell in a rage.[28] Most of the others, notably "Deep Sea" Johnson, treated the islanders as though they were feudal workers who owed the superintendent personal allegiance. All the superintendents seized and destroyed any liquor they found. Liquor, in fact, was the subject of one of only nine rules made up for island behavior. "No spirituous liquors shall be sold on the Island, nor any brought or received by any of the members of the staff of the island, nor by any of the crew of a vessel or vessels that may be on the island, and no drinking of spirituous liquors shall be allowed at the depot or place where the crew reside while on the Island." Island staff were docked a month's pay if they were caught sneaking a drink, while visiting crew forfeited their right to salvage.

At times the population dwindled to around a dozen people, at times rose to more than forty, occasionally as high as sixty. Janet Carnochan reported that the superintendent (McDonald) had taken to calling himself "Governor," and that this governor ruled, when she was there, no fewer than six stations and a total population of twenty men, twenty-four women and children.[29] Boutillier sometimes summoned a preacher—or preachers—to minister to the spiritual needs of the islanders, and the Anglican minister, the Reverend J. Ruggles, and the Catholic, Father Moriarty would alternate their trips out on the government steamer. Boutillier also hired a schoolteacher, who suffered from the schoolchild-delighting name of Miss Ancient. She herself was the daughter of an Anglican clergyman, the Reverend W. J. Ancient of Halifax.[30] There was no entertainment other than that they made for themselves, but they did their best, and it wasn't uncommon to hear the strains of Mozart and Brahms echoing across the sand dunes on a summer evening.[31]

Isolated as the life was, most of the children who grew up there hated to leave, and couldn't wait to return. James Farquhar wrote years later that he had become terribly homesick when he left. "I would have given anything to go back to the place where I had spent so many happy years of health and perfect freedom."[32]

The wrecks, meanwhile, accumulated in the logbooks, and stand out now only when they somehow violated convention or became attached to a particularly poignant or memorable story. Such, for example, was the American ketch *Commerce,* inbound for Boston from Messina, in Italy, with a full cargo of lemons. It was stranded in 1855 while laying-to during a strong northerly gale and "took the ground" on the north side of the east bar, about five miles east of the eastern station. But the *Commerce* was a lucky one; after most of the lemons were removed (dumped into the sea), it floated free of its own accord and made it safely to Halifax.[33] The following year, in September 1856, the brig *Alma* was stranded; all were saved but one of the lifesaving crew, washed out of the bow of the lifeboat by a sudden breaking wave.[34] The same thing happened in 1864, when the

William Bennett went down, and the captain, his sister, and crew were brought ashore in a gale so strong the men had to shovel sand into the beached boats to keep them from blowing away. In the confusion and terror of the rescue the woman's child, just a baby, had been left on board, and a sailor fastened a line about himself and made it through the waves to effect the rescue. Not all the lifesavers survived. For years afterward, until it too was taken by the winds, a small wooden headboard stood in the Sable graveyard, with the inscription: "Sacred to the memory of Henry J. Osborn, who died December 20, 1864, while saving passengers and crew of the brig *Wm Bennett*, aged 37 years."[35]

A mere two months later, the story of the *Eliza Ross,* dismasted and dragged into the shallows about four miles east of the main station, was spreading through the island and the fishing fleet, for while all hands and the single passenger were saved by the lifeboat *Victoria,* it was only with the help of a spectral crewman: The *Victoria* was short one man, and there was no time for a replacement. "The bow seat of the lifeboat was empty. As they rowed out to the schooner, the head of what looked like a man bobbed out of the water. The specter grasped the gunnel and pulled itself in, and sat on the empty seat. It then grasped the missing man's oars and with the others rowed out to the stranded vessel." Apparently, the apparition rowed back with the crew without once acknowledging anyone. When the lifeboat reached the place close to where the specter had appeared, it dropped its oars and, "like some creature of the sea, slipped over the side." The *Eliza Ross's* lifesaving ghost reappeared many times after that; those who saw it said it appeared "human, but not alive."[36]

The captain, crew, and sixteen passengers of the brig *Argo* (sometimes called the *Arrow* in the records) were not so lucky. All perished despite heroic efforts to save them; the only thing that washed ashore was a capstan and a single bucket.

Then, on July 12, 1879, the memoirist Janet Carnochan, the schoolteacher from Niagara Falls on her great adventure to Europe, was stranded on Sable when her vessel, the steamer *State of Virginia*, under Captain Moodie, grounded in eighteen feet of water (the ship drew twenty-two feet) in thick fog. One hundred and fifty survived. Four women and five children died.

Her recounting of the incident has a nice air of immediacy.

> Suddenly we felt a slight jar, then another, but not violent enough to move a chair. . . . We have run ashore; the ship is not moving, and where we are God only knows! We heard a grinding, crushing, grating noise such as one might suppose would arise from striking on rocks. . . . It was caused by the breaking of the rudder chain. Though our ship had struck the sandbar bow on, it had been gradually swinging round till her stern also struck hard. . . . What strange sounds . . . the straining, creaking, and grinding of the timbers, the roar of the surf, the lapping of the water on the sides of our poor ship. . . . During a momentary lifting of the fog . . . we made out a lighthouse looming through the mist, and then a low sandy shore at a distance of apparently half a mile.

Carnochan "went off safely," as she put it, in the first lifeboat, but the second was not so lucky.

> They came on slowly, hesitating as it were on the edge of the surf, then tossing about helplessly. While we gazed with bated breath, we saw the boat with its living cargo, one moment on the top of an immense wave, the next moment hurled end over end, and all the passengers struggling in the water. The horror of that moment cannot be forgotten, to see the people falling out and black specks tossing about, and to know that these were our late companions and that we had just escaped so dreadful a fate.

Less than an hour later, as the survivors still sat shivering on the shore, at Carnochan's feet lay "two dead bodies, washed up, with the white foam on their lips."[37]

By the time Boutillier took over as superintendent in 1884, Sable Island was under the jurisdiction of the still-new country of Canada. Under the Canada Shipping Act, the Department of Marine and Fisheries was assigned responsibility for all marine navigation, lifesaving stations, vessels, and shore bases; its chores included the government of Sable Island and operation of all lighthouses, lightships, and floating lights, buoys, beacons, radio aids, and everything else maritime it could think of.[38]

In 1885, when she was only five years old, Superintendent Boutillier's daughter Trixie moved out with her mother to live on Sable Island. She was to spend the next twenty-five years of her life there, and in a way became the island's unofficial chatelaine—keeping the island's logbook, giving musical recitals in the "Blue Room" on the island's only piano (which had been laboriously wrestled through the surf from the government supply boat), observing the men at work, sailing a dinghy (named *Trixie* and salvaged from a wreck) on Lake Wallace, riding the wild horses, helping with gathering berries and vegetables, recording the thirty-three wrecks that happened on her father's watch, learning to operate the newfangled device called a "Marconi wireless," and sending coded messages to the mainland. "We even had school sometimes, with Miss Ancient," she wrote later, rather dismissively. She also took photographs. She was given a Brownie box camera as a child and recorded everything she could, including some of the shipwrecks. Years later she recalled being hoisted in a bosun's chair to get a better view of the wrecked ship *Crofton Hall,* which went aground on Sable in April 1888.

Alexander Graham Bell, who visited Sable Island in 1898 on a hunt for the bodies of friends lost when the liner *La Bourgogne* went down south of Sable Island, was obviously taken with the self-possessed young woman, and presented her with a plate camera, which she used for many years, even experimenting with early color photography, and she left behind many images of Sable life.[39]

Her diaries and girlish letters deal mostly with the small matters of domestic life, but they contain numerous glimpses into the daily difficulties of life on an isolated island. For example, how complicated it was to keep in touch: "My sister Berna died while working in Boston and it was 6 weeks before we heard," she wrote. Berna was a nurse who caught some unknown virulent disease; her Christmas gifts to her family arrived at the same time as news of her death. Trixie's father once tried using carrier pigeons to take messages to Halifax, but it just didn't work. "In 1875 we got telephones, but they were only for talking among the life-saving stations. We couldn't talk to the mainland. We got a telegraph station on the island in 1905." The life was generally healthy, though Boutillier kept a stock of opium pills on hand for emergencies. Visiting steamers often brought colds and fevers with them, "steamer colds," as they were called.[40]

Farm animals, as we have seen, had a long history on Sable, dating back to the early 1500s. Cattle were on Sable Island much longer than horses. Cloven hoofprints have been found in sand formations old enough that they seem to confirm the presence there of the red bulls of Fagundes and the subsequent landings by the Barcelos family, while no one has found any credible signs of horses prior to Le Mercier. The Portuguese also landed hogs on the island, but by 1598 they seem already to have disappeared, for the La Roche colonists made no mention of them.

John Rose of Boston had mentioned only cattle and foxes, though there is no record of how foxes got there, or why, unless it was to control rats. In 1738, when Le Mercier settled his animals on the island, only the foxes were present—there was no mention even of rats. Le Mercier added pigs, cattle, and sheep, but after the American Revolution neither cows, pigs, sheep nor even foxes remained. The Humane Establishment brought back all of them, even the foxes.

The nineteenth century taught many lessons in the complications of managing a closed ecology. Rabbits were imported as food by the first superintendent, James Morris, and rapidly ran wild, as did rats that escaped from shipwrecks. They were both supposedly controlled by importing cats. Some of the rats, however, not only killed rabbits but even attacked the cats. Rabbits were brought back in 1809 and were promptly eaten by snowy owls, occasional visitors to the island. Again, they were imported, and by 1850, workmen building a lighthouse (never finished) reported that the island seemed overrun with both rabbits and rats. By 1848, the island staff had to suspend the provisions stored in refugee huts from the ceilings and walls to keep them from the rats. The same rats again prevailed against the rabbits, which again vanished. The station persisted, and rabbits were let loose in 1882. They rapidly became a nuisance—so much so that seven cats were sent from Halifax to control them. Another thirty cats were loosed in 1890, but they themselves became a problem for the birds, and seven foxes were imported to deal with the cats. They finished off the cats and the rabbits in a single season, but then they turned on the birds. So dogs were brought in to control the foxes, which were also hunted and shot. When the foxes disappeared, the dogs were kept on to kill the rats. They did keep them under control but failed to get rid of them, and by the 1950s rats were still common. It wasn't until the 1960s that they were finally "eliminated."

Mice, however, were a problem until recently. Gerry Forbes recalls that, in the 1990s, a barn fell down and released a population of mice to the wilderness. "To the gulls, they were manna from heaven. None—we think—survived."

No snake ever made it to Sable Island, perhaps by the luck of the Irish. There have been rumors on the mainland of bloodsucking bats on Sable, but, like many such rumors, this one is untrue. Every now and then an occasional silver-haired bat or red bat is seen around the buildings, but they don't last and don't multiply. Nor are there leatherback turtles. Although stories are current that they are occasionally found, none of the island staff has seen them.

Insects, of course, abound, and not just the benign sort, like bees (probably imported). Periodic plagues of grasshoppers occur. There are also millions of mosquitoes, blackflies, beach fleas, ordinary fleas, and great swarms of horseflies.

Hancock's sheep died off within a decade. The Humane Establishment imported more in 1802, but they died too, apparently from eating plants poisonous to their systems.

Pigs did somewhat better. The island was stocked with swine by Portuguese fishermen, although they disappeared by 1598. Both Le Mercier and Hancock reintroduced them, but none remained by 1776. Morris brought in more in 1801. They rapidly became feral, and eventually they were almost all shot, mostly for their unnerving relish in devouring human corpses washed up from the wrecks. In 1814, as we've seen, nature took care of the problem, and the remainder died in a particularly bad winter. After a few years the island was restocked, and this time the pigs were kept in pens. By 1884 the staff was producing eight thousand pounds of pork annually. Pickled pork was sometimes shipped to the mainland.[41]

By the end of the twentieth century the only four-footed mammals remaining on the island were the horses.

Despite the first superintendent's difficulties in rounding up the horses, they were tamed readily enough and were used for food when necessary, as draft animals, and for transportation around the island, in later years pulling the island's "truck" to wreckage sites. In the middle of the nineteenth century, live horses and barrels of horsehair were shipped to the mainland to help pay for the upkeep of the Establishment, which was perennially short of money; their short stature made them ideal as pit ponies in the mines of Cape Breton and mainland Nova Scotia. Several times during the century, too, breeding stock from the mainland was introduced to see if the horses, which were sturdy but small, could be improved for draught work and general labor, but none of these infusions of new genetic material took. Even when breeding did take place, the horses remained small and retained their characteristic thick, short necks, thick legs, and flowing manes and tails.

The feral horses seemed to reject everything from the mainland. When bales of hay were brought in during lean years, they refused to eat it, and the stallions urinated on it defiantly.

They were still being used as a primary labor source a hundred years later. In the 1950s, remembers Norman Campbell, "the wild horses were a delight. They were all over the island and several of them were tamed. They would pull the boats out of the water on wagons. When we moved house, I remember sitting in the wagon being hauled by these wild horses, wondering how wild they were, because they were never far from wild really. Our drivers were Fred Stone and a man with a wonderful name, Ozz Cribby; Fred would whack the horses and the wagon would go up over the dunes and down the dunes, with no attempt at roads." One day in winter, Campbell saw two gangs of horses confronting each other. After much posturing and stamping, a dominant stallion emerged from each herd. They came closer and closer to each other, then one whirled and lashed out with its hind legs, kicking the other a brutal blow. "It was quite a thing to see that kind of warfare still going on." In the spring, he says, you could sometimes see the bodies of older horses that had not survived the winter, nature's culling of the herd.

Not infrequently the more brazen of the fishermen from Nova Scotia's south shore would sneak onto the island and snaffle themselves a "pony" to take home to the kids.

CHAPTER THIRTEEN

Its Savage Storms

Appalling storms tear away at the island,

and fishing fleets are battered by the furious

Gales of August

The one constant thread that ran through all the superintendents' journals was the weather. The kind word for it was *unpredictable*, with storms of discouraging suddenness and appalling ferocity.

In the late 1860s, to take one example of many, a terrific gale struck the island. Its melodramatic effects were reported a few weeks later in the Halifax newspapers, courtesy of Susan Kelly, wife to the coxswain of the lifeboat at what was then the south station. If the gales were strong, so, on the evidence, were the people. Kelly's prose was matter-of-fact, the antithesis of melodrama. Not so the action itself.

She was alone at the station when the storm hit. Her husband, Joseph Kelly, and other staff were fifteen miles away, attempting to rescue sailors from a barque stranded on the bar. They later reported that the winds from the east-southeast were so strong that they, like others before them, had to shovel sand into the boats to prevent them being torn away from the beach into the interior. They were forced to a crawl to be able to move at all.

Back at the station, Susan Kelly reported that the first things to go were the two flagstaffs, ripped from their moorings. The roof of the earth cellar was then torn off and disappeared into the Atlantic. Enormous ocean waves surged over the south beach to the outpost and smashed into the stable. Because the shrieking wind threatened to carry off the whole stable building, she flung open the doors to allow a crosswind, so there'd be less resistance to the gale, opened the stalls of the five horses in the building, and let them run free. The lifeboat was in the same building, and she made it ready in case it was needed. If the house were destroyed, she said later, she was determined to run the boat to Lake Wallace and try to cross over to the main station. But the wind was so fierce that she, too, was forced to crawl on her hands and knees from the house to the stable and back again. She also crawled out to the dairy hut and propped it up with planks to prevent it from being thrown against the house. By this time the sea had washed in through the doorway of her home to fill it with two feet of water. She waded in with an ax and chopped holes in the floor to allow the water to drain.[1]

Clearly, Susan Kelly would be a good person to have on your side in an emergency.

And at sea?

On the fourth of July 1883, the schooner *J. W. Russell* left Mahone Bay for Quero Bank, off Sable Island. It baited twice at Canso and fished on the southern end of the bank until July 27, when it hauled up and started for home with 450 quintals [hundredweights] of codfish. It encountered a gale just after sighting the light on Sable Island. In a terrific wind, a huge sea struck the schooner and hove it on its beam ends—that is, turned it over—and it lay on its side, wounded but still afloat. The same sea took the captain, Allan Ernst, his brothers Hibbert and Edmund, and Henry Weinacht, one of the hands, and swept them overboard. They were not seen again.

Three men were below or in the fo'c'sle when the wave hit, and scrambled up through the water, clinging to whatever they could find. Two of them were just boys: Ezra Mader, sixteen, and Willie Schnare, seventeen. All three clung to the forerigging to prevent being snatched away by the battering waves. Another of the hands, Benjamin Kaiser, tried clinging to the same rigging, but there was not enough room. He tried for one of the ship's dories and managed to launch it and scramble in. As he pulled away, he yelled at the others, "If any of you are saved, tell my poor wife I'm gone." Then he too vanished in the storm, and his wife and five children never saw him again.

Three more men were in the main rigging. Only one survived, by threading his arm between the lanyards. The other two disappeared when another wave came, taking the shear poles and much of the main rigging with it. The survivor crawled onto the bulwarks and lashed himself there. "There I stopped till near daylight, when both spars went out of her nearly together, and then she went bottom up, and the other three who were forward let themselves run out on the bottom by a line."

All day they clung to the ship's keel and, toward evening, preparing for another night, lashed themselves tight. And there they stayed, through the night, in the dark and dangerous seas, just waiting. One or two of them actually slept, but toward morning, when the wind again rose and the sea broke over them, they had to be wakened. At eight in the morning they finally saw another schooner bearing down on them before the diminishing wind, and rigged a signal with a broken piece of the bulwarks and a pair of pants. The rescue vessel sent out two dories with five men in heavy seas and took them off. The savior was the American schooner *Flora Dellaway*, with Frank B. Wright as master, from Gloucester bound for the Grand Banks.

Eight of the thirteen men aboard the *J. W. Russell* were lost.[2]

On Sable Island, not knowing the drama taking place only a few miles away, the staff had barely noticed the storm. The logbook entry was routine. It was just more of the same, pretty much weather as usual.

And so too with storms in recent times. One of the most frequently asked questions of Sable staff these days has been, *What was the weather really like on Sable Island during the Perfect Storm?* The Perfect Storm of book and movie fame, which was called the Hallowe'en Storm in Nova Scotia and was really the intersection of three storm systems, lasted about forty-eight hours on Sable Island, from 6 PM on October 28 to the evening of October 30, 1991. The temperatures were steady at around eight degrees Celsius (forty-six degrees Fahrenheit), and the peak wind was from the northeast at eighty miles an hour. Total rainfall was just over one and a half inches. It wasn't, in fact, a particularly bad storm for Sable, and the logbook recorded it without comment. A few times a year most years there are more powerful storms than that.[3]

It is the collision of wind- and ocean-temperature gradients that produce the North Atlantic storms, these "personifications of the wrath of god,"[4] the type of furious gale that "attacks [a man] like a personal enemy, tries to grasp his limbs, fastens upon his mind, seeks to rout his very spirit out of him."[5] But what's really interesting about them is not their animus but the mundane and mechanically simple nature of their origins. The western edge of the Gulf Stream is where these storms are made. As the current snakes its way past Cape Hatteras on the coast of North Carolina and turns back out to sea after a close swipe at land, it mingles briefly with the cold tongues of the southbound Labrador Current. In winter, when a dome of high pressure from the Arctic drifts southeast, it may come to the edge of the Gulf Stream and stall. If there is a core of warm air off the coast, just east of the Gulf Stream, and if the jet stream is flowing toward the northeast, the two air masses collide, the cold air fighting to move east, the warm air prodded by the jet stream. A pocket of turbulence develops in the crook between them. Wind flows east, then is bent quickly to the north. Unable to resist the centrifugal force, it begins to move full circle, creating a system of low pressure that deepens violently.[6]

So commonplace are these violent winter storms that the load lines painted on modern ocean vessels denoting the depths to which they may safely be loaded always have as the lowest line, the lightest loading, a line marked WNA—Winter North Atlantic.[7] Storms strong enough to rip containers off a ship happen on average about once or twice a year, particularly in the wintertime.[8]

Peter Barss, in his wonderful collection of oral histories of men at sea, has assembled the testimony of fishermen and sailors who have lived through some of these winter gales. "I'll tell you, sometimes it looked bleak. Well I had a suit o' Black Diamond oil clothes. An' that was a Saturday afternoon that we cut the cable. On Sunday mornin' the only t'ing left was just the collar around my neck. That's true as I set here. Oil clothes was tore off me." And again:

> We was fishin' that day out there to the south'ard o' Sable Island in twenty-nine fathom o' water. An' there was seas I'm safe to say a hundred feet high. An' in the afternoon when we was out in our dories we was up to the wind'ard o' the vessel. An' when she would go down in a swell, you could just see her topmast truck . . . the main top truck. Well the mainmast is ninety feet an' that was up thirty feet more. That shows how much swell it was.

And: "Oh my, oh my, the sea was vicious. An' blowin'! It was wicked to the world—blowin', you. That was the biggest storm ever I was into."[9]

Wicked to the world and blowing, as the seaman said, the wind driving little seas down over the towering cliffs of slate-gray water of the bigger ones, the men and gear and everything that could be lashed down fastened tight, the wind vibrating the stays and sheets and halyards and even the spars themselves, making an ungodly howl in the rigging, the vessel riding the swells up, up, up, forty, sixty, eighty feet, tipping over the edge into the trough, far below.

Fishermen took what precautions they could, developed what emergency remedies they could. Sometime in 1846, for example, the schooner *Arno,* a fishing vessel whose home port was not recorded, was stranded on the bar off Sable in rough seas. Its skipper, Captain Higgins, hurled blubber and barrels of fish oil overboard to calm the waters and was able to launch a dory, in which he successfully made his way ashore, where he was picked up by Darby's men and taken to the station.

It seems scarcely possible, given the massiveness of the seas and the savagery of the weather, that a little oil—even several barrels of oil—could have the desired effect, but experienced sailors believe it works. And Higgins's experience wasn't the only time lives were saved off Sable by the same trick. In 1926 a schooner called *Silver Thread* under Captain Murdock Getson was being battered by monstrous following seas, and a crewman used oil to extricate the vessel from the most immediate peril. Now remembered only by the name of Carl, the crewman recounted the story years later: "Well, I poured oil on the deck an' that run off t'rough the scuppers—made a ca'm [calm] slick. The sea wouldn't break. Oil smoothens it, see . . . that it comes a'roll all right, but it don't come no sharp rolls an' cut—don't roll up an' smash down. An' that's the way you ca'med it down." Getson and his crew all credited Carl with saving their lives.[10]

These storms would come up with fearsome speed. Norman Campbell recalls the day he left: "The weather was deathly calm, strangely calm, the water was not moving, nothing was moving, the air was still. We went out to the [transport ship] *Bernier* in the surf boats, and [suddenly] as we went the sea started moving, up and down, up and down, and there was a storm coming." In the few minutes the boats took to reach the supply ship, the swells were already a dozen feet high. "As our boat got alongside the *Bernier* we could only get off one at a time, each person had to grab the Jacob's Ladder and pull himself up, and you'd grab the ladder and suddenly you were twelve or twenty feet high." An hour later the swells reached fifty feet, and the banshee wind was tearing through the rigging.[11]

In a great storm, the island felt like a giant jelly: "We had oil lamps then," one of Sable's superintendents, Donald "Deep Sea" Johnson, wrote in a journal years later, "and when the seas hit Sable, well, you could see the oil in the lamps just quivering from the vibrations of a thousand tons of water hitting the south beach. I've seen forty feet of the bank go in one storm."[12]

After one severe storm in 1863, an island resident came upon the exposed skeleton of a young man who had probably starved to death years before. With the body he found some old British coins dated 1760.[13] On another occasion, after a severe gale that shifted a great deal of sand, one of the island's young people found cannonballs, musket balls, swords, a brooch with plaited hair in it, cuff links, and human bones—all of which had been fully thirty feet below the surface.[14] No wonder that the novelist Thomas Raddall, who spent some time on Sable as telegrapher and who set one of his novels there, once remarked that to walk across Sable's dunes was like walking over a big tomb.

All through the existence of Sable Station, the superintendents routinely reported large sections of the island under their care being torn away in storms.

During the four years between 1809 and 1813, four miles were removed from the western end, and the signal station had to be moved inland. In 1813, a single gale trimmed away an area approximately forty feet wide and three miles long. In the thirty years prior to 1833, eleven miles of the western end disappeared, and the signal station there was moved three times. At least five of the eleven miles must have been from the outer part of the west bar, where the waves formerly broke.[15]

On June 5, 1815, Superintendent Edward Hodgson contacted the commissioners in Halifax: "The west end of the island is washing away at such a pace, that it is near the house at the west end settlement and we shall have to remove the dwellings this summer or lose them entirely."[16] Later he sent a letter to the mainland telling them that he and his men had pulled down the west-end house and relocated it at what he called Haulover Ponds, about three miles to the east.

Still the sea continued to advance, and during the winter storms, it made inroads on the sand cliffs at the western side of the island and radically changed the dune topography of the interior. By 1833, the sea had swept so much of the island away, so rapidly, that it was within half a mile of the buildings and new ones were being erected a further four miles east.[17]

A procession of ferocious gales hurled themselves on the island in the winter of 1881, removing large areas of sand; one such storm destroyed an area seventy feet by a quarter of a mile, and a month later, thirty feet of the whole width of the island disappeared in a matter of a few hours.[18] The terrified lightkeeper reported that the lighthouse was in danger; he could feel it shudder from the wind and huge waves. The next week the light was dismantled and the superstructure moved. Days after that an enormous bank of sand vanished into the ocean, taking the lighthouse foundation with it.[19]

The new location didn't fare much better, for in 1882 "an unusual storm" bringing very high tides removed an embankment within forty feet of the lighthouse keeper's barn and threatened the new light itself. The station staff were appalled, for the light was on a grassy knoll in a protected area, and they'd believed it safe. The cattle were dragged from the barn to the lighthouse porch, and everyone stood by, watching as the waves ate away at the bank, almost as though a huge knife were dragged through the sand; another quarter-of-a-mile piece of beach, fifty feet wide, simply fell away into the sea. By morning the barn had disappeared altogether, and the sea was within twelve feet of the lighthouse.

For a brief period, there was calm, and the seas subsided. But then the ocean once more started its relentless advance on the lighthouse. The lightkeepers moved everything from the structure that they could. A heavy ground swell that had set in from the southeast helped undercut the whole embankment, giving the lighthouse itself an alarming list. After an hour or so of this, the whole thing came crashing down.

In a report to the commissioners in 1884, Superintendent Duncan McDonald laid out for his masters the ravages the island had undergone in the eighty years since the station was set out: "In my second paper," he wrote, frustrated that he had had no reply, "I called your attention to the vicissitudes this island has undergone from storm and current, [which] according to Admiralty surveys, had within 80 years reduced its area from forty miles in length and two and a quarter in breadth, to twenty-two miles in length and less than a mile in breadth, its height from 200 feet to 80 feet."[20]

In 1888 the light was set up again, a mile to the east, but the sea continued its assault, and the light had to be moved yet again, a full two miles eastward.[21] This time crews erected an octagonal ferroconcrete tower on the top of a large dune, ninety-seven feet high with wing buttresses for support. But in 1915, the superintendent, by then Captain V. W. Blakeney, reported that "the island is now again in danger of being washed away,"[22] and the following year, 1916, the light was itself toppled, ferroconcrete, buttresses, and all, by erosion and the battering waves. Yet another new structure, 110 feet high, was erected a quarter of a mile farther east, on a broader part of the island. The erosion was too severe, however, and it too went down, making it the fourth west-end lighthouse to be destroyed in forty years.[23]

On the other side of the island, matters were a little more stable. The eastern light shone from a wooden octagonal lighthouse 123 feet high, built in 1873. It was replaced only once, in 1917, by a steel skeleton, mostly because of salt corrosion.

And in 2004? The erosion zone, a bare area northeast of the east light but before the eastern end of the dunes, used to have dunes, but they eroded away to nothing. This area is no more than six feet or so above sea level, and during severe storms, the ocean sometimes washes right through. There was once a bald dune there, but it marched into the sea. The island at that point is probably only thirteen hundred feet wide, and the erosion zone is about two thousand feet long. The western end is stable—more or less.

In all the long and bleak history of Sable Island there were no storms worse than the Gales of August of 1926 and then again the following year. In no other years were the Sable-Bank fishing fleets and the small communities from which they came so struck by multiple tragedies. The storms of those years were so intense, and that of 1927 struck so suddenly and without any warning, that experienced seamen had no time to prepare, and many went down with their ships. A few survived, and their testimony of improbable escapes from the raging seas now fill to overflowing the file drawers in the archives of Lunenburg's Fisheries Museum. Many vessels survived only by the desperate expedient of actually driving themselves across the Sable bars into the lee on the other side; then—because these were hurricanes, and the wind reversed after the eye passed—they'd find themselves in peril there too. On the Lunenburg waterfront, near the ships' chandlers Adams & Knickle, there is a granite monument to the men who died when they went down to the sea in ships. The lists of names from the years 1926 and 1927 are much longer than any other—more than 150 men and boys, from just a handful of tiny villages. One woman alone, Mrs. Granville Knickle of Blue Rocks, lost her husband, three brothers, and two brothers-in-law in a single storm.

The 1926 storm, a mere prelude to the gale of the following year, struck Sable waters a little before midnight on August 7. It lasted all night and much of the next day, fourteen or fifteen hours of high drama, terror, and destruction: *Sylvia Mosher,* lost with all hands. *Sadie Knickle,* lost with all hands. *Mary Pauline,* lost two men overboard. The *Mary Ruth,* the *Golden West,* and the *Silver Thread* miraculously survived, having been driven, or having saved themselves by sailing, right across Sable's fearsome bar.

It was a Force Four hurricane, with winds that circled the compass as it passed through. A strong tide was running toward the island.

On the mainland, just a hundred unreachable miles away, it was a beautiful day.

Ernest Baker was a crewman on one of the lucky vessels, the schooner *Annie Conrad.* He was a doryman out on the sea with his hand lines when word came to head back to the mother ship.

They fired off the swivel (a small cannon) for us to come back on board. After we dressed our catch we started to prepare for the storm. All the loose gear was put down below in the hold, the hatches put on and battened down. Then we reefed the foresail (which is your main sail in a storm because it stands in the center of the vessel, and set a little sail aft, what they call a riding sail), so we were well prepared. As the wind increased we kept paying out [our anchor] cable until we had 240 fathoms [1,440 feet] out and only a few fathom left on deck. We were still in the lee of the island but she was really bobbing into it. Around midnight there was a thud as she pulled her anchor out of the sand and went adrift. She fell off across the cable, which acting like a drogue kept her head up to the wind and sea. After she struck adrift the wind hauled into the west and kept on increasing. It must have been blowing eighty miles an hour and we couldn't carry any sail at all. As we drifted clear of the island we struck the really heavy seas, 60 or 70 feet high. We took bags of cod oil and hung them over the side to keep the seas from breaking so bad. She drifted all night and the next day, until she hooked herself on the southwest edge of Middle Ground in 26 fathoms of water. The only damage we had was one of our shrouds parted in the heft of the gale.[24]

Three days after the storm, the fishing schooner *Mary Ruth* limped back into port, with nine of its crew seriously injured; its captain, Harris Conrad, had a broken shoulder, its sails were torn, all dories were gone, and even the cabin stove was smashed to pieces. The storm had driven the vessel onto the northwest bar of Sable Island, and the surf had swept it clear of everything that was left on the decks. Then, as though by a miracle, it was lifted by a massive wave and hurled free of the sandbar into clear water on the other side. There it lay to, "until the crew could sufficiently recover themselves to set sail for their home port, which they reached in a most exhausted condition."[25]

The *Marion Elizabeth* also made it home safely, though during the storm it had parted its cables, and its riding sail was torn to shreds, and its foresail also badly torn. One of the crew was struck by the sea and washed overboard, but fortunately caught hold of a rope, and the next sea carried him on board again. The huge seas broke over the vessel throughout the night; there was a very strong tide running toward the island, and it was all they could do to keep clear.

The *Golden West,* from the LaHave River, was fishing on the south side of the island, several miles off, when the storm struck. It was one of the three vessels to save themselves by the desperate means of deliberately sailing over the bar into deep water beyond. Herbert Getson was the mate, and his brother was skipper.

> The bar runs out there twenty miles and we crossed it in two places. My God, it was an awful sea. It was breaking on the bar and breaking right over the vessel—we lost 11 dories out of the 21. She only struck the one time and then the sea lifted her clear, and being a brand new vessel it didn't hurt her any. Then we got clear of the bar, got clear of everything and it was some better.

Getson's other brother was the master of the *Silver Thread,* and, although the vessel was thirteen years old and loaded with fish, it also managed to cross the bar into the relative safety of the deep water beyond. It was the *Silver Thread* that had "ca'amed" the sea by throwing barrels of fish oil through the scuppers.

As they approached the bar, the mate went down to the forecastle and stood in the doorway. All hands looked at him standing there. "You got any friends home now," he said, "it's time to t'ink on 'em. Everybody on deck, if she strikes the bar we're all hands gone. It's every man for himself and the devil for us all."

The devil let the *Thread* and its men go, but not so the *Sylvia Mosher,* under its twenty-five-year-old skipper, John D. Mosher.

On August 9, a telegraph arrived from the Sable Island Station: LUNENBURG SCHOONER SYLVIA MOSHER TOTAL WRECK ON OUTER BAR NORTH SIDE NEAR NUMBER 4 STATION, LYING ON SIDE. NO SIGN OF CREW.

Two days later the *Halifax Herald* carried a still-hopeful story.

> The schooner *Sylvia Mosher,* high-liner of the Lunenburg Fleet, and named in honor of the skipper's two-year-old daughter, lies wrecked on the outer bar on the north side of Sable Island, the mariners' dread. She was sighted there Monday morning by members of the island lifesaving staff. But of the crew there was no sign. Last night came word to Halifax that six empty dories, supposed to belong to the schooner, had been washed ashore, [but] Lunenburg last night was hopeful that the missing fishermen will turn up. It was pointed out that if they abandoned the vessel they would take only eight or nine dories, three men in each boat. . . . Saturday night she may have had a comfortable lee at anchor two or three miles north of the island, but the next day the wind swong [*sic*] round and blew a gale from the north. It was then, mariners say, that the schooner was swept on shore.

Alas, no such luck. Captain John Mosher and his brother Aubrey Mosher were lost; so were the brothers William, Ladonia, and Kenneth Whynacht and Kenneth's son Donald; so were brothers Caleb and Guy Baker, and Carman, Caleb's son, and so too brothers John and Warren Wagner.

The warden of the LaHave Islands, Gordon Romkey (later Speaker of the Nova Scotia legislature), telephoned the newspaper the next day.

There is now no hope that any of the men were saved. We have accepted what seems to be the inevitable. The oldest fishermen here, men of years of experience of the sea, say there is nothing to do but meet the situation. Business is at a standstill, so shocked are the people. LaHave Islands has suffered the most because nearly half of the crew of the *Sylvia Mosher* were from that part of the country. What makes the loss so poignant is the realization that the best and brightest of our youth are gone.[26]

Soon after the storm abated, the coast guard's brand-new radio service instructed the direction-finding wireless stations at Canso and Chebucto Head to broadcast a request to the trawlers to watch for signs of the La-Have schooner *Sadie Knickle,* "which it is feared perished with her crew of twenty-two men in the recent storm along the Atlantic coast." There was no response. That schooner too had been fishing off Sable Island.[27]

A year later, on August 7, 1927, the fishing fleet, with its men from Lunenburg, Blue Rocks, Stonehurst, LaHave, the LaHave Islands, and Shelburne were again out on the banks, hard by Sable Island. On the mainland, the families prayed that this time the devil would stay in his hellhole and leave their men alone, and he seemed to do so, for the week passed without incident, the weather calm, the fishing good. But the devil is nothing if not devilish, and he was just waiting for the tension to soften into relief, and for the relief to spread through the islands and fishing ports up and down the coast. He waited two weeks. Until the twenty-fourth.

The hurricane struck with appalling ferocity and startling suddenness. There was virtually no warning.

"It was a fine afternoon, couldn't a been nicer." Thus said Fred

Crouse, who was "second hand" on the fishing schooner *Partana* out of
Lunenburg.

I was with Frank Meisner an' our bait was all [that is, finished]. So he
said we'll try to git in Canso see if we kin git squid bait. There was no
power then, just sails, and we hoist all the sails. Well there was just wind
enough that she went along about three, four miles an hour. Before dark
we was all turned in. He [the captain] come down an he said, "Fred, I
never seen a sunset like this in my life. I can't believe it but we're goin'
a have somethin' of this." He said, "Call the gang out an put the gear off
the deck."

We all laughed at him and when we had the gear put in the hold I
just said to him for a joke, I said, "What shall we do, batten the hatches?"

He said, "You better do."

"About the sails how 'bout them?"

He said, "I t'ink you better haul down the mains'l an tie up the jib
. . . put the storms'l on."

So we done that an it was still fine weather. The crew all laughin' at
about what in the name a Lord he was about. Well nine o'clock that
evening we wasn't sorry we done it! It come right the same as you emptied it out o' a bag. It blowed.

He said, "I don't know if we'll clear the bar on Sable Island or not."

Then he said, "We're standin' a poor chance. Fred, there's only one
t'ing that I would know that we got a chance . . . to swing her off and
run her on the bar. Maybe if we run her on, she might jump it. . . . can
you get two men that will volunteer to take the wheel?"

An' two fellas, Johnny Knickle from the Rocks [the community of
Blue Rocks] and Billy Tanner said they would take the wheel, and I
lashed 'em to the wheel and they swung her off. We sailed I'd say 15 minutes or somet'in' . . . well then there was a sea boarded us. How much

water went over that can never tell but when he swung her he told the crew, he said, "It's every man for himself. . . . you can go below and shut the companionway, you can go in the riggin' or you can stay on deck, but it's every man for himself."

When that sea hit her it took everythin' it cleaned everythin' off o' her. There was fellas in the riggin' well, the next mornin' they said how high they was and we measured it an it was sixteen feet from the deck up to where they was . . . an they had their boots filled, they filled their boots up there.

After the sea went over we got across the bar an it was smoother. One fella on the wheel, he was as black in the face as the stove. It must a been where the sea hit him so hard. We carried him in the cabin an' got him on the floor and worked with him an he come to. It blowed that night, you couldn' walk from one end o' the vessel to t'other, you couldn' walk agin' the wind. We had a rope run and the only way you could git from one end to t'other was holdin' on t'the rope an pull yourself along. Because we had boards, bait boards we used to call 'em, on the cabin house for cuttin' bait on an they were two-inch spruce planks nailed right solid on the cabin house an I had sixteen five-inch galvanized spikes in 'em, nailed solid, an the next mornin' after that sea hit us, the boards was gone. . . . the sixteen spikes was drawn right through the boards, drawed the heads through.[28]

The skipper of another schooner, Leo Corkum of the vessel *Maxwell F.*, dictated his experiences to his wife after he made landfall, stressing the same point about the suddenness of the storm.

We were fishing off Sable Island when the glass suddenly began to drop. I must say, in all my thirty-nine years as a skipper, I never saw anything like it. I blew the distress signal and the dories hauled their trawl as quickly as possible. The first men on board helped to hoist sail and the remainder we picked up under sail. It was a beautiful morning with just a nice breeze. We sailed away from Sable Island as quickly as the wind would take us. Everything was lashed fast, and then the wind started. The mainsail and the foresail were lowered and the storm sail set none too soon. The wheel was lashed firm and everyone ordered below deck. Then the hurricane struck. Only those who were in a similar situation know the awful fear and the terrible pounding. It lasted about an hour [sic]. Not a word was spoken. Twenty-five men waiting, for what? Then a great silence seemed to fall over the vessel. I opened the companion-way hatch and looked out. Beautiful blue sky, flat calm and the deck of the vessel as clean as if it had been holy-stoned . . . not a dory nor a shred of any kind of a sail remained. The boom was as clean as if no sail had ever been there. White sand filled every crevasse. Without hardly a word being spoken, extra sails were brought out and set in a manner and I steered a course for Canso.[29]

Those were some of the survivors. Others didn't make it through the night. But it was many days before the real toll was known.

On Saturday, October 1, 1927, the *Halifax Herald* finally produced an issue detailing the grim news. In a headline style normally reserved for the beginning or ending of wars, the paper blared: "Over Eighty Lives Lost in Great Disaster. Lunenburg Fishing Fleet Suffers Most Appalling Tragedy." The subtitle was as charged with emotion as the headline: "Pall of sorrow spreads over fishing communities as captains and crews of four gallant vessels are given up as lost—Pathetic loss of bread winners in Nova Scotia towns and villages—In some cases lives

of three members of households are blotted out—Pathos Unutterable—
Dread toll of Sable Island sands."

The article, which took up the first two pages of the broadsheet, included a photograph of Sable Island, another photograph of Blue Rocks (a
village that lost two-thirds of its young men to the hurricane, three of
them brothers, and left a dozen weeping widows), an anti-Sable poem, and
details of the lost vessels and their crews.

Lost with all hands were the schooners *Clayton Walters,* whose wreckage was never found, the *Mahala,* the *Joyce M. Smith,* and the *Uda Corkum,*
all grounded on the south side of the west bar, and the *Columbia* from
Gloucester, Massachusetts, whose wreckage was later discovered in shallow water twenty-three miles northwest of Sable. The vessels that made it
home were the *Marshal Frank,* which reported two men lost at sea, the *Al-
berfolite,* the *Andrava,* which survived by going over the bar, the *Bluenose,*
badly damaged, the *Partana,* which also found safety by driving over the
bar, and a dozen others. Eight out of ten Newfoundland boats fishing on
the Grand Banks were lost in the same storm.

Crossing the bar was a desperate act, not one that any skipper would
contemplate unless there was no other course open. As we see, a couple of
the lucky ones made it. Judging from where the wrecks of some of the
others were found—on the south side of the west bar—they, too, had been
trying that same desperate move, and had failed. They were the *Sadie
Knickle* (1926) and the *Mahala,* the *Uda Corkum,* and the *Joyce M. Smith*
(1927).

Rollie Knickle, the *Andrava's* thirty-nine-year-old skipper, had been
reading in his bunk when mate Lemuel Isnor roused him. "The sky looks
peculiar, Captain, I think we're going to have a breeze." They were then
about four miles south of the western lighthouse but decided to change
course and seek the shelter of the north side. By seven-thirty the wind was

already at hurricane force, and they had to shorten sail, taking in the jib and mainsail and two reefs in the foresail and hoisting the storm trysail. At nine-thirty a gigantic sea swept down, carrying away the storm trysail and half the jumbo, burst the foresail, broke the main gaff in three places, and swept the dories off the deck. It even smashed the chain tackles holding the main boom, washing three hundred fathoms of hawser overboard. At around eleven a tremendous wave heeled the ship far over, and water poured down the companionway. A crewman later reported that the vessel "was on her beam end, with her cross trees in the water, from 11.30 to 11.38 by the cabin clock; her cabin lamp, in gimbals, swinging completely [vertical] to the cabin wall."[30] In desperation, the crew decided they'd have to cross the bar in a run for safety. Isnor lashed himself to the wheel, turned the vessel to the bar, and in great lurches, keel grazing the bottom, pumping desperately to keep afloat, they made the other side.

Rollie Knickle was well into his nineties when he told his story again to the authors. It had in the meantime grown a little in the telling, though it hardly needed embellishment. He had a small bottle of sand on his mantelpiece, collected from the deck, Sable Island sand that had been swept on board in the storm. He kept it for luck.

The *Mahala,* the *Andrava,* the *Marshal Frank,* one of which was lost, the other two saved, shared one East Coast fishing characteristic: The vessels had three *A*s in their names, which was commonly thought lucky, the *A,* with its three strokes, representing the Trinity. Three *A*s were better still. Similarly, many good men would not sail on a ship with thirteen letters in its name, and so the *Elizabeth Ward* became the *Elizabeth Warde* before attempting to recruit a crew.[31]

The *Bluenose* was perhaps the most famous of all the vessels of the North Atlantic fleet, for it was undefeated in a dozen international races with American schooners, and was captained by the legendary Angus Walters. In later years, there were reports that the *Bluenose,* too, "went over the bar," but Walters never said so, and it is doubtful. He was too canny a skipper to have approached too close to Sable, for he was quoted in the aftermath as saying that "[there was] no chance, really, after it shoaled to fifteen [fathoms]. The seas break from the bottom then." It was at this point that he made his crucial observation about Sable: "It is by seas breaking from the bottom that Sable Island destroys the fishermen afar off."

Walters was anchored sixteen miles off the west light of Sable Island with a thousand feet of cable down and the treacherous island invisible under the horizon, which would have put him in twenty-seven fathoms of water.[32] Even so, the *Bluenose* limped home with its sheer poles lying in the water.

The weather on the mainland: hurricane-force winds, crops destroyed.

CHAPTER FOURTEEN

Its Wild Creatures

The peculiar fauna of the island and its

ocean neighborhood, and the now-feral

horses, finally left to fend for themselves

In a dusty little three-inch tray in the Philadelphia Academy of Natural Sciences museum you can see an unremarkable little scallop. Less than two inches across, it is the classic fan-shaped shell of scallops everywhere, though on closer inspection it is prettier than most, a light creamy beige at the base shifting through a spectrum of delicate blues, with a sea-gray ridge at the fan's edge. In the museum's meticulously careful catalog, the shell is # ANSP 290900, and is labeled *Argopecten irradians sablensis*, a subspecies of Bay Scallop. It was donated to the museum by "Andrewschuk, Mrs. F.," who had picked it up on the north beach of Sable Island in 1962, "at 43.59 N, 60.00 W," as the label locates it. There is no record of who Mrs. Andrewschuk is, or was, or whether she was a scientist or merely a curious amateur. And so there is no way to know whether she knew the shell's history or anything about its character.

If you walk along the north beach, there are plenty of similar shells, in a variety of subtle colors. Some are almost pure white; others show a range of roses and corals. On a shelf in our Lunenburg office there now sits a scallop shell from Sable Island marked with concentric circles, ranging from tan through sepia; its fan edge is a darker red, almost the color of dried blood. These shells are not exactly thick on the ground—there are no middens of them—but they're not uncommon either, which is curious enough, because the *Argopecten irradians sablensis*, sometimes called the *Aequipecten irradians sablensis*, which was unique to Sable Island, has been extinct for at least two thousand years and probably a great deal longer, being a species that lived and died with the shifting glacial ice. The scallop, along with an oyster called *Crassostrea virginica*, was a warmwater animal and thrived in Sable's lagoons and surrounding waters when temperatures rose after the Ice Age receded; but it died out as the climate cooled again. The oysters became extinct about five thousand years ago; the scallops apparently clung to existence for another three thousand years after that before succumbing.[1]

Once there were walrus along these shores too, the so-called sea horses of the early explorers, but like the scallops, they have vanished, victim this time not to climate change but to human predation. They're not extinct—they are still found in the Arctic, east of Greenland, and are still relatively common in Russian waters—but they haven't been seen in non-Arctic waters of the Atlantic since 1798. From early accounts, they were once plentiful. The hapless colonists of the marquis de La Roche hunted them for food and skins. English and French fishermen also killed the walrus, extracting oil from the fat and leather from the hides. "The tusks, being of good ivory, brought the men four dollars a pair."[2] Later, in 1633, John Rose of Boston reported "a great store of sea horses," and, in 1642, the Boston Merchants' Expedition carried away four hundred pairs of walrus tusks, having massacred the animals they were attached to. No more living walrus were recorded on the island, although during the mid-1800s, many hundreds of tusks were collected as they washed out of the sand.[3]

But anyone strolling along the beach won't lack for companionship. There may no longer be the walrus (and their companionable grumping, which sounds for all the world like the wheezing of an emphysemic old man), but there are seals aplenty, lying in "families" of fifty or sixty individuals at many parts of the beach. These are mostly gray seals, which will disperse rapidly and slip into the water if you get too close. There, they'll bob up and down, their long, doglike faces looking oddly worried. Grays have found sanctuary on Sable that they don't always find on the mainland; fishermen tend to shoot them on sight, because they are the prime vector and terminal host for a nematode, which at an intermediate stage is the codworm, which encysts in the flesh of cod, making it more expensive to market. The other common seal on Sable is the harbor seal, which seems considerably less worried about human incursions; as you pass, they'll raise their heads and tails in that curiously endearing smile-shape they make, and go back to sleep. Harbor seals have small, round heads, slightly upturned noses, and a distinctive white mottling. Children tend to find them charming, but gray seals intimidating. Gerry Forbes's "commuters" were harbor seals; they'll cross unconcernedly in front of visiting pedestrians and even ATVs.

Harbor seals are great travelers. Young seals tagged at Sable have been recovered from Manasquan, New Jersey, a straight-line distance of 916 miles.[4]

With no human predators on Sable, the seals might be thought to have an idyllic existence. But lurking in these waters is their only natural enemy: sharks. Gerry Forbes's joke about the seals inviting humans in for a swim as a tasty diversion for sharks has a kernel of grim truth. Newborn seal pups can swim within a few hours of birth, and by the end of their second day will go regularly into the sea, where they fall easy prey to sharks attracted to the large breeding groups. Dead pups, severely mutilated by sharks, are a common sight on Sable Island; in a three-day period during the 1980 breeding season, sharks killed twenty-three pups along a five-mile stretch of the beach, and those were just the ones that washed ashore to be counted.[5] In the early 1990s, the number of seals killed by sharks in the waters around Sable Island went up sharply, and every year since then, a few hundred carcasses of shark-killed gray, harbor, harp, hooded, and ringed seals are found dead on the beaches. However, only about a dozen actual attacks have been witnessed in the last twenty years or so, mostly by oil-company technicians on seismic survey boats. None of the oil people were able to identify the shark species involved, but from wound patterns, including score marks on bone and tooth fragments, several species seem to have been at their grisly work, including great whites. Most of the dead seals on the beach, on the other hand, showed bizarre wounds, with the blubber having been peeled off in a spiral or corkscrew shape down to the midsection. These wounds didn't look at all like those inflicted by great whites. Also, the attacks occurred mostly in winter, when the great whites were down south, presumably harassing swimmers in the Caribbean and Florida. Shark researchers in other parts of the world, who were sent photographs of the wounds, confessed themselves perplexed. It appeared that the scale and nature of shark predation around Sable was unique.

Then a Sable Island study begun in 1993 by Lisa Natanson and other scientists from the Apex Predator Program on Rhode Island and by the Canadian Shark Research Laboratory, along with a Discovery Channel crew, attributed the hundreds of mutilated bodies to the elusive Greenland shark,[6] which fishermen have seen in the waters around Sable. Zoe Lucas, who has been involved in the seal-mortality studies, acknowledges that, until such attacks are actually witnessed, the evidence will remain circumstantial, and assigning the role of perpetrator to the Greenland shark is still a matter of speculation, "albeit well-founded speculation."[7]

Other sharks are present in these waters too. Basking sharks, also called bone sharks, elephant sharks, sailfish sharks, and big-mouth sharks, grow up to forty feet long and weigh up to seven tons, and are common enough around Sable. But although they are the closest living relatives to the great white shark, they are really harmless (unless you're a plankton or a baby fish; one basking shark can process 1,500 gallons of water an hour, the size of a small swimming pool, and can be deadly to several tons of plankton a day). Great whites have been seen in Nova Scotia waters, but although they seem to have killed seals around Sable, no one has yet caught an actual glimpse of one.

Whales are another story. Fifteen species of whales and dolphins have been found in Sable waters, and in and around the Gully, and cetaceans commonly strand themselves on the shores of Sable—as they occasionally do on the mainland. Some have speculated that the bewildering currents around the Island may account for the large number of strandings on Sable's beaches, though it seems implausible that an animal that passes its whole life in the sea is so easily confused by its environment. Theories have been put forward that the cetaceans' apparently suicidal dashes may be caused by human-created noise pollution: underwater explosions, sonic probes from geologists mapping the seafloor, and sonar pings from submarines. Hal Whitehead, a cetacean scientist at Dalhousie University in Halifax, has suggested that multiple strandings somehow involve the social nature of whales. He points out, for instance, that if a group or family of whales is stranded, it will do no good to get one back into the water. You have to get them all back, or the rescued whales will simply rejoin their stranded cousins. And if one whale strands itself, possibly because it is ill or dying, their strong group instinct will often doom a whole family to a similar fate.

The numbers are not trivial. A study by Zoe Lucas and Sascha K. Hooker presented to the International Whaling Commission's Scientific Committee in 1997 reported that forty-nine stranded cetaceans of ten species were recorded on Sable between 1990 and 1996. The same researchers, writing in the *Canadian Field Naturalist* in 2000[8] tracked 267 stranded cetaceans of seventeen different species in 102 "events" between 1970 and 1998. In many cases (eighty-four) only a single whale was involved; nine involved two animals; eight involved three to ten; and one extraordinary event involved over a hundred and thirty. The most common whale to be stranded was the long-finned pilot whale (173 animals). Group strandings almost always happened in winter, and most often on the north side of the island. Single individuals stranded themselves throughout the year, on both sides.[9]

The number of strandings has been going up, too—which, if there is indeed a link to underwater activity by humans, would not be surprising. Between 1970 and 1989, there were fewer than two strandings a year; whereas from 1990 to 1998, the end of the study, there were more than seven. Mass strandings of multiple male sperm whales have occurred three times (all since 1990).

At the other end of the physical scale of Sable's curiosities are creatures almost too small to be seen. "One of the most striking phenomena connected with the island," the Reverend George Patterson wrote in 1894, "is the phosphorescent light of the sea, of which there are here sometimes the most magnificent displays. The Ocean will appear at times to be in a blaze, or, when the sea breaks high, it will rise as a great fire, it may be to the height of fifteen or twenty feet."[10] These great crashing walls of pixilated fire do not appear every day, even on Sable; Gerry Forbes, who has lived there for more than three decades, has scuffed up a phosphorescent glow when walking along the beach yet has never seen anything like what Patterson described. But if you sit on the beach at night, perhaps to listen to the sea's restlessness and to imagine yourself into its life, you will occasionally see a sudden swirl of luminescence, a spiral, a curl, a quick burst of busy light that vanishes as quickly as it arrives. In a prehurricane sea, with the waves crashing on the beach, there will be a sudden flicker of silvery light across a wavetop, and if the wind is right a glowing plume of pearl will flick back from the top of the breaker, a curtain of fiery mist. No wonder the ancients, as long ago as 500 BC, when it first appears in literature, thought of such phosphorescence as fairy dust or the breath of luminous spirits, or as liquid fire, for it moves even sobersided scientists into unexpected displays of emotion. "In my memory," wrote the deep-sea explorer William Beebe, after witnessing a spectacular display of bioluminescence in 1934, "it will live throughout the rest of my life as one of the loveliest things I have ever seen."[11]

Of course, in our reductive days we now know that the basic production of bioluminescent light involves nothing more than a chemical reaction between a compound called luciferin and a catalytic enzyme, luciferase, the same reaction that lights fireflies. But there are still wonders in the deeps even for *Homo scientificus*, who tends to decode all mysteries into the basic vocabulary of chemistry or physics. Almost every one of the species (90 percent, by some reckoning) that make their lives in the deep ocean produce their own light, small and lonely beacons for themselves and their fellows. Over the long ages they have evolved an array of structures called photophores, luminous organs that range from simple skin glands in the more primitive creatures to intricate body parts with intensifying lenses, color filters, and movable covers. Some species even host bioluminescent bacteria in their translucent bodies or in specialized depressions in their bodies. These bacteria produce a constant light, steady and unblinking, so their hosts have typically adapted methods to cover or conceal it. In consequence, they can turn it on and off at will; the light then becomes a controlled code used for navigation, communication, or reproduction.

The most spectacular and easily accessible display of bioluminescence is that produced by tiny organisms called dinoflagellates, a light-producing microscopic algae, a type of phytoplankton. Dinoflagellates thrive not only near shore and on Sable Island but across the surface of all the oceans, and they account for the glow in ships' wakes at night, that romantic sight so beloved of honeymooners—and even for the less-romantic-but-still-interesting luminescent toilet bowls in ships that use seawater for sanitation. No one, of course, thinks a gang of dinoflagellates is intelligent, or even necessarily aware, but they do seem to behave somewhat like a marine neighborhood-watch program. After all, while they drift at the whim of the currents and accumulate close to shore, they become bioluminescent en masse when disturbed, either by a breaking wave, a hungry fish, or the sweep of a hand or foot. One plausible theory of why they do this: to alert predatory fish to the presence in the neighborhood of dinoflagellate-grazing crustaceans, thereby getting the creatures that are eating them eaten in turn.

There is also, alas, a downside to this marine pixie dust, at least for humans and some marine creatures. In certain cases—for instance, when concentrations of nitrates in the water rise, perhaps through runoff from polluted rivers—the dinoflagellate population explodes and blooms take place, resulting in red tides. (The redness comes from a concentrated mass of pigmentation, visible even in daylight. At night, red tides glow blue.) Red tides are toxic to fish and can cause neurological damage in humans who swim in them. Not just neighborhood watch, then, but neighborhood vigilantes too.[12]

In October 2001, after intense lobbying from environmentalists, oceanographers, and others—and with a strong assist from telegenic cetacean scientist Hal Whitehead—the Canadian federal government promised to turn the Gully just to Sable Island's east, "Nova Scotia's Grand Canyon of the Sea" as it was referred to in journalese, into Canada's first Marine Protected Area. This was supposed to happen sometime in 2002, but it didn't. A discussion paper with proposed regulations was published late in 2003, but the politics were still confused by conflicting reports of what the offshore exploration teams from Big Oil wanted, and the proposed regulations never explicitly prohibited oil and gas exploration or seismic testing. At times the gas companies professed themselves thrilled by the dizzying prospects of unlimited undersea gas reserves around Sable; at others they sounded skeptical that there was anything there worth extracting at all, a position that cynics interpreted mostly as signaling to local governments that they had better not exclude any place, including the Gully, from exploration permits. In the end, the Gully was protected—but only just. Seismic exploration and drilling were permitted on the very edge of the protected area, too close for the environmentalists, much too far for the oil companies.

The push to declare the Gully a protected area was inspired partly by its extraordinary topography. (As we have seen, it's a steep-walled, almost V-shaped canyon more than twenty-five miles long and ten miles wide, and more than eight thousand feet deep in places.) And partly because it supports a rich diversity of marine life, some of it found nowhere else at these latitudes, "and is home," as the newspaper in Halifax put it, "to two charismatic groups of creatures, marine mammals and deep-sea corals."[13]

The Gully is ecologically separate from Sable Island, although contiguous and in some ways inseparable from it, for as we have also seen, some of Sable's sand is already seeping into its depths. The Gully's currents bring in—and keep churned up—a steady supply of rich nutrients and small creatures into the canyon, which provide food for fish, which in their turn provide food for seals, birds, dolphins, and whales. This creates a classic, if contained, food chain, assisted by the huge amount of organic detritus that pours into the Gully from the adjacent banks. Clustered around the canyon are other creatures: fifteen species of whales and dolphins, mostly living around the rim and some of them diving to great depths to eat squid; seabirds that fish from the surface; marine worms living in soft mud; and corals. Because of the canyon's configuration, shallow-water and deep-water species live here in unusually close proximity. The Gully also seems to function as a nursery for many species, including halibut, shrimps, cancer crabs, lobsters, white hake, cusk, tilefish, and others.

Perhaps the most interesting of the newspaper's two "charismatic" species is a small population—maybe just 130 animals—of rare northern bottlenose whales, which use the Gully as a larder for squid. Bottlenose are not found anywhere else in the North Atlantic except off Labrador, an 870-mile jaunt away, and the Gully is essential for their survival. They're interesting animals, even if not particularly charismatic. They're between twenty and thirty feet long and weigh from six to eight tons, have prominent bulbous ("big-dome") foreheads and unexpectedly small, narrow beaks, and they are known for deep, long-lasting dives, in which they routinely descend three thousand feet or more. The Gully population doesn't migrate but remains in an area of about sixty square miles, the Gully's core. They're easy to see: Hal Whitehead's group found that more than forty of them "hang out" in a fairly small area of ocean, about five by fifteen miles. "We think [they're there because] they're eating a species of squid called Gonatus (G. *fabricii* or G. *steenstrupi*) found at the bottom of deep North Atlantic waters, and deep in the Gully itself."[14]

One of the curiosities of the Gully is the sheer volume of squid that appear to be available there for the bottlenoses to eat. The supply is obviously not inexhaustible, but it sometimes appears to be, for, to sustain their large bodies, each bottlenose must put away at least 300 squid each day. Even multiplied by the minimum population of 44 animals, that's a pretty astounding 13,200 squid a day, and the real number is probably much greater. This means that currents must be sweeping the squid in from outside the canyon, for that many animals would be unlikely to exist amicably otherwise in such a small space. One theory is that they move into the canyon to breed, but, as Whitehead points out, that wouldn't account for a steady year-round population.[15]

Northern bottlenoses are considered vulnerable to extinction and have been placed on Canada's Species at Risk list. And yet, from this small population, to the fury of Hal Whitehead and others, young whales often get entangled in the floating longlines used by the swordfish and tuna fishery. "If only three or four newborns are dying of longlines each year, that's enough to create a serious problem," says Whitehead, bristling behind his beard.[16]

Big Oil, mindful of its political Ps and Qs, is aware that marine wildlife frequently become entangled in floating debris, like plastic bags and other discarded packaging, and has declared a zero-discharge policy for garbage from its offshore projects. Gerry Forbes, for one, believes the policy is working well, and entanglements are diminishing. But that's as far as good citizenship of the sea goes.

A zero-tolerance policy for sonic probes and undersea noise would be another kettle of cetaceans altogether; without those, exploration would hardly be possible, and so, of course, they are ongoing. Research vessels studying the whales report that, even to the less-finely-tuned human ear, the noise from exploration and drilling is easily audible thirty kilometers from its source. The explosive arrays towed by the exploration vehicles are, effectively, surface mines; when they detonate, anyone listening to whale noises with earphones risks having his ears damaged, and there can be no real doubt that the explosions are both painful and disorienting to cetaceans. In the spring of 2003, moreover, a consortium of medium-sized oil companies announced its intention of drilling new wells 6.2 miles (ten kilometers) north of the existing Venture field, which if you examine the charts, places it right at the head of the Gully's feeder canyons, although just outside the new Marine Protected Area. The consortium's self-congratulatory press release made no mention of what this activity would do for and to the whales.

Sometimes, technology and conservation go hand in hand, but it is seldom as simple as that. Technology tends to give with the one hand but cross its fingers with the other. A case in point is a new device used by scallop draggers for finding their quarry. A Nova Scotia–based fishing company, Clearwater Fine Foods, is using a technique called multibeam data sets, developed by Canada's Seabed Resource Mapping Program, for imaging the sea bottom. These data sets, which give an almost photographic picture of the ocean's floor, with resolutions down to three feet, use a mix of multibeam sonar, backscatter imagery, and high-speed computer programs. According to Gary McLeod, one of Clearwater's skippers, the old way (dragging) was "like trying to find our way around a dark room with a pen flashlight. [Now] someone turned the lights on, and we don't have to bump into the furniture anymore." The upside: Draggers are towing their arrays over 70 percent less area than they used to, with better results. The downside: It will make it possible for them to clean out the very last hidden scallop beds and deplete the resource that much earlier. Also, the technique does use sonar, which disrupts the whales, albeit at a much less destructive level—

so much less that the World Wildlife Fund itself used the technique to help map the Gully.[17]

The other animal that attracts conservationist attention (the Halifax paper's other "charismatic") is the deep-sea coral, a close relative of the sea anemone. The Gully's corals typically live at depths around one thousand feet, and some of them are estimated to be anywhere from five hundred to fifteen hundred years old, as old as the oldest trees.

Corals are in many ways unlovely creatures—they're basically polyps with tentacles. But their skeletons are a different matter. The coral skeleton is a stonelike substance that can grow in a glorious assortment of colors and a bewildering array of shapes, giving beds of coral an ethereal, otherworldly appearance. Many brightly colored coral fronds can be found in the Gully and its neighborhood, more than fifteen species of them, some with what sound like undergraduate-inspired names: bubble-gum coral, popcorn coral, the very rare spider-hazard coral, and bamboo coral. Not all corals form reefs. In fact, most of the Gully's corals are soft-shell corals and don't—but some do. The spider-hazard coral, found near (but so far not in) the Gully, is one of the rarest and most beautiful. It is a creamy white, fingerlike protrusion with tentacles and can construct reefs up to 110 feet tall and 1,600 feet long. Since it grows only about a thirtieth of an inch a year, about a quarter as fast as its tropical cousins, constructing a colony can take hundreds, and even thousands, of years.[18]

It would take only a fraction of that time to destroy them all. All it needs is one industrial accident. Declaring the Gully a Marine Protected Area would surely be helpful. But even so, drilling would be permitted within 1,100 yards or so (a kilometer) of where the bottlenose whales dive three thousand feet for their daily helpings of squid. Even with careful management and scrupulous attention to the concerns of the Gully's environment, that's perilously close.

There are also living curiosities on the island itself. A species of freshwater sponge, *Heteromeyenia macounii,* found nowhere else on Earth, lives and breeds and dies in Sable's lakes and ponds. There are a few other creatures unique to the island too: two insects, according to the Nova Scotia Museum of Natural History, and "three moths, a beetle, and a nematode" (worm), in the lists of Zoe Lucas.[19] Not very many, you might think, when six hundred invertebrates and more than three hundred species of birds have been catalogued on the island. But all the rest are imports—brought here by winds, ocean currents, birds, as parasites on imported animals, as stowaways, or through deliberate action by humans. Few as they are, though, the origin of the endemic species is nevertheless puzzling. Some biologists think they survived on the Sable Island Bank during the Ice Age, when the rest of their kind perished under the glaciers. But how? There is considerable geologic evidence that the Sable Island Bank was flooded after the glaciers melted. If the island formed since the Ice Age, it could not have been a refuge for land creatures; if it formed before, how did the creatures survive the ice itself?

A little bird, the Ipswich sparrow, a pale subspecies of the Savannah sparrow, breeds only on Sable, though how it got to the island is, of course, no mystery at all. It provided its own transportation, and the Sable sparrows still winter in the Carolinas and Georgia, thereby mimicking many of their human Canadian compatriots. (Not all of the sparrows go south, though. Gerry Forbes estimates that only about a third make the trip, "and the rest wish they did.") The Ipswich is large as spar-rows go—six to six and a quarter inches—a sandy gray with a pale yellow eyebrow stripe; the Peterson bird guides, in their colorful way, describe its voice as "a dreamy lisping tsit-tsit-tsit, teseee-tsaaaay."[20] It summers on Sable in the dunes, making nests in the beach grass. The population during the last real census, in the 1970s, was about 2,300 adults in the late spring and about 10,000 in the late summer, and though the bird can have three and even four successful broods in a single season, it is regarded as vulnerable to extinction. The Canadian Wildlife Service has undertaken a long-term project to study their survival, and has noted, rather primly, that "a few errant females" have nested with male Savannah sparrows on main-land beaches in Halifax County, Nova Scotia.

Many other birds make Sable their temporary home. A survey in 1972 reported over three hundred species passing through or resident, including black ducks, red-breasted mergansers, sandpipers, Leach's storm petrels, blue-winged teals and green-winged teals, terns, and gulls, and even a snowy owl or two.[21]

The island still supports large colonies of nesting waterbirds, some of them in globally significant numbers. Once, almost certainly, there were more than there are now. The shipwrecked Ontario schoolmarm, Janet Carnochan, wandered around the dunes after her rescue and remarked on how many she saw.

> We sat down on a little hillock of sand. At once innumerable birds began flying wildly about our heads, flapping their wings, uttering peculiar sounds of defiance and fear or astonishment at such an invasion of their domains. We soon saw the reason: the ground around us was one vast succession of nests. We could hardly stretch out our hands without touching either their eggs or the young birds, little downy things, some just hatched out.[22]

These would almost certainly have been terns—a few roseate terns but mostly Arctic and common terns—which still use the island to breed in significant numbers, possibly around 5 percent of the North American tern population. But at the time Carnochan was trying to find a place to sit among the nests without crushing the "little downy things" she mentioned so fondly, there would have been many more; the Canadian Wildlife Service estimates the tern population would have been closer to a million. There were still considerable numbers on the island in 1945. Norman Campbell recalls having to make

> a vicious thing we called the tern-whacker, a piano wire and a whip, and you'd whack it in the air to drive them off, because they'd drive you mad. They thought they were defending their turf, but they'd have laid their eggs up in the dunes and we'd walk along the beach near the shore level, miles from their eggs. They'd dive at us, like a Hitchcock [movie], and they'd dive at the horses; it was not a very comfortable experience.[23]

By 1995, however, a survey was able to identify only 2,570 nesting pairs. Their decline seems to have had nothing to do with the presence of humans on the island—except indirectly, for it may be caused by diminishing fish populations in the neighborhood. The real reason seems to have been the population explosion among competing birds, primarily herring gulls (two thousand nesting pairs, 1 percent of the North American population) and the aggressive great black-backed gulls (six hundred pairs in 1998, also 1 percent of the North American population).

Roseate terns, for their part, are today a threatened species. A mere sixty adult birds were found on Sable in 1985, and there are now even fewer—in the 1990s nesting roseates ranged from a high of four pairs in 1993 to a low of one pair in 1997 and 1998.[24] Other small breeding colonies exist on a couple of islands closer to the mainland (Country Island in Guysborough County and the Brothers Island in Yarmouth County), but the species was listed as threatened in 1985 and reclassified as endangered in 1998.[25]

Researchers from Dalhousie University have been visiting Sable in the past few years to see if there are any conservation-management techniques that might encourage more terns to return to the island.[26]

Of course, the management techniques of some of the past human inhabitants of Sable would have given those researchers from Dalhousie heart attacks. In their season, curlews, plovers, bluewing ducks, and sandpipers came to the island in the thousands. "About the middle and end of August, they would leave the Labrador, where they had spent the summer, and arrive at the island on their way south. They gave Mr. Dodd [Philip Dodd, then the island's superintendent], who was an excellent shot, plenty of sport." This, of course, was a common enough approach to wild things, very much in tune even with the "conservationist" notions of the time. (Didn't Teddy Roosevelt turn up in Africa at about that time, and come home with a shipload of trophies, among them dozens of rhino, which no doubt gave him great sport too?) It was perhaps not surprising, therefore, that when James Farquhar returned to Sable many years after he'd lived there as a boy, he found that things were just not the same. "In 1913 I paid a visit to my old home, and found great changes. There were very few curlew and plover compared with seventy years ago."[27]

These days, environmental fretfulness is built into every human activity, even so apparently benign an affair as a decision to erect wind-power generators. In 2002, Sable's managers launched a preemptive "bird-strike study," to see how the generation towers would affect the bird population. Two guyed towers were then present on Sable Island, both located near the west light. One was a microwave transmission tower belonging to Maritime Tel&Tel, 200 feet high and supported by three sets of guy lines (nine in all). The other was a tower that belonged to Saint Mary's

University. It was 105 feet high and supported by four sets of five lines (twenty lines in total). For two months, the island staff diligently poked about the base of the towers every third day for dead or injured birds. None were found. For the previous fifteen years, less-formal surveys had found a total of a dozen bird carcasses, mostly greater shearwaters, Leach's storm petrels, and herring gulls, at the base of the towers. These were re-assuringly low numbers, though the researchers prudently suggested that perhaps a few more might have survived a damaged wing and walked away, or that their bodies had been scooped up by scavenging gulls, few of which scrupled to eat their dead fellows.[28]

Now that the last of the mice have (probably) per-ished, eaten by owls or gulls, the horses are the only mammals, apart from a few humans, still living on Sable. It was a close call, though—the horses were almost removed for good. In 1960, the year after the Humane Es-tablishment was shut down, and the weather-station crews that remained had converted to diesel-driven ATVs for their transportation, the federal Crown Assets Disposal Corporation put Sable's horses up for sale. Little was known about them at the time, or at least not 1,500 miles away in Ot-tawa; it was simply assumed that they were small because of inbreeding and a lack of food. Without thinking about it too much, the Ottawa bureau-crats decided that they would take the horses off Sable Island "before they starved to death" and use them for something properly productive, such as dog food or glue.

The notion kicked off a minor uproar and brought together an unusual but effective coalition of sentimentalists and traditionalists. In a nice pop-ulist touch, schoolchildren were organized in a write-in campaign, and letters poured into the office of the then-prime minister, John Diefen-baker, himself something of a populist renegade from the prairies. Dief, as he was widely called, knew a politically painless issue when he saw one, and intervened on the horses' behalf. The following year an amendment was published to the Canada Shipping Act, which still governed the island. Section 258, paragraph 5d now states: "No person shall, without prior written permission of the Agent, molest, interfere with, feed or otherwise have anything to do with the ponies on the Island."

It's hard, now, to walk anywhere on the island without seeing at least one family of horses. From 1989 the horse population has varied between a high of 360 to a low of 158; in 2003 there were upwards of 350 horses, in family groups ranging from eight to ten or perhaps twelve individuals, maybe thirty to fifty families. Such a group "may consist of one dominant stallion, one or more mares and their offspring, and occasionally one or two subordinate males. Males who are not in family bands form loosely organized bachelor groups, or, particularly if they are older, live as solitary stallions." At any given time, roughly a third of the males in the population are not members of family bands.[29]

Sometimes, the horses pay the passing humans no mind, which seems odd, because horses are naturally inquisitive animals. If you're walking along a sand road in the interior and a horse comes plodding toward you, you might stand aside politely (perhaps scrambling up onto the bank to give the animal enough room to pass), and it will amble past with nary a sideways glance, a toss of its head, or a tiny whicker of acknowledgment. You might as well be an inanimate post.

One October afternoon, on the sandy road from the station, where a bank of bayberry had eroded, its long, coarse roots exposed to the sunshine, a passing stallion extended its neck along this natural comb and then, without a by-your-leave, raised its tail and rammed its haunches back and forth across it. Itching duly scratched, it resumed its amble, grumbling quietly to itself as it passed, paying no attention at all to the human interloper. It was small, perhaps a stout thirteen hands, a glossy black with a small diamond-shaped white blaze on its nose, its sun-bleached reddish mane blowing forward over its eyes, which were completely hidden in the tangle. On an island without trees, the horses will scratch where they can, which is the main reason that beacons, posts, rain gauges, landing lights for the helipad, and anything else that can be broken by a horse's heft are fenced in. The hair they slough off mostly just blows away, but a fair amount can be seen attached to scratching posts like guy anchors.[30]

On other occasions, if you're crossing the heath toward a group of horses, they might amble slowly aside, but they might keep grazing and hardly lift their heads from the grass to watch you pass, or perhaps one in a group will swivel to watch as you go by. But usually they will be more inquisitive. A whole group might watch as you pass, in curiosity and not alarm, looking at you intently, as though mulling the peculiar fact that you have only two legs where there should be four. And if you come across a couple of young bachelor horses in an amiable mood, they might follow you cautiously, peeping over banks and around dunes, like great big children clumsily playing hide-and-seek. Once or twice, if you sit in the lee of a dune and wait awhile, you might look up to see a great, long-lashed horse eye peering at you over the edge, so close that you can hear the wind in its owner's shaggy mane and hear its little snorts and breathy breathing.

The station staff, busy with their chores, sometimes think of the horses as pests. If you leave a gate open, you will very soon find a horse inside the compound, checking it out, and if there is sensitive or delicate equipment within its reach, it will be rubbed and scraped—the horses always seem to itch—and often damaged. "The grass is *always* greener on the other side of whatever fence or gate or building there is," Gerry Forbes grouses. One of the first instructions he gives to newcomers is: Don't let the horses in.

They almost always seem to have their heads down. Like horses every-where, those on Sable spend most of their time grazing, usually in the lush grasses on the dunes and the sheltered inland dunes. In summer they gain weight and build up body fat for winter. As early as August, their coats start to thicken, and by November they're shaggy with new hair. Through the winter they lose weight, and in the spring their ribs are clearly visible. This is when mortality is greatest, in late winter through early spring, when the food is most meager. In really bad winters, a quar-ter of the population has been known to succumb to the cold and poor diet, and on rare occasions over the past two centuries the herds shrank to a few dozen animals, not even as many as were deposited there in 1756.

In winter, particularly, the horses seem to eat all the time, cramming in as much dried marram as they can, compensating in sheer volume for the poor nourishment the grass yields. That they're able to do this has helped their survival. Cattle and the smaller ruminants had much greater trouble on Sable, being limited to the amount of food their multicham-bered stomachs could process.[31] There's almost always enough fresh wa-ter to drink, even in the coldest weather, but in really severe frosts the horses will munch on snow. Winter also mutes the horses' competitive nature. Stallions put aside their obsession with sexual rivals to focus more on survival, and families sometimes huddle together in the lee of a dune in bad weather.

In late May and June, the animals look mangy, with the old winter hair sloughing off in matted chunks, but their body weight is improving as the new growth of beach grass, marram, and beach pea spreads across the dunes.

Like horses elsewhere, Sable's mares reach puberty at about a year, though they're seldom successfully mated until at least double that age. They're polyestrous—that is, if not bred in the spring, they are fertile at regular intervals until the end of summer—and when they foal they generally produce one, or at most two, young. The gestation period is between eleven and twelve months. They seldom produce an infant every year.[32]

The biggest dietary problem for Sable's horses is sand. Everything on the island is coated with sand, even the grass, and horses ingest great quantities of sand as they graze. The hard quartz grains don't do their stomachs any harm, passing through without difficulty, but they are deadly to their teeth. Like other grazing herbivores, horses have developed a set of strong, high-crowned teeth, suited to grinding tough grasses. Young horses shed their milk teeth at about age two and a half, and the permanent teeth, thirty-six to forty of them, are completely developed by age four to five years. These include twelve incisors that cut and pull at grasses, and twenty-four grinding premolars and molars. (Curiously, the stallion has extra teeth seldom found in mares: four carnivore-style canines, remnants without function in the modern horse.) Horse teeth keep growing until about age six, so tooth wear is not a problem early in their lives. But older horses may starve when their worn teeth can no longer grind the marram, and life expectancy on Sable is therefore far lower than the twenty-five or even thirty years and more found elsewhere—Sable horses commonly die after a decade.[33] In earlier days, before the current no-interference policy was instituted, station staff used to feed crushed oats to the older horses, especially those they used as riding or draft animals. Gerry Mader, who spent six weeks on the island with her meteorologist husband in the 1970s, said they used to feed them bananas. "They just *loved* bananas."

Only occasionally is the body of a dead horse seen on Sable. They seem mostly to just fade away, picked at by the gulls, and cleaned up by the elements. Sometimes in the spring, a new tuft of marram, or sandwort, or cranberry will appear, a horse's only memorial.

But a horse's lot is far from only grimness and death. Witness the joie de vivre of the foals in spring, long-legged and endearing, scratching

their ears with their hind legs (something no adult horse can do), galloping madly about for no purpose but sheer exuberance, dashing off after
birds and sometimes seals, playing chasing and catching games with others of their kind, or simply racing across the slopes for the sheer pleasure
of running.

When they're not grazing or simply snoozing in the Sun, the adults
will sometimes join in these games, chasing the foals and dancing
around them. The stallions, too, race each other in furious gallops
down the beach, jostle and push and wrestle and get into mock fights,
teeth bared and biting, eyes rolling, legs flying, but no damage seems to
be done and when it is over, all is amiability again. You can see the evidence in the sand—dancing, pawing, circling—and if you're lucky, you
can see them at play, manes flying and long tails swirling, coats glisten-
ing with sweat. Roberto Dutesco, a New York fashion photographer
who became fascinated with Sable's horses, captured them at play in
stunning still and video images, including footage of a father and son
wrestling in the sands.[34]

All the early commissioners on Sable Island commented on the horses'
remarkable adaptation to the conditions there. They were fleet-footed
and very much at home in the deep island sand that lamed so many of
the other horses introduced to Sable between 1801 and 1830 with the
stated intention of improving the breed. (Almost all these interlopers
were later killed by the native stallions.) Barbara Christie quotes an observer, writing in 1885 about the horse drives that had been instituted on
Sable (rounding up horses to ship them to the mainland for sale, one of
the Humane Establishment's fund-raising efforts):

> The horses trot, jump, gallop, paddle, rack, prance, shuffle and waltz. . . .
> They will carry a stranger anywhere without the slightest inconvenience
> to themselves . . . and in the wild round-ups . . . need no urging whatever

to race uphill and down, turn, double head round, take a flying fifteen feet [*sic*] leap over a gulch and drive back any who make a desperate struggle for their freedom. . . . The chase over . . . the jaded little Tartars desired no stable or groom, but as soon as their saddles and bridles were removed, they started off for a roll in the grass, a drink at the pond, and the wild freedom of the [sand hills] until their services were again required.[35]

Occasionally through their history on Sable, the horses have faced perils other than the weather; what nature has given, nature can take away, especially in a place as small and vulnerable as Sable. August 1894, for example, was an unusually scorching and dry summer, and a plague of grasshoppers landed on the island, brought from the mainland in a gale. "The hordes destroyed all the vegetable gardens and stripped a vast portion of wild grass making it impossible to secure enough fodder for the stock during winter. The cows, because of damaged pastures, began to fail in their milk." The superintendent was forced to contemplate the wholesale slaughter of the horses. "In a month," he wrote, "the whole island will look as though fire had run over it." The only respite from the pests were high winds that blew many of them out to sea and kept the rest from moving, but as soon as the winds died, the swarms were back and resumed their assault on the island's vulnerable wild-pea and marram-grass fields. When the pests were finally driven off or died, well into September, "the relief was immense, and damage horrendous."[36]

In this instance, the horses themselves were nearly the victims. But one of the tricky ecological questions facing Sable's managers is whether the feral horses themselves, which by regulation are now strictly left alone to thrive or die without human intervention, are effectively destroying the environment on which they so intimately depend. By consuming vast quantities of marram, are they destabilizing the dune system and encouraging the erosion of the island? Are they, quite literally, eating themselves out of house and home? So far, there is no simple conclusion. A report at the beginning of this century admits that

> the relationship between the horses and the island's vegetated terrain . . . is poorly understood. Although simplistic views hold that the impact of grazing on the island may reduce the stability and integrity of grazed areas . . . [and] grazing and trampling may result in increased erosion in some areas . . . these activities also recycle nutrients and create habitats for certain plant species and thus may compensate for erosion.[37]

In other words, they're eating the stuff but are also providing the fertilizer that encourages it to spread. This is a decent if not spectacular example of hedging your bets, but then—*pace* that *simplistic*—it's not really surprising if a bit of benign denial is going on. In any case, the island staff carefully removes piles of horse dung for their gardens only from those places where they would otherwise do no good, such as the sandy roadways. Dung in the grasses is dung that will stimulate plant growth, after all.

The effect humans have had on Sable is far less ambiguous. Records kept since a continuous human presence began on Sable, in 1801, show that over the last two hundred years the island's vegetation cover has been sharply reduced. A number of studies indicate that after the lifesaving station was set up, destabilization of the dune systems accelerated. The erosion was largely caused by intensive cultivation and by pasturing for the horses; the damage to the vegetation allowed loose windblown sand to advance over large areas where it had previously been absent.

By and large, Sable's human inhabitants ignored the ecological damage they themselves were causing. But island superintendents often expressed concern about drifting sand and wasting dunes, and made sporadic attempts to put a stop to it.

Most of these early attempts involved planting programs. They imported, for example, tussock grass from the Falkland Islands in a vain hope that it would help bind the sand; instead, it died. In 1901 a tree-planting project was undertaken, using rootstock supplied by an experimental farm in Ottawa. A substantial number of trees were shipped to the island and strategically planted—69,000 evergreens, 12,500 deciduous trees of various persuasions, 1,000 willow cuttings, 600 fruit trees and bushes and a collection of rhubarb roots were planted. About 55 pounds (twenty-five kilograms) of pine seeds were sown. None of it worked. Everything but the evergreens were slashed to pieces in the winds and perished. By 1913, only thirteen evergreens survived, and a decade later only a single mournful pine remained, very likely the same plant that still clings to life by the helipad.

In 1973 attempts were made to enhance the sand accumulation on the spits at each end of the island. Two parallel rows of wood-lathe snow fencing were installed down the center of the spits, trapping the wind-blown sand. It worked, too: Within a few years the western spit gained four feet in height, enough to prevent high tides washing over it and drastically altering it. The sand was stabilized enough to encourage colonies of sandworts to take root.[38] By 2002, the western spit was still well vegetated, but the vegetation cover on the eastern spit had again been taken out by storms and flooding.

These snow fences were used elsewhere on the island too, to encourage sand accumulation and marram-grass plantings. But since about 1984 their use has been discouraged, because the wire used to bind the slats together remained after the wood deteriorated, and was both an eyesore and a hazard to the horses.

In 1987 the Canadian branch plant of Mobil Oil, eager to drill in the neighborhood and therefore also eager to curry environmentalist favor, sponsored a new approach to stabilizing the sand, experimenting with importing discarded Christmas trees and using them instead of snow fencing. Rows of balsam firs, stripped of bunting and ornaments, were placed to capture sand and protect plantings of native species like marram grass and beach pea. The first year, 900 surplus trees were used, and the following June, 6,500 more were imported. The trees left no hazardous debris after they decayed, and proved effective three-dimensional sand traps that worked well whatever the wind direction. Within the first two months the tree-fences accumulated as much as five feet of windblown sand in previously eroding areas. More than 8,500 clumps of marram grass were collected from areas of healthy growth and good cover, separated into clumps of eight to ten stems, and transplanted at the restoration site.[39]

The Christmas-tree initiative, however, has now been abandoned—it was too expensive, and Mobil had made its gesture. But the planting of native species like marram and beach pea goes on, and the island's stewards are now much more careful to avoid careless construction, like unnecessary road building. There are also efforts to protect other vulnerable sites such as dune lines and the freshwater ponds, and to protect rare plant species.[40]

CHAPTER FIFTEEN

Its Confusing Politics

The Establishment is shut down,

Sable's usefulness is disputed, its

governance confused, its future uncertain

In 1939, Donald S. Johnson, aka "Deep Sea" Johnson, became the last superintendent of the Sable Humane Establishment. It was a time of rapid change: The telegraph had given way to the radio, Canada was at war, and, apart from its meteorological services, which remained important, the Sable Station's main task was to watch for enemy submarines and any suspicious activity by foreign vessels. From 1939 to 1945, the occasional aircraft refueled on the island, and for a while a small-fleet air arm called Walrus was stationed there, and the population swelled. In 1941 the island experienced the first of another kind of wreck, when a Hudson bomber hit a steel mast in heavy fog and crashed, killing all aboard. It wasn't the last such accident. Norman Campbell, whose tenure on Sable lasted from 1945 to 1946, later recalled a chance meeting on the train he had taken from Toronto to Halifax on his way to the island for the first time.

"I met a young airman, a little tipsy and having trouble getting into his upper berth, and I gave him a hand and had a chat with him.

"'Where are you going?' he asked.

"'Sable Island, do you know it?'

"'Know it? Hell, I crashed on it!'

"He'd been flying up from Bermuda and developed some kind of engine trouble. They were coming down in fog and rain, the rain streaking past their windshield; they hung on but thought they were finished, thought they were coming down in the ocean. But then there was a screech from the undercarriage. . . . They had come down on the western bar of Sable Island. They looked outside and, to their astonishment, saw a stream of lights coming out toward them—the station had been alerted to an aircraft in trouble. When I got to the Island, I went out to visit the plane, which was still lying there on the bar, a great eyeless bird. There were masses of seals around it. I went into the plane and up toward the flight deck, with the wind howling through the holes in the fuselage. The controls were still there; they hadn't taken them away. It was a strange feeling. And suddenly I heard a noise and I looked back, and there was this face looking at me; a big seal had humped itself up onto the floor of the plane."

Late in the war, a Canso aircraft with a wing commander on board as a VIP passenger came in to refuel, landed on Lake Wallace, and got stuck. It couldn't get out of the lagoon, which was then too short for a takeoff, and although it had wheels, it was really a ship's hull, and so it couldn't maneuver itself out onto the land either. The wing commander and the airplane's crew stayed the night at the station, and the station staff afterward gossiped about a high muckety-muck doing the dishes, sleeping over on the carpet, and eating up their rations, which then consisted of powdered egg yolks and dried cod. The next morning, the men cobbled together a skid made of planks torn from an old barn, and Sable's wild horses were pressed into service, laboriously hauling the aircraft out of the lagoon onto the beach, where it was prepped for takeoff. Some days later they heard a noise, looked up, and saw a plane circling overhead. "Out comes a parachute and a case of something, and it lands on a nearby sand dune," Campbell later recalled. "It was a big case of steaks, tomatoes, fresh vegetables, everything, courtesy of the air force. *That's* gratitude."

Sable's meteorological station was then separate from the lifesaving establishment. It generated its own electricity from a Delco wind turbine and was supposed to send daily reports to Halifax. Mostly it did, but as Campbell explained, the head of the station, an old Maritimer, was not always as diligent as he might have been: "He would measure wind direction, he would read the temperature on the surface, and the humidity. He was supposed to do all this every hour, or every two hours, but I can remember him sitting by his key in the office, and if it was too cold to go out he'd just sort of look at the window and make up the figures as he went along."

Like most of the other superintendents in Sable's history, Deep Sea Johnson was quite a character. His sobriquet came from his having spent some years as a diver in Halifax, and he kept his gear with him at Sable— an old-fashioned copper helmet and rubber hoses, just like the kind you see in the old Hollywood movies in which divers are inevitably attacked by ravening squid the size of school buses. Instead of experts, Johnson brought in dozens of teenagers from Cape Breton homes for delinquents to "straighten them out," and he ruled them with an iron fist. He treated the station very much as though it were his personal fiefdom and the boys his personal servants—building fences around his house, cultivating his garden, improving his residence.

The difficulty was, they weren't very good at rescues.

On Christmas Day, the last Christmas of the war, the station heard on the radio that an American trawler, the *Gale*, was in trouble. Norman Campbell, a member of Johnson's meteorological staff, later recalled how his boss handled the crisis.

Deep Sea decided he'd go out and rescue them, so he organized his troops of boys into the surf boat, but they'd had no training, they'd been too busy building his fences, and these poor kids rowed out there and the sea was terrific; it was just smashing in, Deep Sea at the tiller. It was like a bizarre movie: him at the stern, and oars going in every direction, and we saw them going out, going out and disappearing with each wave.

The actual rescue was performed by another American vessel that had thrown a line to the *Gale*. The Canadian corvette *Petrolia* had been standing to about a mile out in the stormy sea, and its crew were obliged to rescue the would-be rescuers. When Deep Sea climbed aboard, he went into the captain's quarters and signed the guest book, *Governor Johnson of Sable Island*. With the storm raging, Deep Sea couldn't get back to the island, so the meteorological staff decided to have Christmas dinner at the radio station. Campbell has fond memories of that meal.

We got a huge turkey platter and a set of [carving] knives and so on and had a tin of Spam plopped on the middle of the platter and a gravy which we made out of raisins. . . . this was our Christmas dinner. *Would you like a slice of dark meat or light meat?* We'd carve off a piece of Spam, as we listened to Bob Hope coming in on the radio from New York. We didn't see Johnson for weeks.

And so the venerable Humane Establishment, begun with such good intentions and executed with such heroism over such a long period, deteriorated into farce.

There were two more real shipwrecks. On April 23, 1947, the steamship *Alphios*, five thousand tons, of Greek registry, cracked up on the east bar but vanished under the water. Seven years later, after a wild summer storm, the ship suddenly reappeared, showing itself upright and almost clear of the sands, looking for all the world as though it were ready to steam away. A station patrol carried the news back to the main station. The *Alphios* was on view for six months and then vanished as abruptly as it had reappeared.[1] And on July 4, the *Manhasset*, bound for St. John's from Newport News under Captain Luis Marangos, foundered and broke apart.

Four years later, in 1959, the government closed the lifesaving station for good.

With the exception of a few stray yachts, ships don't run aground on Sable anymore. Most oceangoing vessels, in any case, still give the island and its deadly neighborhood a very wide berth, even with modern navigational gear and command centers that can locate a vessel to within a few feet. (So computerized are modern vessels that the skipper can tell from the bridge exactly what is functioning and what isn't, even to deciding whether the chef's freezer is a few degrees too warm.)[2] A few fishermen still trawl the waters around Sable, but with GPS systems aboard, better weather forecasting, and reliable diesels, the risk is small. Which leaves only the drilling rigs to worry about, and the hazard of an industrial accident to one of the nearby gigantic mobile platforms. In the basement of one of the Sable Station buildings is a chilling reminder of what might happen if there was a major disaster: Piled in neat stacks is a substantial quantity of emergency equipment and supplies, including racks of body bags. But in essence, the human presence on Sable, which had existed there with such tightly focused purpose for more than two hundred years, began by the 1970s to seem superfluous to need.

Even the lights didn't require a human presence anymore; Sable's lighthouses were fully automated in the 1960s. The lightkeepers had doubled as weather reporters, and that function was taken over by the Meteorological Branch of the Ministry of Transport, later transferred to Environment Canada, which still keeps a weather station on the island—that too now largely automated. The staff of Environment Canada's Atmospheric Environment Branch, with the exception of Gerry Forbes, who remained, still rotated out to Sable for short periods to conduct studies of the upper air, essentially becoming agents of the coast guard, which was nominally in charge.

The main station in 2003 consisted of the Forbes residence and another building that served as a social center for rotating workers, with an apartment on the second floor that slept eight, and in the basement the emergency rescue equipment. There was a gaggle of other buildings: three row houses for occasional staff, a machine and generator shed, a weather balloon building, and the office and laboratory building, where the computer systems and the other weather monitoring devices were housed. All the buildings were painted white, with black roofs, but were, to put it kindly, nondescript; none would ever likely grace the pages of a design magazine. The diesel storage was up on a nearby dune; gravity took it where it was needed. The road connecting the south and north beaches passed by the machine shed. The whole compound was surrounded by a four-foot fence to keep the pesky horses out.

There used to be a lightkeeper's house to the east, but it became buried in sand. For a while, a family lived on the second floor, the first having filled with sand, but that whole building has now disappeared in the dunes. Other ruined buildings are scattered about, periodically reappearing from the sand, and then submerging again.

Jurisdiction seemed as confused as the station's purpose. From 1962 the coast guard was officially in charge; the Canada Shipping Act was updated to reflect the government's reorganization, and the Sable Island Regulations were passed. These stated that "the island is under the control, man-agement and administration" of the coast guard's Dartmouth base. The coast guard provides ship transportation and supplies for the base on Sable and maintains a helicopter pad (a second, smaller pad is owned and main-tained by the oil rigs), a radio beacon, and navigation lights at the east and west ends of the island, and an emergency base. At the western light is a straggly collection of yet more nondescript buildings: a Quonset hut be-longing to the coast guard, a small cottage for the use of Maritime Tel&Tel personnel when they visit to service the microwave transmission towers (put up at great expense in the vain hopes of capturing the oil-rig com-munications business), and the lightkeeper's house, now vacant, which is used by Department of Fisheries and Oceans people on their rare visits to the island. Despite all this, the meteorological service of Environment Canada was effectively in charge; at least it had someone in situ.

Only two people were living permanently on Sable at the start of the millennium: station manager Gerry Forbes, who was paid by Environ-ment Canada, and Zoe Lucas, both of whom had been there for decades and showed no signs of ever wanting to leave.

Lucas had no official position, but she had been there so long, and had contributed so steadily to the island's environmental studies, that no one seemed to question her presence (and in any case she apparently attracted more revenue to the island through research grants than she cost to main-tain). Lucas is a slender blonde, elusive to the rare visitors, and is usually spotted with her hair wrapped in a scarf and haring off somewhere on her ATV. In 2003 a movie was released starring Jane Seymour, set ostensibly on Sable Island and portraying a Zoe Lucas–like character living alone amid a herd of wild horses. Seymour's reclusive and somewhat antisocial curmudgeon-with-sort-of-a-heart-of-gold perpetrated something of a li-bel on Lucas, who is well known for charming schoolchildren on the mainland with her passionate portrayals of Sable's unique environment.

(The movie was not shot on Sable but in a provincial park in Ontario; the trees in the landscape were somewhat of a giveaway, but then that's the movie industry. The movie of Sebastian Junger's *The Perfect Storm* also showed Sable with trees, and an American-style wooden lighthouse.)

For the rest, Sable's population swings from a handful to a dozen or more, as scientists and meteorologists visit for short- to medium-term projects.

In an attempt to sift through the jurisdictional muddle into which Sable was sinking, a group of stakeholders got together in the mid 1990s, determined to form a Sable Island conservancy to head off what one participant called "a foul-weather siege of politics" since the advent of oil and gas exploration. And so, on April 16, 1998, about a hundred people from public and private corporations, academies, and government agencies listened to an annotated slide show put on by Zoe Lucas and voted on the spot to set up a conservancy and trust fund. A year later this mutated into the Sable Island Preservation Trust, whose function it was to run the island on behalf of all the confusion of people who had been doing it hitherto. Gerry Forbes, whose employer had been Environment Canada, transferred to the new agency. He stayed on as station manager.[3]

Even so, matters remained somewhat confused. It is far from clear, in fact, who actually owns Sable Island. By a law of May 4, 1836, the island was annexed to Nova Scotia, in order to bring it within the jurisdiction of the local courts.[4] But did this annexation persist past the creation of Canada in 1867? The province of Nova Scotia, which puts up about a tenth of the island's million-dollar annual budget, still claims territorial rights, but a tenth doesn't carry with it much heft, and in any case, a legal opinion, derived after drilling permissions were sought by oil companies, found the province's claims murky. Sable (or so said the legal opinion) is under the direct legislative authority of the Parliament of Canada in Ottawa, a state of affairs enshrined in the British North America Act that assembled Canada. Confusingly, it nevertheless remains part of Nova Scotia, because the colony that joined the confederation in 1867 explicitly included the island. (The Council of Nova Scotia in 1785 declared that Halifax County "includes all the Townships and other granted and ungranted lands within the Province not comprehended within any of the aforesaid Counties—also Sable Island.")[5]

There are even a few diehards who maintain that the Hancock family of Massachusetts might still have a legitimate claim to ownership. The family are the heirs of the famous John Hancock, who inherited much worldly wealth from his uncle, who in turn inherited all Le Mercier's goods and chattels, and Le Mercier, after all, had been given de jure control of the island, and had later attempted to sell it (or those rights), but there is no record that he ever did so. It is a well-known fact of Nova Scotian life that squatter's rights can be transferred into permanent title, under certain circumstances. But the odds are very long, and no one would advise any of the current Hancocks to rush over to the island to stake their claim. The squatter's law requires, among other things, that to acquire proper title an individual and his assigns must actually use the island continuously for a minimum of sixty years (only recently reduced to forty), which by itself lets Le Mercier and Hancock out. In any case, they would have had to pay taxes on the property, which would by now amount to a nifty bill, stretching as it does from 1738 to the present. Never mind that a revolution and the War of 1812 occurred in the interim, or that the Humane Establishment was directly administered by the municipality of Halifax through its Board of Works.

Sable is still connected to the wider world, just as it is shaped and maintained and changed by the same planetary forces that affect all of us. In some more or less discouraging ways, this is simple to see. Notoriously, on July 5 each year, wind-borne debris reaches Sable's dunes and beaches, a depressing aftermath of patriotic celebrations up and down the U.S. East Coast; helium-filled balloons, particularly, drift onto the island in disturbing quantities. But litter arrives every day, not just on the day after the Fourth. In a study in the 1980s, Zoe Lucas found that plastic litter was washing ashore at a monthly rate of roughly two hundred items every six hundred yards—which means that more than eight thousand items per month were washing up on these pristine, isolated beaches. Anecdotal evidence indicates that not much has changed since then.

But Sable is also connected in ways that are less a product of a wasteful industrial civilization than of its peculiar geography. Because it is in the center of the East Coast storm track, Sable Station has been in the thick of studies aimed at better predicting and managing responses to major storms, including two studies called Experiment on Rapidly Intensifying Cyclones in the Atlantic (ERICA) and Canadian Atlantic Storm Program (CASP). Sable operates an around-the-clock aviation weather program, with data collected automatically and transmitted to the mainland by satellite uplink. In 2003 work was under way for the installation of a series of five wind turbines at the end of the road from the station to the south beach—and at first sited, bizarrely enough, in the very center of the island's tern sanctuary. The windmills were to have blade lengths of thirteen feet and be installed on eighty- or one-hundred-foot towers; they would have an output of 7.5 kilowatts each and would produce about a quarter of the island's power demands. The purpose was partly for research, to see how wind power could best serve remote locations, and to see how modern turbines coped with the savage weather. (Institutional memories can be oddly short. Environment Canada seems to have forgotten that in the early 1950s there was a wind charger on the island, providing a good deal of what were obviously much tinier power demands. This charger, too, was on a high tower. Norman Campbell doesn't remember how high, but it was high enough. "I had to climb up one night to free the frozen propeller, a scary thing to have to do." There was also a generator for those days when the wind failed—"no more than three days like that, all the time I was there," asserts Campbell.)

The station has also collaborated with other agencies, most notably the National Oceanic and Atmospheric Administration (NOAA), based in Colorado, and Princeton University. The focus for most of these studies has been a better understanding of winds and storms, and accumulating data on pollution (including global warming and airborne contaminants). Airborne-pollution projects have included studies of acid rain, atmospheric aerosols, organic contaminants, background carbon-dioxide levels, hydrocarbons and halocarbons, carbon monoxide and ozone, oxides of sulphur and nitrogen, and the toxic components in fog.[6]

Other, somewhat grimmer projects than "mere" pollution and ocean dumping are ongoing in the waters around the island. The Department of National Defence is spending $10 million or so trying to locate—and then, with any luck, destroy—the thousands of tons of munitions and chemical and biological weapons that were dumped into the sea after the Second World War. Canada was, for example, a major manufacturer of mustard gas, and in one notorious instance immediately after the war, Canadian navy crews used cannon fire to sink a barge filled with barrels of the compound. The barge holding twelve hundred barrels full of mustard gas was towed out by tugboats to the waters just south of Sable, and in a first try at sinking the barge, the HMCS *Middlesex* fired three depth charges at it. Alas, the attempt failed, partly because the convoy was in the grip of one of the island's

across the Scotia Shelf to Country Harbor on the mainland, whence its destiny is the insatiable maw of the North American energy grid. This fragile pipeline runs the full length of Sable's south beach, a mere mile or two offshore. The Thebaud processing plant is also perilously close to the Gully. Environmentalists can be forgiven their palpitations.

In 2003 natural gas off Sable had a virtually unlimited future, with more than 3 trillion cubic feet of proven reserves. Or it was rapidly running dry. It depended on whose figures you believed. Or on when they were issued, and with what motives.

Oil and gas exploration in the region dates back to the 1960s, when test well-probes were put down on Sable Island itself and in the shallow waters that surround it. As we have seen, nobody protested or seemed concerned. The word *environment* was not yet shorthand for rigorous conservation but merely meant the milieu in which exploration was conducted. That Sable Island itself might be damaged by the drilling and its attendant operations never entered into anyone's calculations. Mobil conducted seismic and sedimentary tests, and produced a rough sketch of probable oil and gas deposits. In 1966, Amaco drilled two test wells off the Grand Banks. Nothing was found, but the signs were promising enough that by 1972, half a million square miles of permits had been issued for offshore drilling and forty wells had been drilled. All of those were dry too, and it wasn't until 1979 that the drilling rig Gulftide confirmed natural gas at the Venture site, near Newfoundland in 65 feet of water, at a depth of 16,250 feet.

Like all petroleum (hydrocarbon) reserves on the planet, the resource around Sable Island was formed in earlier geologic times. In Sable's case, it long predates the geologic origins of the island itself. Indeed, by these measures the most-recent glaciation was a last-minute affair.

Gas begins with living things, especially plants. About 150 million years ago, rivers flowing from the proto-North America carried with them heavy loads of silt and mud sediments, together with great quantities of dead leaves and stems of plants. The St. Lawrence basin was a major source of this organic soup. The sediment gathered on the ocean floor, and because the ocean at those depths was then rich in oxygen, the plant matter decayed and rotted, as it would have on the surface. But as more and more rot accumulated, the oxygen levels diminished, and eventually the organic silt simply piled layer upon layer, without decaying. Eventually, it became buried and covered in layers of nonorganic silt. As the layers continued to accumulate, the pressure cemented the silt into rocks called sandstone and shale. As the silt layers got deeper, the ocean waters no longer cooled them, and the pressure caused the temperature to increase. Once the pressure was great enough and the time period long enough, the organic material was converted into either oil or natural gas. Geologists, for once eschewing their penchant for a jargon-rich technical vocabulary, called the process *cooking*. The amount of cooking determined whether oil or gas was produced as a result. Small amounts of cooking typically produced natural gas; more cooking produced oil. (Curiously, yet more cooking would then produce natural gas again.) A second factor determining oil or gas was the nature of the sediment. Marine sediments (plankton, sea plants, fish) usually became oil. Terrestrial plants swept into the ocean normally became gas.

Sable's gas is contained in porous sandstone layers, which is one factor that encouraged the prospectors. Under pressure, natural gas acts as a liquid would: The pressure forces it to move, generally toward the surface, so the nature of the rock in which it is found is critical. If it is not porous enough, and has very few cracks, the gas won't accumulate into reservoirs.

Too porous, and the gas will simply dissipate. Even if the porosity is just right, the rock mustn't be too close to the surface, or the gas will escape into the atmosphere. The sandstones deep under the Sable basin are perfect, porous enough to make good reservoirs, and relatively far down.

But one more thing is required for commercial-sized deposits to accumulate: a layer of impermeable rock lying over the porous sandstone. Shale normally does this work, but to be effective it must completely cover the reservoir like a shallow dome, as it does, for example, in the Gulf of Mexico. Geologists, still adhering to their newfound fondness for giving things easily understood names, call these domes *traps*, and the petroleum or gas so trapped are *pools*. All natural-gas exploration is essentially a search for these traps, and hence the pools.

Sable's traps were unusual in that they were formed not by domes of shale but by a single flat layer of igneous rock. This layer was then fractured by geologic stresses, creating separated pockets of natural gas. The distribution pattern has become clear through the 125 test wells that have been drilled in and around Sable Island, at depths varying from three thousand to thirteen thousand feet and more. But exactly how many of these pockets there are, and how much gas they contain, was still a matter of some dispute in the petroleum industry by 2003. It could be over 3 trillion cubic feet, in which case the industry is viable until 2025 or thereabouts, or as few as 700 billion cubic feet, in which case the wells will suck air a decade earlier.

Environmental concerns about these wells have been fairly muted in Nova Scotia, a part of Canada that has always been industry-shy and could use the employment that gas processing provides. Nevertheless, in early 2003, a regulatory board held hearings into the Deep Panuke Project, southwest of Sable, owned by a newly formed Canadian energy giant called EnCana. The company's plans were to spend

$1.2 billion deploying three energy platforms to recover and process the gas before piping it ashore to the community of Goldboro, more or less paralleling the SOEP line. At the time, EnCana was estimating the recoverable reserves of Deep Panuke at about 90 billion cubic feet. Deep Panuke was the first East Coast gas project to envisage processing so-called sour gas, which contains substantial amounts of hydrogen sulphide. Environmentalists told the board, predictably, that the environmental review of the project had been "fundamentally flawed."[8]

Among their worries: drilling muds that could wash up on Sable's beaches or, worse, seep into the Gully, where they would overwhelm the filter-feeding organisms on the ocean floor; and something called *produced water*, a by-product of gas extraction, which is simply dumped back into the sea. Produced water is a complex soup of heavy metals such as arsenic and mercury, radioactive materials, and droplets of oil and grease that could not be removed by treatment. It also contains defoaming and anti-corrosion agents used by the oil rigs in the drilling and pumping process. The industry's position is that it can't do any harm, because it so rapidly becomes diluted. Still, it is known that produced water has a feminizing effect on male marine creatures and therefore inhibits breeding. It is also fair to say that no one really has a clue whether it does long-term harm to the ecosystem.[9]

Also, the pipeline trenched along the seabed south of Sable is vulnerable to cracking as the sand underneath it erodes. It is too expensive to bury the pipeline completely, and the extraction companies are reduced to keeping their fingers crossed. ("Are they in denial?" an engineer who has examined the data was asked. "Only to the public," was the reply.) Even if the pipeline breaches, this wouldn't necessarily be an environmental catastrophe, of course. Gas is not oil, and would bubble to the surface instead of fouling the water, resulting in a lot of very surprised fish and seabirds, but not much further damage.

Another possibility is that extracting billions of cubic feet of gas could cause subsidence in the surrounding seabed—subsidence that would take down Sable Island with it. Subsidence has happened, for example, in the North Sea, where drillers suddenly found themselves in deeper water than they had started with, costing them millions of dollars when they had to resort to jacking up their rigs. The oil-company engineers believe the risk is small in the Sable area, but the potential remains. As the geologist Ned King puts it, "If you had [only] two meters of subsidence, that's basically a catastrophic event [around Sable]."

Much more worrying were the sonic probes the oil companies were still using in 2003; the regulatory agency (the Canada–Nova Scotia Offshore Petroleum Board) was allowing a company called Marathon Oil to do seismic testing within six hundred yards of the Gully Marine Protected Area, despite full knowledge that it would place the rare population of bottlenose whales at risk. Hal Whitehead and his Cetacean Laboratory at Dalhousie were both furious and heartsick, but though their protestations cropped up regularly in the press, the regulators paid them scant attention. Not that the exploration companies had it all their own way. The Department of Fisheries and Oceans set up the Centre for Offshore Oil and Gas Environmental Research (COOGER), based at the Bedford Institute of Oceanography, which tactfully declared in the summer of 2003 that the drillers "have cooperated fully." Whether they had or not, the center was conducting a full range of studies into the way seismic probes affected ocean populations, with the declared intention of using the data to regulate oil and gas exploration.

Perhaps it would all become moot, in the medium if not short term. A flurry of optimistic stories late in 2002 and early in 2003 ("Deep Panuke has reserves of almost a trillion cubic feet"; "Chevron Canada expects to complete drilling its $76-million exploratory well near Sable Island in a few days . . . its projected depth of 20,900 feet"; "Marathon Oil of Houston is drilling one that is almost completed"; "The pace of exploration will continue for 25 years") was followed less than a month later by a note of caution: "EnCana Corp. of Calgary announced Thursday it is abandoning its latest exploratory well off Nova Scotia. This is EnCana's fourth dry well in the region in the past two years. . . . Drilling exploratory wells off Nova Scotia can cost from $30 million to $80 million. . . . [The company] remains optimistic about the East Coast." The same story revealed that Shell had abandoned its exploratory Onondaga well just southwest of Sable Island because there wasn't enough gas. (The well cost $90 million and was $30 million over budget.)[10]

Caution soon turned to pessimism, when EnCana announced a year-long "time-out" for Deep Panuke (February 15, 2003), followed by an announcement just a few weeks later by EnCana's president, Gwyn Morgan, who said that "another gas discovery would have to be made at the Panuke fields to make the project feasible" (March 3, 2003). The very next day Shell revealed that its offshore production was declining and wouldn't last beyond 2010 "in the absence of significant exploration." Then a pipeline operator was quoted as saying bluntly, "No one has [new] gas offshore." This was Wayne Lewis of Lewis Engineering, part of a pipeline consortium. "We've taken it as far as we can," he said. "Now we will have to wait until they find gas and we find out the composition of that gas." Just a week later, a consortium of smaller energy companies announced plans to drill yet more wells, depressingly close to the Gully.

Even if the more optimistic predictions of the exploration companies turn out to be true, the gas fields will be exhausted in twenty years. And so, if no environmental disaster happens in that brief span, Sable Island will be safe, at least from that particular man-made hazard. If the pessimism proves more prescient, of course, the hoped-for jobs will have fled to more promising domed traps, and Sable Island will be, once again, left to its own devices.

CHAPTER SIXTEEN

Its Very Existence at Risk

Sable may be growing, or it may be

shrinking, but in the long term it is

probably doomed to disappear

But will those "devices" allow Sable Island much of a future? Is the island really shrinking, as many have asserted?

If you measure what has happened to Lake Wallace, it would seem so.

In the 1750s, the period when Sable horses arrived on the island, the pond was a slender arc about fifteen miles long. This was when Le Mercier graciously approved Providence's gift to him of opening up the Great Pond to the sea.[1]

In 1763, a very reliable mapmaker named Joseph Frederick Wallet Des-Barres showed the pond filling the center of almost the full length of the island. DesBarres was a skilled surveyor and cartographer, whose charts of the eastern seaboard of North America have become classics of their kind. He spent two years surveying Sable and its vicinity, and almost drowned there himself. The result was a meticulous survey that not only produced charts and sailing directions for the shoreline, complete with many soundings, but also provided information on wind direction and speed, climate, vegetation, and the speed and direction of ocean currents. The result was so complete, and so accurate, that no one bothered to survey the island again for a hundred years.

In 1801, when the Humane Establishment lifesaving service was set up, Lake Wallace was still open to the north, about two miles west of the current Sable Station, near the cut through the dunes that Gerry Forbes now calls Dead Horse Pass, which would be the first gap from the end of the western dunes. The lake ran south of the current station and to the west. The northern entrance was sealed off by a storm in 1833. Janet Carnochan, in her notes compiled a decade or two later, wrote that "it is said that two vessels were closed in there in 1836."[2]

In the 1870s the reference books were indicating that Lake Wallace was about six miles long.[3]

In 2003 it was a shrunken thing, less than seven hundred yards long and a mere fifty yards wide; its depth was uncertain, as no one had waded across it for some time or bothered with its close measurement (a few years before that it was about six feet at its deepest point, a few inches elsewhere). It is still salty, although now closed to the ocean; wave overwash in storms keeps it that way.[4]

As for the pond, so for the island.

The classic 1911 edition of the *Encyclopaedia Britannica* asserts that

> the island is constantly changing in shape, owing to the action on the sand of wind and wave, and tends to diminish in size. Since 1763, when taken over by Britain, it has shrunk from 40 miles in length to 20, from 2½ in breadth to 1, and from 200 feet in height to 85; since 1873 the western lighthouse has thrice been removed eastward. . . . The Canadian government has planted thousands of trees and quantities of root-binding grass, and the work of destruction has been somewhat stayed.[5]

An engaging book called *Natural Wonders of the World* (1980), of which Sable is one, asserted, as though there was no dissent, that "waves continually wear down its western tip and add new deposits of sand at the opposite end, causing the island to move gradually toward the east. The western end has retreated approximately six miles in the last two centuries."[6]

In 1899 the highest elevation on the island was 110 feet, on the north coast. In 2003 the highest point was 85 feet.

Well, all this seems clear enough. Sable Island is getting smaller and flatter, and its lakes and ponds are filling in. Or is it and are they? In fact, the data are not nearly so unambiguous, and the trends not nearly so linear. The Canadian Hydrographic Service has conducted numerous studies on the island, and the reports and discussions these studies have generated over the last few years have centered on three crucial questions: How stable is Sable? And how much has the island itself actually moved, and in which direction? At first glance, and without factoring in dates, the conclusions drawn are far from consistent.

A 1965 study by the geologist Harcourt Cameron surveyed the historical data from the early maps of the mid-1700s to photographs taken in the 1950s, and concluded, even after allowing for margins of error on the part of the mapmakers, that the island had migrated steadily eastward over the period in question. In particular, both the east and west spits moved eastward toward the end of the continental shelf and toward the Gully. But Cameron's study also showed that between 1955, when the photographs in question were taken, and 1964, both east and west spits migrated again, only this time to the west. Another study by the Halifax firm Evans-Hamilton in 1972 found that Sable was neither drifting to the east nor rapidly washing away as had been predicted. Some erosion was occurring, but its long-term and even medium-term effects were uncertain.

The geologist Terry Hennigar, somewhat with the benefit of hindsight of these studies, concluded that the changes occurring on Sable are not necessarily all destructive or final.[7] He even suggested that the long-term movement trends of the island, especially considering the past two hundred years of record, may be cyclical. He quoted the Evans-Hamilton study as indicating that between 1900 and 1947 the east spit eroded by a few miles, but that between 1947 and 1955 it increased in length again, by about four and a half miles. By 1960, however, all that had been added was lost once more. A series of aerial photographs taken between 1959 and 1973 showed that the west spit increased by about a mile and a half, which supported either a westward drift (unlikely) or a cyclical movement, which was more probable, or perhaps just the effects of one aberrant storm. Zoe Lucas has seized on this cyclical notion, clearly with some relief: "Changing sea level inevitably affects the size and shape of the island, though recent research indicates that long-term sand movement may be cyclical. Sable may not be drifting inexorably eastward toward the deep Gully, or washing away as rapidly as once thought."[8]

In 2002 a Halifax newspaper reported a new study.

> Researchers say Sable Island is growing but they're not sure if the change is a permanent one. The sandy island off Nova Scotia is eight kilometers (4.96 miles) longer than it was 36 years ago. The researchers from the College of Geographic Sciences in Lawrencetown compared their GPS measurements with data from 1966 and aerial photos from 1996. Most of the additional length is on the eastern tip of the island. As part of the research program the team is looking at landscape changes to find out if the island actually is getting bigger, moving, or if it's losing part of its vegetation.[9]

The geologist Ned King introduces a note of caution into this debate: "It's a matter of whether it [the equilibrium effects on the island] can keep up with climate change and the global sea-level rise. . . . Maybe it will drown, but I don't [yet] have a good sense of that."[10]

What, then, is the best guess? That the ever-malleable island is buffeted by forces larger than it can withstand, by shifts in the tides, by currents, by winds and storms. That these forces are by their nature variable, and some of them cyclical in ways not yet understood, but nevertheless have long-term predictability. That the island residents may be, to a degree at least, in perfectly understandable denial and have seized on the notion of cyclicity with a certain relief. That in the long term, Sable Island is probably self-destructive. That it may, indeed, slide into the abyss we now call the Gully; or may simply flatten and widen, until it is nothing more than a sandbar, still treacherous, but no longer home to anything other than aquatic creatures. This may not happen for a very long time. Or it may happen catastrophically, as Ned King conjectures: "[The island] maintains itself, and all processes are slow, but all of a sudden you get a big storm. It breaches and maybe can't rebuild itself."[11]

But there is a decent chance it may not happen at all.

Its Endless Gales

The horses are still there,

humans come and go,

the gales still blow, the storms

still wound, Sable endures

In 2003 the Sable Island Preservation Trust itself seemed vulnerable to dissolution. While the effort to declare a Marine Protected Area around the Gully inched its way through the federal political process, grumblings about the trust were increasing. Its operations were paid for by a multiplicity of stakeholders (the province, the oil and gas industry, the federal government through the coast guard and Environment Canada), all of whom thought they paid too much and received too little for their money. Environment Canada was under pressure to close weather stations across the country; Sable was just one on a long list. It got to the point where the staff, including Gerry Forbes, actually received layoff notices. The crisis was papered over, but it was bound to recur. And so, after 250 years of occupation, the human presence on Sable Island was as uncertain as it had ever been. If the humans depart and the island is abandoned to the planetary forces that sustain it and carve it and shape it, the seals and the seabirds will, of course, remain, and so will the horses. For a generation the horses might even notice the absence of the two-legs and their peculiar artifacts and loud noises. But unless horses keep legends alive in their dreams, the memories will soon fade. Only the wild storms will remain, and the harsh winter cold and the sweet summer grass, and the eternal rhythms will resume.

Two stallions, galloping along the north beach. They had been wrestling in the soft sand of one of the blowouts to the interior, and the sand was as churned as though an army division had passed through. There had been shrill whinnying, biting and butting, manes and tails flying, hooves flailing, and spittle spraying, big horse teeth in a lipless grimace. It looked as though there would be serious damage, blood and wounds and broken bones, but it was all in play, a black stallion and his son the bay, and when the wrestling was done, with energy still in reserve, they turned and raced each other down the beach, long tails trailing behind them in the wind, Pegasus on the sands of Sable, creatures out of legend, the very symbol of freedom and muscular joy.

A gaggle of Preservation Trust members and their families sat on the sand in the lee of a dune to eat their packaged lunches—not bad, lobster sandwiches and plastic cups of champagne brought from the mainland. Earlier, when one of the women had approached the black stallion, he had been guarded, snorting imperiously as she neared, but he'd trotted off and found his son, and the intruder was forgotten in the art of games. Other animals in his troop gathered around, curious; one of the horses, a mare, blew softly through her nostrils and lightly, gently, briefly, laid her head on an apprehensive human shoulder, then backed away, shaking her mane, peering benignly at the giggling creatures on the ground; then she trotted off, her little herd with her.[1]

Perhaps they *will* miss the humans when they are gone.

The humans left that night in their little soft-tired fixed-wing plane, bound for Halifax. They needed to get out. The barometer was falling, and a storm was coming. In the morning, no doubt, another notation would go into the Sable Island logbooks and be uploaded to the satellites. James Rainstorpe Morris, the first superintendent of the Sable Island Humane Establishment as far back as 1803, would have understood perfectly. He could have written the entry himself. "Gale today," the logbook would read. It would need no amplification.

NOTES

See bibliography for full citations.

PROLOGUE
Its Mysterious Presence

Descriptions of the island come from personal visits. Unless otherwise specified, quotes from Gerry Forbes are from conversations with him and now from printed sources. (Forbes was, it should be said, good-humored and patient with what must have seemed at times endless inquiries.) The list of questions posed toward the end of the prologue is derived from our own contemplation of Sable's fate.

[1]Berton, *Seacoasts*, p. 204.

[2]Published in Dawson, *The Mapmaker's Eye*, as the frontispiece.

CHAPTER ONE
Its Disputed Discovery

Information on the Norse voyages of exploration is taken from a Penguin edition of the Vineland sagas, published in 1965 but hardly bettered since. Mark Kurlansky's wonderfully readable history of the Basques is a prime source for much of the information about those intrepid mariners. One quote in this chapter, as well as others in later chapters, is from Lyall Campbell's 1994 book, *Sable Island Shipwrecks*, which is not a history but an engaging compilation of legends, tales, and recountings of stirring deeds. Campbell also published an earlier book, *Sable Island, Fatal and Fertile Crescent*, in 1982. Citations here are from the later book.

[1]*Phantom Islands*, p. 47.

[2]Magnusson and Pálsson, *The Vineland Sagas*, pp. 17ff.

[3]Ibid.

[4]J. Bernard Gilpin, "Sable Island, Its Past History, Present Appearance, Natural History & etc, & etc" (lecture).

[5]Kurlansky, *Basque History*, p. 56.

[6]Ibid., p. 58.

[7]T. W. Hennigar, *Water Resources & Environmental Geology*, p. 13.

[8]Presumably this name had something to do with the apocryphal martyred virgins of Cologne, who at least had a connection with the sea. (According to the legends, they had been blown about the ocean for three years before making landfall in Europe, where they were massacred by the Huns.)

[9]Information on the Barcelos family comes from a paper by Dr. Baptista De Lima of the Historical Institute of Terceira, presented at the First International Congress of the History of the Discoveries (1960).

[10]Campbell, *Sable Island Shipwrecks*, p. 10.

[11]Ibid., p. 11.

[12]Slafter, Voyages of Samuel de Champlain.

[13]Winthrop, *History of New England*.

CHAPTER TWO

Its Glacial Origins

Information from the geologist Ned King, cited here and in other chapters, came from interviews with him in 2003. (Ned's father, Lewis, was a pioneer on geology in the region.) Similarly, the natural scientist Allan Ruffman was generous with his time. Silver Donald Cameron has been sailing Nova Scotia waters for many years; his book *The Living Beach* is so readable that it's easy to overlook how richly detailed it really is. Other useful sources include the publications of the geologist Terry Hennigar, who maintains a keen interest in Sable Island; the oceanographers Robert Rutherford, Derek Fenton, and Heather Breeze; and the writers Jack Zinck and the Keoughs, Pat and Rosemarie, whose pictorial book *Wild and Beautiful Sable Island* appeared in 1993. There is also one citation in this chapter (and others in later chapters) from Barbara Christie, the reigning queen of writing about Sable Island's horses; we are indebted to Christie for her historical research. The edition of the ever-reliable *Encyclopaedia Britannica* we have used, unless otherwise specified, is the fifteenth.

[1] Interview with Ned King.

[2] Lewis H. King, *Surficial Geology*, p. 4.

[3] The Tertiary period ranged from 66 million years ago to 1.6 million years ago.

[4] T. W. Hennigar, *Water Resources & Environmental Geology*, p. 15.

[5] Cameron, *The Living Beach*, p. 42.

[6] *Encyclopaedia Britannica*, 16:740.

[7] Interview with Ned King.

[8] *Encyclopaedia Britannica*, 16:739.

[9] Ibid., 16:742–3.

[10] Lewis H. King, *Surficial Geology*, p. 5.

[11] Interview with Ned King.

[12] T. W. Hennigar, *Water Resources & Environmental Geology*, p. 15.

[13] Keough and Keough, *Wild and Beautiful Sable Island*, p. 5.

[14] The discussion of Sable's various names draws from Dawson, *The Mapmaker's Eye*, pp. 5, 7, 11.

[15] *Boston Weekly News-Letter*, August 11–18, 1737.

[16] Harcourt Cameron was a geologist well known in the region, and colleagues have cheekily named a cut in the elevated plateau thirty-two miles off Sable's west bar extension Harky's Pass.

[17] Rutherford and Breeze, *The Gully Ecosystem*, p. 1.

[18] Interview with Ned King.

[19] Zinck, *Shifting Sands*, p. 5.

[20] *Encyclopaedia Britannica*, 2:6.

[21] Johnson, *Phantom Islands*, p. 72.

[22] Simon D. McDonald, "Sable Island, Its Probable Origins and Submergence."

[23] Thoreau, *Cape Cod*.

[24] Cameron, *The Living Beach*, p. 51.

[25] *Encyclopaedia Britannica*, 7:685.

[26] T. W. Hennigar, *Water Resources & Environmental Geology*, p. 16.

[27] Ibid., p. 7.

[28] Christie, *The Horses of Sable Island*, p. 12.

[29] Patterson, *Sable Island, Its History and Phenomena*, p. 5.

[30] Carnochan, *Shipwrecked on Sable Island*, p. 19.

[31]Cameron, *The Living Beach,* p. 68.

[32]T. W. Hennigar, *Water Resources & Environmental Geology,* p. 16.

[33]Ibid., p. 19.

[34]Reader's Digest, *Natural Wonders,* p. 169.

CHAPTER THREE

Its Feckless Colonizers

Stories of the luckless "colonists" of Sable Island were derived from many general and regional histories, and more specifically from Bruce Armstrong's history of Sable, written in 1987. Armstrong is a terrific storyteller, and his book is well worth searching out. M. A. MacDonald's *Fortune & La Tour,* used as a source here and in recounting the Acadian story, is a well-written popular history.

[1]Christie, *The Horses of Sable Island,* p. 13.

[2]T. W. Hennigar, *Water Resources & Environmental Geology,* p. 13.

[3]MacDonald, *Fortune & La Tour,* p. 2.

[4]Levot, *Dictionary of Breton Biographies.*

[5]Mahaffie, *A Land of Discord,* p. 21.

[6]The La Roche story comes from multiple sources. The words in quotation marks are from *A History of Maritime France* published in Paris in 1910 (Ch. de La Roncière, *Histoire de la Maritimes française,* Paris, 1910 volume 4; it was this volume that the Simoneau family Web site (www.simoneau.ca) used to recount their version of the story. The story is also recounted in a Canada Fisheries and Oceans publication, *History of the Coast Guard,* which can be seen at www.ccg-gcc.gc.ca/usque-ad-mare/chapter07-02_e.htm.

[7]The Simoneau family Web site alleges that the survivors were Jacques Simoneau, Jacques Simon dit Larivière, Olivier Delin, Michel Heulin, Robert Piquet, Mathurin Saint-Gilles, Gilles Le Bultel, François Provostel, Loys Deschamps, Geoffroy Viret, and François Delestre.

[8]Public Archives of Nova Scotia Web site.

[9]Armstrong, *Sable Island,* p. 20.

[10]A book called *The Pseudo-Turpin Chronicle,* written in the 1200s, recounts how Charlemagne was said to have had a vision of such a headless Frenchman, who revealed how the stars of the Milky Way pointed toward the tomb of St. James in Compostela, a somber image that supposedly was an omen of Charlemagne's own death.

[11]Ibid., p. 22.

CHAPTER FOUR

Its Serial Shipwrecks

Lunenberg's Fisheries Museum is one of the prime sources for regional historians. Curator Ralph Getson's filing cabinets are stuffed with treasures, not the least among them his own conversations with sailors, some of whom survived the great Gales of August of the 1920s. Getson himself exemplifies the best traditions of curators; he is always willing to share his files and his knowledge with researchers. There is one citation in this chapter from his copious files, but there are many others in later chapters.

[1]Allan Ruffman, in *Divers Free Press,* vol. 10, no. 3, p. 18.

[2]*Halifax Chronicle-Herald,* March 10, 1928.

[3]*Sailing Directions to Accompany the Chart of the North American Coast from Belle Isle to Boston.*

[4]Ibid.

[5]Slocum, *Sailing Alone*, chapter 3, 36.

[6]Unattributed news clipping in Ralph Getson's files.

CHAPTER FIVE

Its Tides and Complex Currents

Translating hard science into lay terms without oversimplifying or condescending is always admirable, and Ernest Zebrowski does it skillfully in his *Perils of a Restless Planet*. Excerpts are used here by permission of Cambridge University Press. We also used as prime sources the endless research at the Woods Hole Oceanographic Institute in Massachusetts, and its companion in Dartmouth, Nova Scotia, the Bedford Institute. R. J. Rutherford, D. G. Fenton, and H. Breeze work out of Bedford.

[1]Zebrowski, *Perils*, p. 143.

[2]Ibid., p. 145.

[3]Some details are from Cameron's *The Living Beach*, pp. 25ff.

[4]Ibid., p. 25, quoting Arthur C. Clarke.

[5]De Villiers and Hirtle, *Into Africa*, p. 266.

[6]Donald S. Johnson, *Phantom Islands*, p. 61.

[7]www.Oceansonline.com.

[8]No, it's not true that the water in a sink or bathtub empties one way in the Northern Hemisphere and another in the south; the Coriolis effects are too tiny to show in small bodies of water.

[9]One of these icebergs has become famous in maritime history for holing the Titanic.

[10]Rutherford and Breeze, *The Gully Ecosystem*, p. 5.

[11]Michael S. McCartney, Woods Hole Oceanographic Institute (www.whoi.edu).

[12]The Smithsonian, Ocean Planet Online.

[13]Sable Island Preservation Trust (SIPT) newsletter, November 2002.

[14]Patterson, *Sable Island*, p. 34.

[15]Farquhar, *Farquhar's Luck*, p. 120.

[16]Voyage of the research vessel *Pelagia*, Netherlands Institute of Sea Research, in collaboration with the University of Cape Town. UCT Web site (www.MCT.AC.ZA).

[17]W. Sean Chamberlin, Fullerton College, Fullerton, California.

[18]T. W. Hennigar, *Water Resources & Environmental Geology*, p. 15.

CHAPTER SIX

Its Gales and Killer Waves

Jan DeBlieu is a poet rather than a scientist, but her book on wind (*Wind: How the Flow of Air Has Shaped Life, Myth, and the Land*), while lyrical, does contain a good deal of useful information. Excerpts are published by permission of Houghton-Mifflin Company. In this chapter Silver Donald Cameron's *The Living Beach* has again proved a useful resource, and so has Zebrowski's *Perils of a Restless Planet*. Other sources include Carsten Stroud, whose real métier is high-grade thriller writing, and Mather Byles DesBrisay, whose "History of the County of Lunenburg," published in 1870, contains endless information, both trivial and fascinating.

[1]T. W. Hennigar, *Water Resources & Environmental Geology*, pp. 8–10.

[2]*Backscatter* magazine, Spring/Summer 2002, p. 8.

[3]DeBlieu, *Wind*, p. 39.

[4]Some of this information is from *Encyclopaedia Britannica*, 1:675.

[5]DeBlieu, *Wind*, p. 39.

[6]*Encyclopaedia Britannica*, 6:543.

[7]DeBlieu, *Wind*, p. 4.

[8]Zebrowski, *Perils*, p. 249.

[9]*Encyclopaedia Britannica*, 2:6.

[10]Ibid., 16:737.

[11]T. W. Hennigar, *Water Resources & Environmental Geology*, p. 19.

[12]*Encyclopaedia Britannica*, 16:738.

[13]Stroud, *Cuba Strait*, p. 212.

[14]Some of this material comes from Cameron, *The Living Beach*.

[15]*Science Frontiers Online*, issue 109, January–February 1997.

[16]R. W. Warwick, et al., "Hurricane Luis, The Queen Elizabeth 2 and a Rogue Wave," *Marine Observer* 66 (1966):134.

[17]DesBrisay, *History*, p. 238.

[18]Cameron, *The Living Beach*, p. 20.

[19]This may have given rise to the completely erroneous and easily disproved theory that every seventh wave is higher than the previous six.

[20]B. S. White, "On the Chance of Freak Waves at Sea," *Journal of Fluid Mechanics* 355 (1998):113–38.

[21]Neall Driscoll, Woods Hole Oceanographic Institute, March 2003.

[22]Zebrowski, *Perils*, p. 143.

[23]Ibid., p. 140.

[24]*Coastal Living* (undated).

[25]Conversation with Gerry Mader. She spent six weeks on Sable shortly after her marriage to the meteorologist John Mader in the 1970s.

[26]T. W. Hennigar, *Water Resources & Environmental Geology*, p. 21.

CHAPTER SEVEN

Its Human Drama

There are endless histories, both popular and academic, of the early settlements of the Sable region and the eastern seaboard of America; the information in this chapter was drawn from a variety of them, plus the ever-reliable Barbara Christie and one citation from Allan Ruffman.

[1]McCreath and Leefe, *A History*, p. 13.

[2]Oliver J. Thatcher, ed., *The Library of Original Sources*, vol. 5, *9th to 16th Centuries* (Milwaukee: University Research Extension, 1907), pp. 342–54.

[3]McCreath and Leefe, *A History*, p. 56.

[4]Armstrong, *Sable Island*, p. 25.

[5]Christie, *The Horses of Sable Island*, p. 12.

[6]Ibid., p. 14.

[7]Razilly's story comes from a variety of sources, including the archives at Ste.-Marie-de-Grâce; the Archives Nationale Paris; Archives des Affaires Étrangères, vol. 4, 112 and 116; H. P. Biggar, *The Early Trading Company of New France* (Toronto, 1901), chapter 2, 508; *Généalogie de la Famille de Razilly* (Laval, France, 1903); E. Lauvrière, *La tragédie d'un peuple* (Paris, 1922); B. P. Candide, *Pages glorieuses* (Montreal, 1927); Az. Couillard-Després, *Charles de Saint-Étienne de la Tour* (Arthabaska, 1930); H. Garneau, *Histoire du Canada* (Paris, 1913).

[8]Christie, *The Horses of Sable Island*, p. 14.

[9]Ruffman, in *Divers Free Press*, quoting Grosvenor, "Safe Landing."

CHAPTER EIGHT

Its Boston Connection

Jon Butler's *Becoming America: The Revolution Before 1776* is an excellent source for life in the eastern colonies in the run up to the Revolution. Bruce Armstrong's *Sable Island: Nova Scotia's Mysterious Island of Sand* is indispensable for anyone interested in the island's lore.

[1] Butler, *Becoming America*, p. 70.

[2] Ross and Deveau, *The Acadians*, p. 38.

[3] Ibid., p. 39.

[4] Christie, *The Horses of Sable Island*, p. 14.

[5] Butler, *Becoming America*, p. 151.

[6] Waldo was second-in-command at the first "liberation" of Louisbourg in 1745, after which he became notorious by pocketing the pensions of soldiers killed there, money supposedly for their widows. He also helped draw up the plans for the second attack on Louisbourg.

[7] Campbell, *Sable Island Shipwrecks*, p. 18.

[8] Armstrong, *Sable Island*, p. 31.

[9] Patterson, *Sable Island*, p. 11.

[10] *Encyclopaedia Britannica*, 10:747.

[11] Armstrong, *Sable Island*, p. 28 and Patterson, *Sable Island*, p. 11.

[12] NSHC (Nova Scotia Historical Society Journal) (1895): 265.

[13] Ibid., p. 37.

[14] Christie, *The Horses of Sable Island*, p. 17.

CHAPTER NINE

Its Acadian Roots

The Acadian story, and the Hancocks' part in it, is derived from multiple sources, among them Barbara Christie, and Ross and Deveau's book on the Acadians. Essential also was Peter Landry, or rather, Peter Landry's wondrous Web site (www.blupete.com). Landry is a lawyer by day, but he has found time to assemble a fascinating selection of Nova Scotia lore and history on his Web site. (Its name, Blupete, derives from the Blue Peter, a maritime signal meaning "Report on board, the vessel is about to sail.") Landry's assemblages on the Web have proved reliable over time and are often used as a shortcut and tracking device by students of local history. Also useful was Winthrop Bell's *The "Foreign Protestants" and the settlement of Nova Scotia*, a magisterial if rather plodding account.

[1] Bell, *The "Foreign Protestants,"* p. 13.

[2] Ibid., pp. 503, 516n.

[3] Ross and Deveau, *The Acadians*, pp. 60ff.

[4] Peter Landry, Peteblu@blupete.com.

[5] Ross and Deveau, *The Acadians*, p. 64.

[6] Bell, *The "Foreign Protestants,"* p. 488n.

[7] McCreath and Leefe, *A History*, p. 252.

[8] Christie, *The Horses of Sable Island*, p. 21.

[9] Andrew Hill Clark, *Acadia: The Geography of Early Nova Scotia to 1760*, quoted in Christie, *The Horses of Sable Island*, p. 21.

[10] Bell, *The "Foreign Protestants,"* p. 489.

[11] Keough and Keough, *Wild and Beautiful Sable Island*, p. 18.

[12] Welsh, "Population, Behavior and Grazing Ecology of the Horses of Sable Island."

[13] *Encyclopaedia Britannica*, 20:648, 649.

[14] Christie, *The Horses of Sable Island*, pp. 24ff.

[15] Ibid., p. 24.

[16] Ibid., p. 25.

[17]*Report on Canadian Archives* 86 (1895).

[18]*Royal Gazette,* July 2, 1834.

[19]At the New England yards, hundreds of these schooners were built, their holds stuffed with white pine boles from the interior. Most of them sailed to England, there to be sold, cargo, vessel, and all, to the great advantage of the traders who built them.

CHAPTER TEN

Its Curious Ecosystem

Zoe Lucas has no official position on Sable, though she has lived there for many years; she is funded, nevertheless, by several government agencies and carries out multiple studies on behalf of a variety of organizations. She is, as we have said in the text, an autodidact in the very best sense: a self-taught scientist whose work is well received by professionals. In addition, she serves as unofficial publicist for the island through her Web site, the Green Horse Society; her visits to the mainland to recount tales of Sable to schoolchildren are anticipated by all for months before they happen.

[1]Zoe Lucas, quoted in Christie, *The Horses of Sable Island,* p. 99.

[2]Ruffman et al., *Historical Records of the Incidences of Sea Ice.*

[3]All ice references are from ibid.

[4]Environment Canada statistics.

[5]Conversation with Gerry Forbes.

[6]Carnochan, *Shipwrecked on Sable Island,* p. 2.

[7]Armstrong, *Sable Island,* p. 31.

[8]Nova Scotia Museum of Natural History.

[9]T. W. Hennigar, *Water Resources & Environmental Geology,* p. 25.

[10]Keough and Keough, *Wild and Beautiful Sable Island,* p. 26.

[11]T. W. Hennigar, *Water Resources & Environmental Geology,* p. 32.

[12]For the technically minded, the relevant equation is this:

$$H_s = H_f \,/\, E_s - E_f$$

Where H_s is the freshwater depth below sea level, H_f is the freshwater depth above sea level, E_s is the density of the salt water, E_f is the density of the fresh water.

[13]Ibid., p. 22.

[14]Ibid., p. 23.

[15]Keough and Keough, *Wild and Beautiful Sable Island,* p. 29.

[16]Ibid., p. 51.

CHAPTER ELEVEN

Its Lurid Rumors

In recounting the often lurid tales that preceded the creation of Sable's Humane Establishment, Bruce Armstrong's book is an engaging and accessible source. So is the very readable book by the Reverend George Patterson, published in 1894, titled *Sable Island: Its History and Phenomena.* Rosalee Stilwell's afterword to Morris's *Sable Island Journals* is unmatched for information on the Establishment's first superintendent.

[1]Berton, *Seacoasts,* p. 206.

[2]Patterson, *Sable Island,* p. 3.

[3]Armstrong, *Sable Island,* p. 33.

[4]Patterson, *Sable Island,* p. 11.

[5]Ibid., p. 10.

[6]Ibid., p. 12.

[7]Armstrong, *Sable Island,* p. 37.

[8]NSHC 1878–1978: 121.

[9]Armstrong, *Sable Island*, p. 40.

[10]Patterson, *Sable Island*, p. 13.

[11]Multiple versions of the story of Mrs. Copeland's ring are extant. This one is credited to Thomas Chandler Haliburton, writing as Sam Slick ("Sam Slick's Wise Saws and Instances") quoted by Campbell, *Sable Island Shipwrecks*, pp. 49ff.

[12]Armstrong, *Sable Island*, p. 40.

[13]Ibid., p. 42.

[14]Patterson, *Sable Island*, p. 13 and Armstrong, *Sable Island*, p. 50.

[15]Grant, *The Tribune of Nova Scotia*, pp. 17–18.

[16]Armstrong, *Sable Island*, p. 83.

[17]Blakeley and Grant, *Eleven Exiles*, p. 36.

[18]Rosalee Stilwell, afterword to Morris, *Sable Island Journals*, p. 162.

CHAPTER TWELVE

Its Eccentric Governors

This chapter could hardly have been written without the journals of James Rainstorpe Morris, the first superintendent of the Humane Establishment. The journals were carefully transcribed from handwritten entries by Rosalee Stilwell and published by the Sable Island Preservation Trust in 2001. Excerpts are used here with permission. The originals are in the archives of the Massachusetts Historical Society, and the transcriptions reside in the Maritime Museum of the Atlantic, Halifax.

[1]Morris, *Sable Island Journals*, p. 116.

[2]Ibid., pp. 94–95.

[3]Ibid., p. 116.

[4]Paul Johnson, *The Birth of the Modern*, pp. 200–206.

[5]Armstrong, *Sable Island*, p. 83.

[6]Ibid.

[7]Paul Johnson, *The Birth of the Modern*, p. 200.

[8]Armstrong, *Sable Island*, p. 83.

[9]Ibid.

[10]SIPT Web site Oct. 2003.

[11]Armstrong, *Sable Island*, p. 86.

[12]*First Things in Canada*, p. 158. Newspaper article from Ralph Getson's file.

[13]Farquhar, *Farquhar's Luck*, p. 109.

[14]News clipping in Ralph Getson's files.

[15]Patterson, *Sable Island*, p. 27.

[16]Carnochan, *Shipwrecked on Sable Island*, p. 20.

[17]Farquhar, *Farquhar's Luck*, p. 114.

[18]Ibid., p. 117.

[19]Ibid., p. 118.

[20]Campbell, *Sable Island Shipwrecks*, p. 105.

[21]Farquhar, *Farquhar's Luck*, p. 119.

[22]Dorothy Grant, *Halifax Chronicle-Herald*, September 29, 2002.

[23]Armstrong, *Sable Island*, p. 76.

[24]Christie, *The Horses of Sable Island*, p. 40.

[25]Armstrong, *Sable Island*, p. 80.

[26]Farquhar, *Farquhar's Luck*, p. 122.

[27]*Sailing Canada* 3, no. 4 (1981).

[28]Ross Mason in *Highway 7 Magazine* (Web based), 2002.

[29]Carnochan, *Shipwrecked on Sable Island*, p. 17.

[30]Armstrong, *Sable Island*, pp. 93–94.

[31]Ross Mason in *Highway 7 Magazine* (Web based), 2002.

[32]Farquhar, *Farquhar's Luck,* p. 114.

[33]Ibid., p. 123.

[34]Armstrong, *Sable Island,* p. 82.

[35]Patterson, *Sable Island,* p. 47.

[36]Armstrong, *Sable Island,* p. 82.

[37]Carnochan, *Shipwrecked on Sable Island,* p. 2.

[38]SIPT Web site.

[39]Information from an article by Victor Cardoza, widely published in 1967.

[40]Nova Scotia Museum of Natural History Web site (www.highway7.com), 2001.

[41]Much of the information on fauna comes from Wright, *Fauna of Sable Island.*

CHAPTER THIRTEEN

Its Savage Storms

The survivors' tales from the Gales of August, in all their colorful and pungent language, were collected (taped and transcribed) by Ralph Getson and now reside in Lunenburg's Fisheries Museum, and also by Peter Barss, as cited in the text. Newspapers of the period were also a fertile source. Some information (stories by Rollie Knickle and Clem Hiltz) were collected by the authors. Others sources are cited below.

[1]Armstrong, *Sable Island,* p. 84.

[2]DesBrisay, *History of the County of Lunenburg,* p. 511.

[3]Gerry Forbes, SIPT.

[4]DeBlieu, *Wind,* p. 4.

[5]Joseph Conrad, quoted in ibid., p. 4.

[6]Ibid., p. 5.

[7]Parry, *Romance of the Sea,* p. 254.

[8]David Jennings, spokesman for the Canadian Coast Guard, *Halifax Chronicle-Herald,* January 28, 2003.

[9]Barss, *Images of Lunenburg County,* pp. 119ff.

[10]Ibid., p. 120.

[11]Interview with Norman Campbell.

[12]Armstrong, *Sable Island,* p. 132.

[13]Berton, *Seacoasts,* p. 208.

[14]Farquhar, *Farquhar's Luck,* p. 110.

[15]T. W. Hennigar, *Water Resources & Environmental Geology,* p. 18.

[16]Zinck, *Shifting Sands,* p. 50.

[17]Ibid.

[18]Ibid.

[19]Armstrong, *Sable Island,* p. 84.

[20]McDonald, "Sable Island, Its Probable Origin and Submergence."

[21]Zinck, *Shifting Sands,* p. 50.

[22]T. W. Hennigar, *Water Resources & Environmental Geology,* p. 18.

[23]Armstrong, *Sable Island,* p. 86.

[24]*Sailing Canada,* 3, no. 4 (1981): 44ff (quoted in Peter Barss).

[25]Fisheries Museum file, no source given.

[26]Undated newspaper article in Fisheries Museum archives.

[27]Unattributed newspaper article, Ralph Getson's file, *Lunenburg Progress Enterprise,* August 18, 1926. Captain Charles Corkum; crew: brothers Walter, Wade, and Parker Wamback, William Wamback,

Perry Corkum, Norman Conrad, brothers Simon and Robert Bush and Robert's son Redvers Bush, Robert Haughn, Andrew Shankle and his son Basil Shankle, John Baptiste, Burns Buchannan, Samuel Firth, Jerry Hemeon, Ross Pierce, Thomas Martel, Horace Rhyno, brothers Joseph and Cyrille Chiasson, Amede Chiasson, Stanislas Muise.

[28]Transcript of interview with Ralph Getson.

[29]Correspondence with Ralph Getson.

[30]*Halifax Chronicle,* March 10, 1928.

[31]Correspondence with Ralph Getson.

[32]"Sands of Sable Is Dust of Death," *Halifax Chronicle,* March 10, 1928.

CHAPTER FOURTEEN

Its Wild Creatures

Much of the material in this chapter came from personal inspections and interviews, most notably with Hal Whitehead, Norman Campbell, Gerry Forbes, and Roberto Dutesco. Zoe Lucas, as always, was a fruitful source, and so was Canada's Department of Fisheries and Oceans and the people at the Bedford Institute, notably Derek Fenton.

[1]Nova Scotia Museum of Natural History Web site, 2001.

[2]Zinck, *Shifting Sands,* p. 6.

[3]Wright, *The Fauna of Sable Island,* p. 77.

[4]Communications Directorate, Department of Fisheries and Oceans.

[5]Ibid.

[6]*Somniosus microcephalus,* Canadian Shark Research Laboratory.

[7]Quoted from Green Horse Society (Zoe Lucas's Web site (www.greenhorse society.com), March 2003).

[8]*Canadian Field Naturalist,* 114 (2000): 45–61.

[9]Blue whale (1 single stranding), fin whale (1 single stranding), minke whale (3 single strandings), humpback whale (4 single strandings), sperm whale (8 strandings, 13 animals), pygmy sperm whale (3 strandings, 4 animals), dwarf sperm whale (2 single strandings), northern bottlenose whale (3 single strandings), Sowerby's beaked whale (1 single stranding), killer whale (1 single stranding), long-finned pilot whale (37 strandings, 173 animals), white-beaked dolphin (1 stranding, 2 animals), Atlantic white-sided dolphin (9 strandings, 13 animals), Risso's dolphin (1 single stranding), striped dolphin (8 strandings, 22 animals), short-beaked common dolphin (4 strandings, 6 animals), harbor porpoise (11 strandings, 13 animals). No other dwarf sperm whale or Risso's dolphin has ever been recorded stranded in eastern Canada; the Sowerby's beaked whale is the first reported stranding in Nova Scotia. Strandings of humpback, minke, and killer whales, and short-beaked common dolphins have not previously been recorded on Sable Island.

[10]Patterson, *Sable Island,* p. 5.

[11]William Beebe, quoted in *Coastal Living,* July–August 1999.

[12]*Coastal Living,* July–August 1999.

[13]*Halifax Chronicle-Herald,* January 26, 2002.

[14]Interview with Hal Whitehead.

[15]Rutherford and Breeze, *The Gully Ecosystem*, p. 1.

[16]*Halifax Chronicle-Herald*, January 26, 2002.

[17]*New York Times*, March 10, 2002.

[18]Interview with Pat Mortensen, marine biologist, Department of Fisheries and Oceans, and World Wildlife Fund, Canada.

[19]Adapted from Zoe Lucas, quoted in Christie, *The Horses of Sable Island*, p. 98.

[20]Ipswich Sparrow, Family *Emberizidae: (Passerculus candwichensis princeps Maynard)*—Wright, *The Fauna of Sable Island*.

[21]Maclaren and Bell, 1972, reported in T. W. Hennigar, *Water Resources & Environmental Geology*.

[22]Carnochan, *Shipwrecked on Sable Island*, p. 7.

[23]Norman Campbell.

[24]Canadian Wildlife Service.

[25]*Progress Enterprise*, December 4, 2002.

[26]SIPT.

[27]Farquhar, *Farquhar's Luck*, p. 109.

[28]SIPT.

[29]Zoe Lucas, quoted in Christie, *The Horses of Sable Island*, p. 100.

[30]Gerry Forbes.

[31]Zoe Lucas, quoted in Christie, *The Horses of Sable Island*, p. 99.

[32]*Encyclopaedia Britannica*, 23:442.

[33]The oldest known horse, preserved in a Vienna museum, was forty-four when it died, although there are reports of horses that lived into their sixties. Nova Scotia Museum of Natural History.

[34]Interview with Roberto Dutesco.

[35]Christie, *The Horses of Sable Island*, p. 33.

[36]Armstrong, *Sable Island*, p. 94.

[37]SIPT.

[38]T. W. Hennigar, *Water Resources & Environmental Geology*, p. 18.

[39]Some information adapted from Zoe Lucas's Web site. She did a good deal of the planting personally.

[40]Adapted from the Green Horse Society Web site, April 2003.

CHAPTER FIFTEEN

Its Confusing Politics

Much of the information in this chapter came from personal inspection and from multiple news sources and interviews. Wayne Walters, grandson of the legendary Angus Walters, skipper of the *Bluenose*, is a sea captain himself and was generous with his advice on things maritime. Zoe Lucas, again, was indispensable for a recounting of the scientific studies under way on Sable.

[1]Armstrong, *Sable Island*, p. 132.

[2]Interview with captain Wayne Walters.

[3]Outdoor Nova Scotia Web site.

[4]Farquhar, *Farquhar's Luck*, p. 105.

[5]Charles Bruce Fergusson (archivist of Nova Scotia), *Journal of Education*, May–June 1969, p. 17.

[6]Zoe Lucas, Green Horse Society Web site, April 2003.

[7]*Globe and Mail*, January 11, 2003.

[8]*Halifax Chronicle-Herald*, January 10, 2003.

[9]*National Post,* November 18, 2002; *Halifax Chronicle-Herald,* January 26, 2002.

[10]*Halifax Chronicle-Herald,* January 10, 2003.

CHAPTER SIXTEEN

Its Very Existence at Risk

The geologist Ned King, who was patient with his time and his explanations, was essential for our understanding of Sable's ultimate fate (and any errors in the material are ours, not his).

[1]Armstrong, *Sable Island,* p. 31.

[2]Carnochan, *Shipwrecked on Sable Island,* p. 19.

[3]*Encyclopaedia Britannica,* 11th ed., 23: 966.

[4]Interview with Gerry Forbes.

[5]*Encyclopaedia Britannica,* 11th ed., 23: 967.

[6]Reader's Digest, *Natural Wonders,* p. 328.

[7]T. W. Hennigar, *Water Resources & Environmental Geology,* p. 18.

[8]Zoe Lucas, Green Horse Society Web site, April 2003.

[9]*Halifax Chronicle-Herald,* 25 November, 2002.

[10]Interview with Ned King.

[11]Ibid.

EPILOGUE

Its Endless Gales

[1]Anecdote from Marcia Harding.

BIBLIOGRAPHY

Armstrong, Bruce. *Sable Island, Nova Scotia's Mysterious Island of Sand.* Halifax: Formac, 1987.

Barss, Peter. *Images of Lunenburg County.* Toronto: McClelland and Stewart, 1978.

Bell, Winthrop P. *The "Foreign Protestants" and the Settlement of Nova Scotia.* Sackville, New Brunswick: Mount Allison University, 1990.

Berton, Pierre. *Seacoasts.* Toronto: Stoddart, 1998.

Blakeley, Phyllis, and John Grant. *Eleven Exiles, Accounts of Loyalists of the American Revolution.* Toronto: Dundurn Press, 1982.

Butler, Jon. *Becoming America, the Revolution Before 1776.* Cambridge, Mass.: Harvard University Press, 2000.

———. *The Huguenots in America, A Refugee People in a New World Society.* Cambridge, Mass.: Harvard University Press, 1983.

Cameron, Silver Donald. *The Living Beach.* Toronto: Macmillan, 1998.

Campbell, Lyall. *Sable Island, Fatal and Fertile Crescent.* Windsor, Nova Scotia: Lancelot Press, 1974.

———. *Sable Island Shipwrecks: Disaster and Survival at the North Atlantic Graveyard.* Halifax: Nimbus, 1994.

———. "Sir John Wentworth and the Sable Island Humane Establishment." *Nova Scotia Historical Quarterly* 6, no. 3 (September 1976): 292–309.

Carnochan, Janet. *Shipwrecked on Sable Island.* Niagara Falls: Niagara Historical Society, 1986.

Christie, Barbara J. *The Horses of Sable Island.* Porter's Lake, Nova Scotia: Pottersfield Press, 1995.

Conrad, Margaret, ed. *They Planted Well: New England Planters in Maritime Canada,* Fredericton, New Brunswick: Acadiensis Press, 1988.

Dawson, Joan. *The Mapmaker's Eye.* Halifax: Nimbus, 1988.

DeBlieu, Jan. *Wind, How the Flow of Air Has Shaped Life, Myth, and the Land.* Boston: Mariner Books / Houghton Mifflin, 1999.

Denys, Nicholas. *The Description and Natural History of the Coast of North America.* Ed. William F. Ganong. Toronto: Champlain Society, 1908.

DesBrisay, Mather Byles. "History of the County of Lunenburg." *Bridgewater Bulletin* (Bridgewater, Nova Scotia), 1967. Originally printed in 1870.

de Villiers, Marq, and Sheila Hirtle. *Into Africa: Journeys Through the Ancient Empires.* Toronto: Key Porter, 1987.

Duncan, Norman. *The Way of the Sea.* Freeport, N.Y.: Books for Libraries Press, 1970.

Dyson, John, and Peter Christopher. *Spirit of Sail.* Toronto: Key Porter, 1987.

Encyclopaedia Britannica, 11th ed., 1911; and *The New Encyclopaedia Britannica,* 15th ed., 1975.

Farquhar, James A. Extracts from the journal of the late Captain J. A. Farquhar. Collections of the Nova Scotia Historical Society, vol. 27. Halifax: Ross Print, 1947.

————, *Farquhar's Luck.* Halifax: Petheric Press, 1980.

Gilpin, J. Bernard. "Sable Island, Its Past History, Present Appearance, Natural History & etc, & etc." Halifax, 1858. (Lecture)

Gordon, D. C., Jr., and D. G. Fenton, eds. *Advances in Understanding the Gully Ecosystem: A Summary of Research Projects Conducted at the Bedford Institute of Oceanography.* Halifax: BIO 1999–2001.

Grant, William Lawson. *The Tribune of Nova Scotia.* Toronto: Glasgow, Brook, 1950.

Grosvenor, Melville Bell. "Safe Landing On Sable: Isle of 500 Shipwrecks." National Geographic, September 1965.

Harrison, W. G., and D. G. Fenton, eds. *The Gully: A Scientific Review of Its Environment and Ecosystem.* Fisheries and Oceans Canada, Halifax.

Hay, John. *The Great Beach.* New York: Ballantine, 1963.

Hennigar, T. W. (Terry). *Water Resources & Environmental Geology of Sable Island.* Nova Scotia, geological report no. 76–1. Province of Nova Scotia, Halifax, 1976.

Hennigar, Ted. *Scotia Spooks, Mystery & Violence.* Including: The Ghosts of Sable Island. Windsor: Lancelot Press, 1978.

Howden, Henry F. *Fauna of Sable Island and Its Zoogeographic Affinities: A Compendium.* Halifax: National Museum of Natural Sciences, 1970.

Howell, Colin, et al. *Jack Tar in History.* Fredericton, New Brunswick: Acadiensis, 1991.

Johnson, Donald S. *Phantom Islands of the Atlantic.* Fredericton, New Brunswick: Goose Lane Editions, 1994.

Johnson, Paul. *The Birth of the Modern: World Society 1815–1830.* London: Phœnix/Orion, 1991.

Keough, Pat, and Rosemarie Keough. *Wild and Beautiful Sable Island.* Fulford Harbour, British Columbia: Nahanni Productions, 1993.

King, Lewis H. *Surficial Geology of the Halifax-Sable Island Map Area.* Marine Sciences Branch, Department of Energy, Mines and Resources. Ottawa: Queen's Printer for Canada, 1970.

Kurlansky, Mark. *The Basque History of the World.* New York: Walker, 1999.

Larson, Erik. *Isaac's Storm.* New York: Vintage, 2000.

Lawrence, Charles A. *Journal and Letters of Colonel Charles Lawrence: A Day by Day Account of the Founding of Lunenburg.* Lunenburg: Lunenburg Heritage Society, 1972.

Levot, P-J. *Dictionary of Breton Biographies.* Paris: n.p., 1857.

Lucas, Zoe. *Wild Horses of Sable Island.* Toronto: Greey de Pencier Books, 1981.

MacDonald, M. A. *Fortune & La Tour: The Civil War in Acadia.* Halifax: Nimbus, 2000.

Magnusson, Magnus, and Hermann Pálsson. *The Vineland Sagas: The Norse Discovery of America.* London: Penguin, 1965.

Mahaffie, Charles D., Jr. *A Land of Discord Always: Acadia from Its Beginnings to the Expulsion of Its People, 1604–1755.* Camden, Maine: Down East Books, 1995.

McCreath, Peter, and John G. Leefe. *A History of Early Nova Scotia.* Tantallon: Four East Publications, 1982.

McDonald, Simon D. "Sable Island, Its Probable Origin and Submergence." Paper read before the Institute of Natural Science, January 11, 1886.

McLaren, Ian A. *Birds of Sable Island, Nova Scotia.* Halifax: Nova Scotia Institute of Science, 1981.

Mitcham, Allison. *Island Keepers.* Windsor, Nova Scotia: Lancelot Press, 1989.

Morris, James Rainstorpe. *Sable Island Journals, 1801–1804.* Halifax: Sable Island Preservation Trust, 2001.

Nova Scotia Historical Review, vol. 5, no. 2 (1985). Public Archives of Nova Scotia.

The Nova Scotia Historical Society, 1878–1978. Belleville, Nova Scotia: NSHS and Mika Publishing, 1977.

Parry, J. H. *Romance of the Sea.* Washington, D.C.: National Geographic Society, 1981.

Patterson, Reverend George. *Sable Island, Its History and Phenomena.* Halifax: Knight, 1894.

Raddall, Thomas Head. "Christmas at Sable Island." *All Sails Set.* Toronto: Copp Clark, 1948.

———. *The Nymph and the Lamp.* Halifax: Nimbus, 1994.

———. *A Pictorial Guide to Historic Nova Scotia: Featuring Louisbourg, Peggy's Cove, Sable Island.* Halifax: Book Room, 1970.

Reader's Digest. *Natural Wonders of the World.* Toronto: Reader's Digest Canada, 1980.

Ross, Sally, and Alphonse Deveau. *The Acadians of Nova Scotia Past and Present.* Halifax: Nimbus, 1992.

Ruffman, Allan, et al. *Historical Record of the Incidence of Sea Ice on the Scotian Shelf and the Gulf of St. Lawrence from 1817 to 1962.* Ottawa: Institute for Marine Dynamics, 2002.

Rutherford, R. J., and H. Breeze. *The Gully Ecosystem.* Canadian Manuscript Report of Fisheries and Aquatic Sciences 2615. Fisheries & Oceans Canada.

Sailing Directions to Accompany the Chart of the North American Coast from Belle Isle to Boston. London: Imray, Laurie, Norie and Wilson, 1911.

Slafter, Edmund F., ed. *Voyages of Samuel de Champlain.* Boston: Prince Society, 1878.

Slocum, Joshua. *Sailing Alone Around the World.* Sheridan House Inc., 1995.

Snow, Edward Rowe. *Ghosts, Gales and Gold.* New York: Dodd, Mead, 1972.

Stephens, David E. *Lighthouses of Nova Scotia,* Windsor, Nova Scotia: Lancelot Press, 1973.

Stroud, Carsten. *Cuba Strait.* New York: Simon and Schuster, 2003.

Thoreau, Henry David. *Cape Cod,* 1865.

Welsh, Daniel E. "Population, Behavior and Grazing Ecology of the Horses of Sable Island." Ph.D. Thesis, Dalhousie University, 1975.

Wentworth, Sir John. *Observations Upon an Establishment*. Report for the Public Archives of Canada, 1895.

———. *Papers Relating to Sable Island*. Report for the Public Archives of Canada, 1895, Halifax.

Winthrop, John. *History of New England* (1630–49). James Savage, ed. Little, Brown & Co., 1853.

Wright, Barry. *The Fauna of Sable Island*. Halifax: Nova Scotia Museum, 1989.

Yetman, Derek. *Midshipman Squibb*. St. John's, Newfoundland: Gooseberry Press, 2001.

Zebrowski, Ernest, Jr. *Perils of a Restless Planet*. Cambridge: Cambridge University Press, 1997.

Zinck, Jack. *Shifting Sands*. Dartmouth: T.&T. Publishing, 1979.

———. *Shipwrecks of Nova Scotia*. 2 vols. Hantsport, Nova Scotia: Lancelot Press, 1977.

INDEX

I

J

K

L